Green Finance and Investment

Clean Energy Finance and Investment Policy Review of Indonesia

OECD
BETTER POLICIES FOR BETTER LIVES

Please cite this publication as:
OECD (2021), *Clean Energy Finance and Investment Policy Review of Indonesia* , Green Finance and Investment, OECD Publishing, Paris, *https://doi.org/10.1787/0007dd9d-en*.

ISBN 978-92-64-42892-8 (print)
ISBN 978-92-64-92351-5 (pdf)

Green Finance and Investment
ISSN 2409-0336 (print)
ISSN 2409-0344 (online)

Photo credits: Cover © Rumagia Bangun Setiawan/Shutterstock.com.

Corrigenda to publications may be found on line at: *www.oecd.org/about/publishing/corrigenda.htm*.

Preface

Indonesia has achieved remarkable economic success over the last two decades, lifting millions out of poverty. The recent COVID-19 pandemic has momentarily halted this economic growth, causing the country's first recession in decades. Yet, the recovery from the pandemic presents an opportunity to build back a stronger and more sustainable economy, helping Indonesia to achieve its commitments under the Paris Agreement as well as the Sustainable Development Goals.

The transformation of the energy sector can play a central role in greening Indonesia's economic recovery. With abundant renewable energy resources and potentia for energy efficiency, Indonesia can become a major clean energy market.

In particular, clean energy investment can be a driving force behind Indonesia's recovery. Renewable energy still accounts for only a small share of electricity generation, and energy efficiency opportunities remain largely untapped. Opening the doors to finance and investment in those clean energy solutions would be a major shift from current trends, in which fossil fuels continue to dominate the energy sector.

Unlocking Indonesia's clean energy potential requires establishing a market framework that enables the mobilisation of hundreds of billions of dollars in private capital over the next decades. This *OECD Clean Energy Finance and Investment Policy Review of Indonesia* aims to support efforts to develop that enabling environment and accelerate the country's clean energy transition.

The report provides a comprehensive overview of the current policy framework, highlighting progress and identifying where changes are needed. It also contains a number of tailored recommendations for the Government of Indonesia and development partners to mobilise private finance and investment for clean energy development.

This *Review* is the result of a constructive dialogue between Indonesia, a key OECD partner, and OECD member countries alongside other clean energy stakeholders. The OECD will continue to support Indonesia in implementing the report's recommendations as the country builds back a stronger, cleaner and more resilient economy. I am confident that this collaborative effort will help in mobilising private finance and investment to support Indonesia's climate action and its overall sustainable development.

Mathias Cormann
Secretary-General, OECD

Foreword

The *Clean Energy Finance and Investment Policy Review of Indonesia* is one of the key outputs of the OECD Clean Energy Finance and Investment Mobilisation (CEFIM) Programme. The CEFIM Programme aims to support governments in emerging economies in South and Southeast Asia as well as Latin America to unlock finance and investment in renewable electricity and energy efficiency ("clean energy").

Building on fruitful co-operation between the Government of Indonesia and the OECD, as well as current policy reforms to facilitate investment and renewable energy development, Indonesia was a natural choice to undertake this first-of-its-kind Clean Energy Finance and Investment Policy Review. The *Review* supports Indonesia's efforts to realise a clean energy transition by providing a comprehensive overview of the current policy environment, highlighting progress and identifying opportunities for strengthening policy interventions that can help to scale up clean energy finance and investment.

The OECD is grateful to the Government of Indonesia for its co-operation in providing information; for the organisation of the virtual review mission (October-November 2020); for the virtual focus group discussions and webinars in 2020; and for the Stakeholder Dialogue held in Jakarta on 8 November 2019. Particular thanks is due to the Coordinating Ministry for Economic Affairs, under the leadership of Montty Girianna, Deputy Coordinating Minister, and the support from his Deputy Assistants, Dida Gardera, Agus Wibowo, Muksin, and their team. CEFIM is also grateful to all the government institutions involved in the cross-agency steering committee specifically formed for the *Review*, including the Financial Services Authority (particularly the International Department), the Investment Coordination Board, the Ministry of Energy and Mineral Resources (particularly the Directorate-General of Electricity; the Directorate-General for New and Renewable Energy and Energy Conservation; as well as the Ministry's Research & Development Agency and Training Centre), the Ministry of Finance (particularly the Fiscal Policy Agency and the Directorate-General of Budget Financing and Risk Management), the Ministry of Environment and Forestry, the Ministry of Industry, the Ministry of National Development Planning (BAPPENAS), and state-owned enterprises such as the Indonesian Guarantee Fund, the national power utility, PT PLN (Perusahaan Listrik Negara), and the infrastructure financing company, PT SMI (Sarana Multi-infrastruktur).

The *Review* was managed by Cecilia Tam, Team Leader of the Clean Energy Finance and Investment Mobilisation Programme. Jeremy Faroi co-ordinated the research and *Review* process. Authors of the report were John Dulac, Jeremy Faroi and Cecilia Tam from the OECD Environment Directorate and Randi Kristiansen from the International Energy Agency (IEA). Aang Darmawan provided in-country support, particularly in facilitating coordination between the Government of Indonesia and the *Review* authors. Dominique Haleva provided administrative support and copy-edited the report. OECD Environment Director Rodolfo Lacy led the dialogue mission in November 2019 and launched the virtual *Review* mission.

Several colleagues in the OECD Secretariat provided input and feedback, including Simon Buckle, Thiana Bule, Ivana Capozza, Alexandre De Crombrugghe, Massimo Geloso Grosso, Eija Kiiskinen, Britta Labhun, Mireille Martini, Jens Sedemund and Stephen Thomsen. We also appreciate the comments provided from Lucila Arboleya Sarazola, Sylvia Elisabeth Beyer, Nathaniel Lewis George and Mike Waldron of the IEA.

The preparation of the *Review* also benefitted from a broad consultation process with a range of stakeholders. We are grateful for the contributions of Bertrand Poche and Nurrahman Waluyo (Agence Française de Développement); Gina Lisdiana (Allotrope); Florian Kitt (Asian Development Bank); Russell Marsh and other colleagues (ASEAN Low-Carbon Energy Programme) as well as Mike Crosetti, Laily Himayati, Damar Pranadi and Rizka Sari (MENTARI Programme); Marsha Sudar (Australia Embassy in Indonesia); Ian Kay and Louise Vickery (Australia Renewable Energy Agency); Trita Katriana (Canada Embassy in Indonesia); Andrew Glumac (Carbon Disclosure Project); Bianca Sylvester (Clean Energy Finance Corporation); Guntur Sutiyono, Jannata Giwangkara and Emi Minghui Gui (Climate Works Australia); Sidonie Gwet (Coalition for Green Capital); Lars Kruse (Cowi); Stephan Skare Enevoldsen (Danish Energy Agency); Raditya Pramudiantoro (Danone); Muhammed Sayed (Development Bank of South Africa); Mylene Celestino Capongcol (Department of Energy of the Philippines); Tom Dreesen (EPS Capital); Marcel Sylvius and his team, Norbert Maas, Satria Wira Tenaya, and Dessi Yuliana (Global Green Growth Institute); Leo Hyoungkun Park (Green Climate Fund); Raphaelle Vallet (Green Investment Group); Mathieu Geze, Dhiah Karsiwulan and Syaifuddin Suaib (HDF Energy); Fabby Tumiwa (Institute for Economic Services Reform); Jinlei Feng, Costanza Strinati, Nicolas Wagner and Badariah Yosiyana (International Renewable Energy Agency); Ogawa Tadayuki (Japan International Co-operation Agency); Dong Joo Kim (Jeju Energy Corporation); Jon Respati and other colleagues (Indonesia's Energy Conservation and Energy Society); Paul Butarbutar, Surya Darma and other colleagues (Indonesia's Renewable Energy Society); Bold Magavan (Mongolian Green Finance Corporation); Sumi Subramaniam and Riri Hijriah (New Zealand Embassy in Indonesia); Sam Kimmins (Renewable Energy 100); Pawan Kumar Bharti (Small, Industry Development Bank of India); Mr. Peter Hobson (Sustainable Development Capital LLP); Katherine Stodulka (Blended Finance Task Force and SystemiQ); Rizkiasari Joedawinata (World Wide Fund for Nature) and other colleagues of the Secretariat and members of the Indonesian Sustainable Finance Initiative; and Bona Raymond (independent sustainable finance specialist). Last but not least, the OECD is thankful to the numerous experts in OECD member country embassies based in Indonesia who were consulted throughout the Review process, with special thanks to His Excellency Bo Larsen, Danish Ambassador, His Excellency Rasmus Abildgaard Kristensen, former Danish Ambassador, Thomas Capral Henriksen and his team (Danish Embassy) for their support on the *Review.* We are also grateful to all the participants in the virtual *Review* mission who provided invaluable input to the *Review.*

This report was made possible through the generous contribution of Denmark. Input to the report from Randi Kristiansen was made possible thanks to the IEA's Clean Energy Transitions in Emerging Economies programme, which received funding from the European Union's Horizon 2020 research and innovation programme under grant agreement No. 952363.

The OECD Working Party on Climate, Investment and Development discussed the draft *Review* at its meeting on 25 March 2021. Special thanks to Gemma O' Reilly, Economist, Irish Climate Change Advisory Council for moderating the discussions.

Table of contents

Tables

Figures

Boxes

Follow OECD Publications on:

http://twitter.com/OECD_Pubs

http://www.facebook.com/OECDPublications

http://www.linkedin.com/groups/OECD-Publications-4645871

http://www.youtube.com/oecdilibrary

OECD Alerts http://www.oecd.org/oecddirect/

This book has...

StatLinks
A service that delivers Excel® files from the printed page!

Look for the *StatLinks* at the bottom of the tables or graphs in this book. To download the matching Excel® spreadsheet, just type the link into your Internet browser, starting with the ***https://doi.org*** prefix, or click on the link from the e-book edition.

Abbreviations and acronyms

AC	air conditioner
ASEAN	Association of Southeast Asian Nations
ATMR	aset tertimbang menurut risiko (risk-weighted asset)
BaU	business-as-usual
Bappenas	Badan Perencanaan Pembangunan Nasional (Ministry of National Development Planning)
BKPM	Badan Koordinasi Penanaman Modal (Indonesian Co-ordinating Investment Board)
BOOT	build-own-operate-transfer
BPDLH	Badan Pengelolaan Lingkungan Hidup (Environment Fund Management Agency)
BPMK	batas maksimum pemberian kredit (legal lending limit)
BPP	biaya pokok penyediaan (average cost of electricity production)
CaaS	cooling as a service
CCUS	carbon capture, use and storage
CFL	compact fluorescent lamp
CGE	central government expenditure
CMEA	Co-ordinating Ministry of Economic Affairs (Kementerian Koordinator Bidang Perekonomian)
CMMIA	Co-ordinating Ministry of Maritime and Investment Affairs (Kementerian Koordinator Bidang Kemaritiman dan Investasi)
CEEE	Clean Energy, Education and Empowerment Collaboration Programme
DEN	Dewan Energi Nasional (National Energy Council)
DG	Directorate-General
DMO	domestic market obligation
DSM	demand-side management
EC	European Commission
ECA	Export Credit Agency
EER	energy efficiency rating
EPC	energy performance contract
ESCO	energy service company
ESG	environment social and governance
FDI	foreign direct investment
FiP	feed-in premium
FiT	feed-in tariff
FTP	fast-track programme
GCF	Green Climate Fund
GDP	gross domestic product
GFM	government force majeure
GHG	greenhouse gas
GW	gigawatt (one billion Watts)
IDR	Indonesian Rupiah
IEA	International Energy Agency
IGA	investment-grade audit
IGGF	Indonesia Infrastructure Guarantee Fund (PT Penjaminan Infrastruktur Indonesia)
IPP	independent power producer
ISO	International Organisation for Standardisation
IUPTL	izin usaha penyediaan tenaga listrik (electricity business licence)
KEN	Kebijakan Energi Nasional (National Energy Policy)
KWh	kilowatt-hour
LCOE	levelised cost of electricity
LCR	local content requirement
LED	light-emitting diode

LMAN	Lembaga Manajemen Aset Negara (State Asset Management Agency)
LPG	liquefied petroleum gas
MEMR	Ministry of Energy and Mineral Resources (Kementerian Energi dan Sumber Daya Mineral)
MEPS	minimum energy performance standards
MoEF	Ministry of Environment and Forestry (Kementerian Lingkungan Hidup dan Kehutanan)
MoF	Ministry of Finance (Kementerian Keuangan)
MoI	Ministry of Industry (Kementerian Perindustrian)
MoSOE	Ministry of State-Owned Enterprises (Kementerian Badan Usaha Milik negara)
MPWH	Ministry of Public Works and Housing (Kementerian Pekerjaan Umum dan Perumahan Rakyat)
MP3EI	Masterplan for Acceleration and Expansion of Indonesia's Economic Development
Mtoe	million tonnes of oil equivalent
$MtCO_2e$	million tonnes of CO_2 (carbon dioxide) equivalent
MW	megawatt (one million Watts)
NDC	Nationally Determined Contribution
OJK	Otoritas Jasa Keuangan (Financial Services Authority)
OSS	on-line single submission
PEEN	Penghargaan Efisiensi Energi Nasional (National Energy Efficiency Awards)
PLN	Perusahaan Listrik Negara (State Electricity Company)
PMR	Partnership for Market Readiness
PPA	power purchase agreement
PPP	public private partnership
PPU	private power utility
PRSF	Partial Risk Sharing Facility
PT SMI	Perseroan Terbatas Sarana Multi Infrastruktur (Multi Infrastructure Facility)
PV	photovoltaic
RAN-GRK	Rencana Aksi Nasional Penurunan Emisi Gas Rumah Kaca (National Action Plan for Greenhouse Gas Emission Reduction)
RAKB	Rencana Aksi Keuangan Berkelanjutan (Sustainable Finance Action Plan)
REC	renewable energy certificate
RIKEN	Rencana Induk Konservasi Energi Nasional (National Master Plan for Energy Conservation)
RKP	Rencana Kerja Pemerintah (Government Work Plan)
RUEN	Rencana Umum Energi Nasional (National Energy General Plan)
RUED	Rencana Umum Energi Daerah (Regional Energy General Plan)
RUKN	Rencana Umum Ketenagalistrikan Nasional (National Electricity General Plan)
RUKD	Rencana Umum Ketenagalistrikan Daerah (Regional Electricity General Plan)
RUPTL	Rencana Umum Penyediaan Tenaga Listrik (Electricity Business Plan)
RPJMN	Rencana Pembangunan Jangka Menengah Nasional (Medium-term Development Plan)
SDG	sustainable development goal
SIDBI	Small Industries Development Bank of India
SOE	state-owned enterprise
SNI	Standar Nasional Indonesia (Indonesian National Standard)
TPES	total primary energy supply
TWh	terawatt-hour
USD	United States Dollar
VA	volt-ampere
VAT	value-added tax
VRE	variable renewable energy
W	Watt

Executive Summary

The Clean Energy Finance and Investment Policy Review of Indonesia supports Indonesia's efforts to realise a clean energy transition. It provides a comprehensive overview of the current policy environment, highlighting progress and identifying opportunities for strengthening policy interventions that can help to scale up clean energy finance and investment. The following is a summary of the assessment and key recommendations from six policy areas that form the framework for the review and that are elaborated in chapters 2 through 7.

Assessment

The Government of Indonesia is to be commended for signalling from the highest political offices that clean energy is an important part of the country's future. Development of Indonesia's abundant renewable energy and energy efficiency potential are critical to meet the country's sustainable development goals and climate commitments. As other countries and corporates pledge more stringent climate actions, Indonesia will also need to accelerate its clean energy transition if it is to remain an attractive investment destination.

Planning and public governance

The adoption of the low-carbon development initiative (LCDI) as part of the 2020-24 Medium-term National Development Planning (RPJMN) reinforces Indonesia's commitment to achieve clean energy and climate change targets and could help accelerate clean energy investment. Co-ordination amongst government institutions and other key stakeholders on clean energy finance and investment still is a challenge. Streamlining the regulatory environment while improving national and regional governments' capacity and resources would improve the delivery of Indonesia's clean energy targets. The global economic slowdown resulting from the COVID-19 pandemic, which has substantially affected the outlook of the energy sector, also will require an update of Indonesia's energy plan, the RUEN. The revision represents an opportunity to support clean energy development as part of the country's recovery programme. This would support efforts to improve energy access and energy security as well as objectives to build back better.

Regulatory framework

The government has put forward a number of important energy efficiency and renewable energy regulations, including measures such as the country's first energy performance standards and the forthcoming presidential regulation on renewable energy. Reforms such as the Omnibus Law on Job Creation help to provide a clearer policy framework that should improve the business environment for renewable electricity, which to date could be difficult to navigate. Corporate sourcing is an important opportunity to accelerate renewables development, but it is hindered by a number of barriers such as lack of clear regulation on power wheeling. There remain other important gaps in energy efficiency policies, including low coverage of energy performance requirements. Work on standards for 10 new appliance categories is very encouraging, and effort should focus on strengthening existing regulations to reflect market realities.

Investment and competition policy

The passing of the Omnibus Law is an important step to improve the ease of doing business. It intends to repeal a number of overlapping regulations and is already easing some restrictions on foreign direct investment (FDI) as well as streamlining business licensing. The long-term impact on the business environment will depend on implementing regulations in other areas, but this should not come at the expense of environment and sustainability goals. While Indonesia's job creation and industry development goals are commendable, the level of local content requirements also tend to stifle solar and wind markets, as local manufacturers often produce at higher costs than international competitors. This affects the profitability of projects and hinders overall investment.

Investment promotion and facilitation

Support for renewable energy investment (including a number of tax incentives) has improved in recent years, with encouraging signs that the forthcoming Presidential Regulation on renewables will facilitate market growth. To continue momentum in promoting investment in renewable energy, perceived risks such as lack of transparency in power purchase agreement (PPA) pricing and uncertainties around force majeure should also be addressed. Government support and incentives equally do not sufficiently target energy efficiency development. Low capacity in the market to propose bankable projects creates a critical barrier to finance and investment, and more targeted support to stakeholders involved in preparing energy efficiency projects is required.

Financial market policy

The recently released, Phase II (2020-24) of Indonesia's Sustainable Finance Roadmap is a key step in resetting the country's finance ecosystem, strengthening the implementation of environmental, social and governance (ESG) considerations and supporting innovation as well as development of financial services and products. Indonesia's financial institutions face a number of challenges to expanding their sustainable finance portfolios, particularly as this pertains to financing renewable energy and energy efficiency projects. Issues include a lack of familiarity with clean energy projects; insufficient information; high-perceived risks; and lack of suitable financing instruments and funds. The creation of a dedicated green finance facility could help to overcome a number of these barriers, helping to improve access to long-term debt, reduce high transaction costs and lower high interest rates.

Crosscutting issues

The government has promoted clean energy Research & Development (R&D) and innovation, but funding is still below commitment levels, and overall energy R&D activities remain focused on fossil fuel technologies, highlighting a major challenge in breaking dependence on hydrocarbons. Indonesia has also made great strides in skill and capacity development for clean energy technologies, as well as sustainable finance. Yet, these efforts have tilted towards technical and operational aspects, and there remains considerable need to develop financing capacity among project developers while equally improving capacity on structuring and due diligence for clean energy projects.

Table 1. Actions for Indonesia to improve its clean energy finance and investment framework

KEY ACTIONS
Near-term
• Undertake an update of RUEN to reflect the impacts of the COVID-19 pandemic on energy demand and take this opportunity to strengthen renewable energy and energy efficiency targets in the country's recovery programme, implementing actions to build back better. • Take steps to ensure more streamlined policies and regulations under the expected presidential regulation on renewable energy, including streamlining PPAs and addressing regulatory gaps for net-metering and power wheeling arrangements. Also, increase efforts to facilitate land acquisition (e.g. drawing from Indonesia's toll road and India's Solar Parks experiences) as land access remains one of the longest lead items for renewable energy projects. • Consider expanding use of financing products like the Kredit Usaha Rakyat, which provides a guarantee scheme and subsidised interest rates for small businesses to help overcome barriers such as high collateral requirements. These types of products can make it easier for businesses to establish or expand their clean energy offerings. • Undertake a detailed market assessment of financing needs and challenges as well as opportunities to identify and scale up suitable financing instruments that meet the needs of the market. Also, consider the use of the SDG Indonesia One Fund to support guarantee schemes aimed at de-risking projects to help project developers overcome collateral requirements while building experience and confidence among financial institutions with clean energy projects. • Expand training programmes to integrate aspects of financial and business development for clean energy projects, including the design of bankable and internationally recognised PPAs as well as development and implementation of public-private partnership models to encourage market growth.
Medium-to-long term
• Develop clear implementing regulations and guidelines for PLN to guarantee a well-functioning procurement process and fair competition in the market. • Plan a transparent shift in coming years to public, competitive tenders to procure renewables, creating predictable and fair processes that attract investors. These have proven particularly successful globally to bringing down the cost of renewable energy. • Develop clear regulatory frameworks and market signals to enable innovative finance and market-based mechanisms such as energy savings performance contracting, open and tradeable energy attribution certificates, and energy-as-a-service models. • Improve clean energy finance and investment data availability to increase transparency and build investor confidence in the market. This can be achieved by setting up monitoring and reporting protocols as well as supporting capacity building among financial institutions. • Establish project finance structures for clean energy projects through collaborations between OJK and commercial banks, standardising contract terms that can be widely replicated.

Table 2. Opportunities to enhance development assistance

KEY ACTIONS
• Assistance from the international community can play a key role in supporting Indonesia to accelerate its clean energy transition and achieving sustainable development goals. The development community is already very active in providing technical assistance and in financing clean energy projects; however support in areas that can have a large multiplier effect will enable more clean energy entrepreneurs and mobilise private capital. • Consultations with project developers, financial institutions and other stakeholders identified strengthening regulatory frameworks as a priority to unleash Indonesia's renewable energy and energy efficiency potential. Development co-operation should enhance efforts to support policy makers in designing and implementing policies to facilitate land access, streamline power purchase agreements, design renewable energy auctions and expand energy efficiency regulation. • Training and capacity development was also highlighted as another priority area and development assistance could allocate additional resources for technical assistance to expand both past programmes such as supporting certification of investment grade energy auditors and develop new programmes aimed at improving financial learning within the energy efficiency and renewable energy sectors, as well as clean energy knowledge within financial institutions. Such training and capacity building efforts should also include developing solutions that can be easily replicated or standardised to facilitate project preparation and due diligence by investors as well as knowledge transfer programmes through partnerships with development partners and foreign investors. • Development funds could also be targeted to support blended finance mechanisms (such as the SDG Indonesia One Fund) that can mobilise private capital from both domestic and international institutional investors as well as commercial lending for clean energy projects. This will need to address not only de-risking of projects to mobilise direct investments but also providing technical assistance to support project preparation as well as setting up suitable investment vehicles that can allow a larger number of investors to deploy capital (e.g. through aggregation and securitisation of projects to meet scale requirements particularly for larger international investors). • Finally, assistance can be targeted at supporting Indonesia to improve clean energy finance and investment data availability and to develop monitoring and evaluation tools. Significant gaps remain in the availability of consistent and reliable renewable energy project performance and detailed resource data that financial institutions require for project due diligence and risk assessment. Tools to help monitor and evaluate energy savings are also needed to support development of the energy efficiency market.

1 Introduction and recent trends in clean energy finance and investment

This chapter examines key trends related to clean energy finance and investment in Indonesia. It provides a brief overview of key macroeconomic, investment and social developments in Indonesia over recent decades. It analyses key trends in energy demand and energy efficiency, as well as in the power sector, highlighting progress against clean energy and climate targets. The chapter also provides a snapshot of Indonesia's clean energy market, looking at recent trends in the cost of clean energy technologies, as well as finance and investment flows.

Introduction

The OECD *Clean Energy Finance and Investment Policy Review of Indonesia* provides a comprehensive assessment of Indonesia's clean energy finance and investment regulations and policies, progress and opportunities for improvements, in a range of key policy areas discussed across its seven chapters. The *Review*'s analysis builds on the OECD's extensive experience undertaking similar reviews such as the *Green Growth Policy Review of Indonesia 2019* (OECD, 2019[1]) the *Investment Policy Review of Indonesia 2020* (OECD, 2020[2]) *and the Economic Surveys 2021* (OECD, 2021[3]), as well as a rich corpus of OECD work on green finance and investment (see Box 1.1). The report reflects latest developments that occurred before 16 April 2021.

Building on strong stakeholder engagement, the OECD undertook numerous consultations and interviews with a range of relevant stakeholders (e.g. government institutions, commercial banks, clean energy businesses and international organisations) in 2019-20 in order to inform the development of the Review's Assessment and Recommendations. Most notably, an extended virtual *Review* mission was organised throughout October-November 2020, consisting of five focused group discussions in important areas (Corporate Sourcing; Skills and Capacity Development; Renewable Energy Investment in Indonesia's Eastern Islands; Energy efficiency Financing; and Green Finance Facility) and three consultation meetings with OECD local delegations, financial institutions and clean energy businesses.

The virtual format benefited from input from around 20 international experts and mobilised a significant number of government officials, project developers, financial institutions, ambassadors and local delegations of OECD member countries, involving over 650 participants. In addition to consultations, a comprehensive Policy Questionnaire was completed and returned by 10 government institutions and the Indonesian national power utility to inform the *Review*.

Box 1.1. Analytical framework of the Clean Energy Finance and Investment Policy Review

The *Review of Indonesia* builds on an extensive corpus of OECD work on green finance and investment that constitutes the main analytical framework of the Review. Specifically, the 2015 Policy Guidance for Investment in Clean Energy Infrastructure provides a starting point for the review structure that was augmented with energy efficiency finance considerations along with aspects of clean energy policy, sustainable finance, skills development and innovation, among others.

Table 1.1. Analytical framework of the Review

	Examples of questions/issues for policy makers' consideration	Overall objective
1. Recent trends in clean energy finance and investment	• Key trends in renewable and energy efficiency development and investment;	Provide an overview of the state of play of clean energy finance and investment.
2. Planning and public governance	• Multi-level governance and policy coordination • Comprehensive clean energy target setting • Role of regional governments	Clear near and long-term clean energy targets are central to the clean energy transition. Strong and well co-ordinated institutions create the right enabling environments for clean energy markets to flourish.
3. Regulatory framework	• Energy efficiency regulation • Renewable energy regulation • Electricity market design	Regulatory quality and policy coherence are two critical dimensions in building investor confidence and the right frameworks.
4. Investment and competition policy	• Non-discrimination of foreign versus domestic investors • Contract enforcement • Competition authority • Public-private partnerships (corporate governance)	The quality of investment policies directly influences the decisions of all investors. Transparency, property protection and non-discrimination underpin efforts to create a sound investment environment. Effective competition policy can help improve economic efficiency, contribute to conditions conducive to new investment and transmit the wider benefits of investment to society.
5. Investment promotion and facilitation	• Carbon pricing and removal of fossil-fuel subsidies • Policy incentives for investment • Licensing	Investment promotion and facilitation measures, including incentives, can be effective instruments to attract investment provided they aim to correct for market failures and are developed in a way that can leverage the strong points of a country's investment environment.
6. Financial Market Policy	• Strengthened local financial markets • Access to clean energy finance • Sustainable finance regulation • Green finance instruments • Role of development finance • Institutional innovation	Well-functioning financial markets can strongly contribute to enhancing investment opportunities for both domestic and foreign investors. Sustainable finance frameworks are needed to transition financial markets towards green finance products and investment practices. Coherent development finance is key to correct market failures, catalyse private investment and support the development of clean energy market.
7. Cross-cutting issues	• Regional integration • RD&D and innovation • Training and skills development • Gender diversity	Achieving a clean energy transition will require regional collaboration, support for developing research capabilities, innovation and skills development as well as targeted programmes to empower women and improve gender diversity.

Key economic trends

Indonesia's economy has grown steadily over the last decades

Indonesia's macroeconomic environment has been robust over the last decade and half. Despite a slowdown since the end of the 2003-11 commodity cycle, real Gross Domestic Product (GDP) has grown at a sustained 5.5% per annum on average over 2005-19 – a rate on par with the Philippines and higher than Malaysia and Thailand. This helped nearly double Indonesia's GDP per capita over the period and place it in the middle range of regional peers (e.g. Malaysia, the Philippines, Thailand and Viet Nam). At 33% of GDP, investment level has been a key driver of GDP growth over the last few decades and has been high by comparison with regional peers (see Figure 1.1).

Ambitious infrastructure plans under the current administration, efforts to improve the business environment and growing (albeit fluctuating) global commodity prices have been key drivers of investment growth in the country.

Figure 1.1. Investment and GDP per capita, 2019

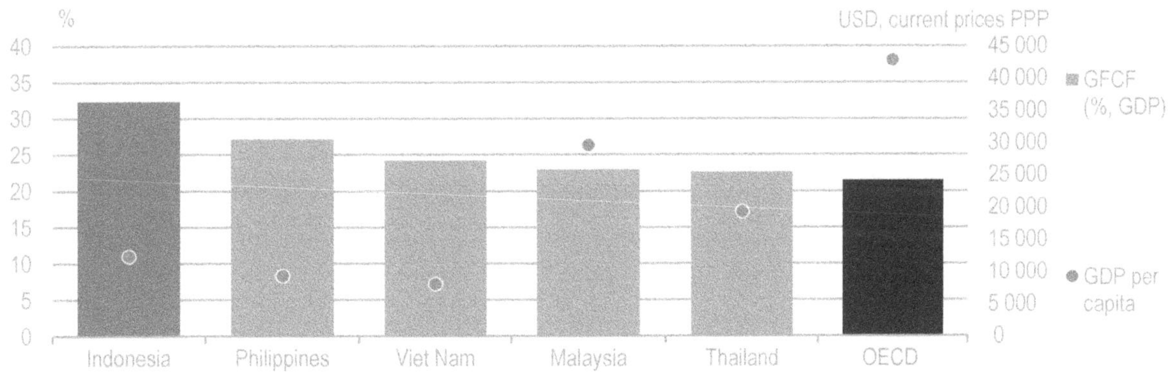

Note: a) Investment is measured by Gross Fixed Capital Formation (GFCF).
Source: OECD (2020), *National Accounts Statistics* (database); World Bank (2020), *World Development Indicators* (database).

StatLink https://stat.link/n8pxys

Nevertheless, Indonesia's economy was hit hard by the global COVID-19 pandemic causing the economy to enter into recession (-2.43% per annum based on OECD data) in 2020, the first time since the Asian financial crisis. The pandemic has had deep effects, causing a spike in unemployment and poverty rates as well as depressing investment and domestic consumption amid growing uncertainties. While the economy is slowly recovering, as domestic and global economies gradually re-open and the Indonesian government rolls out its COVID stimulus packages, socio-economic consequences are likely to be long lasting. By end of 2021, the OECD projects that GDP would be 10% below where it should have been under a business-as-usual scenario (OECD, 2021[3]).

Inwards foreign direct investment (FDI) has historically contributed little to overall investment in Indonesia, but has a great potential to support Indonesia's economic recovery. Most notably, FDI can bring much-needed financing, modern technologies and organisational practices, access to global markets, and improved working and environmental conditions (OECD, 2021[3]). Yet, in spite of an increase over much of the last two decades, FDI inflows have been declining since 2016 (both in absolute and relative terms) against the backdrop of rising trade tensions and protectionism, China's economic slowdown, as well as a tightening US monetary policy that caused significant capital outflows throughout 2018. Strengthening the enabling conditions will thus be key to scale up FDI (see (OECD, 2020[2]) for more detailed information on FDI trends; **see Chapter 4**).

Indonesia has set a high level of ambition for its economic development. After falling short of the 7% GDP annual growth target over 2015-19, Indonesia renewed its economic development goals through defining a new GDP growth target range of 5.2-6.2% per annum over 2020-24. While more realistic, the current COVID pandemic could make this target hard to attain. Looking forward, the country has defined the "Vision of Indonesia 2045", which, most notably, sets the goal to rank Indonesia among the world's top five largest economies by 2045 (from 16th position in 2019).

Growth has improved livelihoods but its fruits remain unevenly distributed

Indonesia has made remarkable progress in improving its citizens' livelihoods and access to electricity. Helped by a near doubling of GDP per capita, Indonesia has slashed poverty rates two-fold since the start of the millennium and has seen the emergence of a dynamic middle class now totalling around 50 million people (out of 264 million inhabitants in total). These improvements have been accompanied by a considerable increase in access to electricity, with the electrification rate sharply increasing from a mere 53% in 2000 to 99.20% in 2020, helped by the provision of rooftop solar lamps, the rural electrification programme as well as other national fast-track programmes for power infrastructure (**see Chapter 2**). However, this ratio remains unequal across islands and around 10 million people continue to lack access to electricity (OECD, 2019[1]). Power outages also remain frequent throughout the archipelago (see Figure 1.2).

Figure 1.2. System average interruption duration and frequency indices, 2020

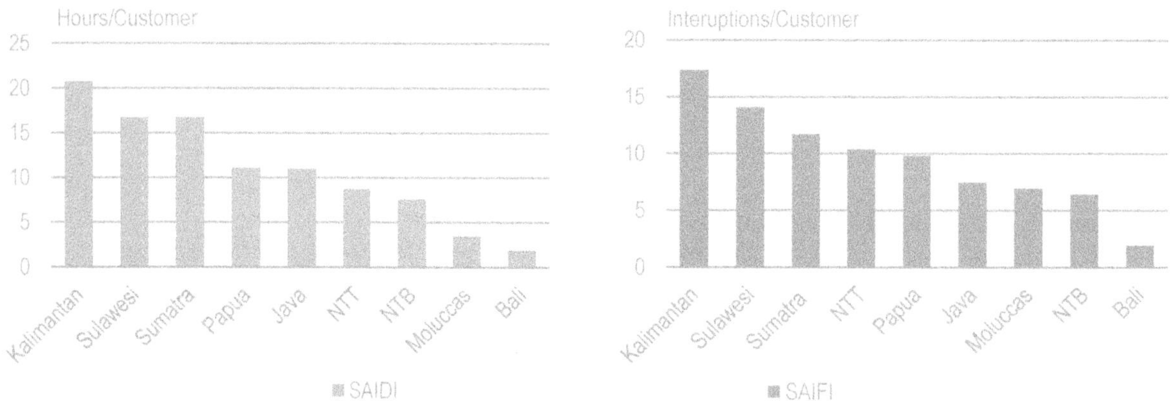

Note: Eastern islands include the Moluccas, NTT (East Nusa Tenggara), Papua and Sulawesi; the System Average Duration Interruption Index (SAIDI) measures the duration of electricity outages per customer in a year; the System Average Frequency Interruption Index measures the number of interruptions per customer in a year. NTB= West Nusa Tenggara.
Source: MEMR and PLN statistics.

StatLink https://stat.link/m5vtkn

Despite this progress, there remains significant discrepancies across and within the country's islands. The island of Java alone concentrates around half of Indonesia's population, 70% of its manufacturing base, and generates close to 60% of the country's GDP. Levels of electricity access as well as infrastructure development on the island are also among the highest in the country. By contrast, the country's eastern islands (e.g. East Nusa Tenggara, Moluccas or Papua) are far less populated and economically developed. These present far lower levels of access to electricity than other islands and have tremendous infrastructure needs, in turn, adding to logistical costs (Oxford Business Group, 2018[4]).

Key energy demand and efficiency trends

Energy efficiency is key to rationalise energy consumption and lower emissions

Indonesia's economy overall is dominated by low-energy intensity sectors. The low-energy intense services sector accounts for around two thirds of value added and has been growing steadily (BPS, 2021[5]). In 2017, tourism accounted for around 4% of GDP and, while it has been among the hardest hit sectors by the COVID-19 crisis, is expected to expand further over the longer term, as Indonesia aims to create "10 new Balis[1]". This could open up market opportunities for clean energy, especially in the hospitality sector (OECD, 2020[6]). Equally, the country's manufacturing sector, which accounts for roughly 20% of GDP (down from around 30% in the early 2000s), remains overall dominated by low-energy intensive sub-sectors – e.g. machinery and transport equipment, food, beverage and tobacco (BPS, 2021[5]). Partly as a result, Indonesia's energy intensity (in terms of energy consumption and supply on both a GDP and per-capita basis) is much lower than that of Thailand and Viet Nam, as well as ASEAN countries as a whole.

Nevertheless, Indonesia's energy demand (in terms of total final consumption, TFC) still represents a third of the region's total and has been growing fast over the last two decades, driven by fast urbanisation, and population and economic growth. In particular, electricity demand has been a key driver of energy demand growth. Over 2005-18, it has more than doubled and could further double by 2030 under a business-as-usual (BaU) scenario; under such a scenario, electricity would even overtake oil as the largest source of TFC by 2050 (DEN, 2019[7]). To satisfy growing electricity demand until 2030, the General National Energy Plan (the RUEN) projects that around 7.5 GW of additional capacity will be needed annually (a third of which would be sourced from renewables), although this number could be an over-estimate (**see Chapter 2**) (MEMR, 2017[8]).

Improving energy efficiency will thus be critical to rationalise fast-increasing energy consumption and hence, power generation capacity expansion plans. Energy efficiency measures will be particularly important in the building sector (covering residential and commercial end-uses) given this sector accounts for two-thirds of electricity consumption (**see Chapter 3**). Energy efficiency will also be important in order to reduce greenhouse gas (GHG) emissions, which have been on the rise throughout much of the last decade. This is of particular importance given that energy use became the largest emitter in 2017 (in large part stemming from fossil fuel-dominated power generation and industry) and has doubled since 2000 (OECD, 2019[1]; Ministry of Environment and Forestry, 2019[9]).

The residential and industry sectors are amongst the largest energy consumers

In 2018, energy use from the residential sector was the largest source of TFC, although this is skewed by the inclusion of traditional biomass (mainly biomass for cooking) (see Figure 1.3 & Figure 1.4). Yet, between 2005-18, residential energy use decreased by roughly 37%, thanks partly to significant energy efficiency gains from government-led programmes to transition from traditional use of biomass and kerosene to LPG for cooking – as 77% of the residential energy consumption is used for that purpose (IEA, 2017[10]; DEN, 2019[7]). Shifts to electricity from other fuel types (driven by a rising rate of electrification) have also contributed to efficiency gains, as have government-led initiatives to shift to more efficient equipment, such as compact fluorescent lamps and LEDs.

Electricity demand from the residential sector has been on the rise, led by population growth, a rising number of dwellings, growing floor area and increasing ownership of household appliances. At the same time, end-use electrification and growing demand for appliances and other electrical equipment, such as air conditioners, will increasingly influence electricity load curves (e.g. during evening hours), as is the case in other countries. This is particularly likely in Indonesia's thriving urban centres, where household purchasing power and energy consumption is typically higher but where on-site or local electricity generation is less common.

Figure 1.3. TFC by sector and industry sub-sector, 2018

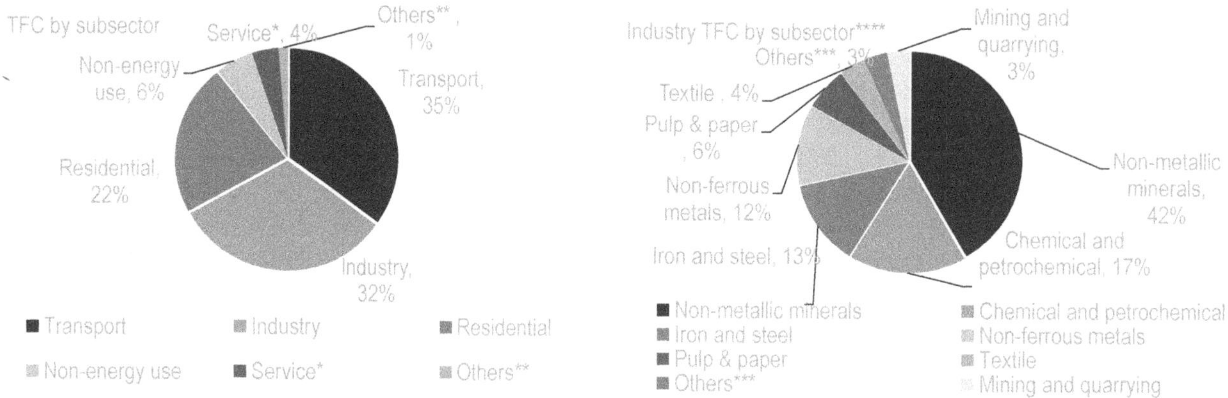

Note: * "Services" covers both commercial and public services; ** "Others" includes unspecified TFC as well as the agriculture sector; *** "Others" includes food and tobacco (2%) while machinery and construction accounts for the remainder; **** Unspecified industry TFC represents more than half of the total and is not included in the figure.
Source: IEA (2020), World Energy Balances (database).

StatLink https://stat.link/joab59

Figure 1.4. TFC by fuel type for selected sectors, 2005-18

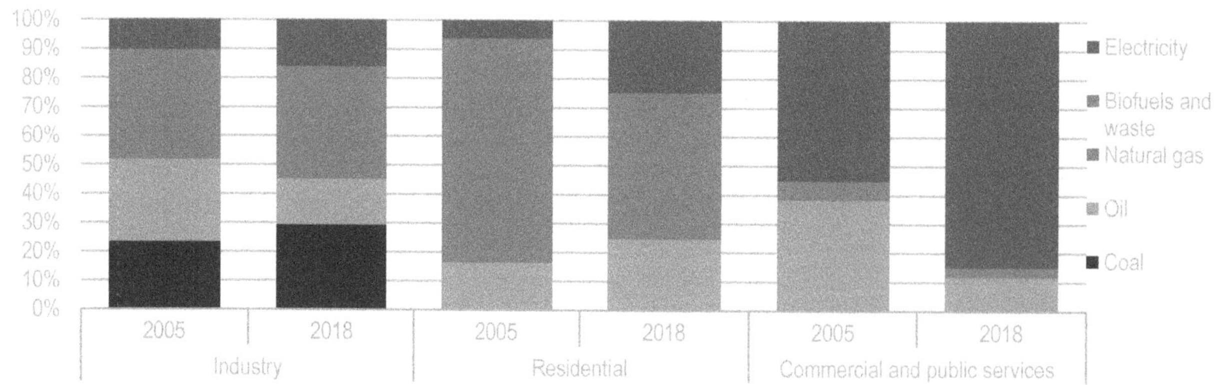

Note: "Biofuels and waste" in the residential mostly covers traditional biomass (most of which is used for cooking).
Source: IEA (2020), World Energy Balances (database).

StatLink https://stat.link/9gfd3c

Energy use in the industry sector has grown at a lower rate than GDP resulting in an improvement (i.e. decrease) of the sector's energy intensity. Energy demand growth from the industry sector has been driven by non-ferrous metals, pulp and paper, chemical and petrochemical, iron and steel and cement (non-metallic minerals) subsectors. Despite their relatively lower contributions to the manufacturing sector's value added, these subsectors accounted for three quarters of industry's total energy use (see Figure 1.3). Given plans to revive Indonesia's manufacturing base, the industry sector's energy consumption is projected to continue increasing and even exceed that of the transport sector by 2030 (DEN, 2019[7]).

Despite a good start, progress towards energy efficiency targets has weakened as of late

National data show that energy intensity decreased (i.e. improved) over 2015-17, exceeding Indonesia's 1% annual reduction target to 2025 (with 2015 a reference year). However, the trend has reversed over 2017-19, in part led by an increase in the transportation sector, largely falling short of reduction targets (IESR, 2021[11]). Hence, Indonesia should continue strengthening energy efficiency measures in all end uses to remain on track to reach targets. In this endeavour, tapping the energy reduction potential of cities will be determinant, as they concentrate more than half of the population and a significant share of economic activity, with the 20 largest cities alone generating close to half of the country's GDP (IEA, 2016[12]). Some cities are already leading the way, the city of Jakarta being a case in point, as the city is committed to reducing energy consumption by 30% by 2030 compared to BaU (OECD, 2019[1]).

Power sector trends

Fossil fuels continue to play a key role in Indonesia's power sector

Indonesia's power system remains dominated by fossil fuels, and more particularly, coal – unsurprising as the country boasts some of the world's largest coal reserves (see Figure 1.5). In 2019, most of Indonesia's power capacity (around 67 GW) was sourced from coal (50%), gas (roughly 30%) and diesel (roughly 7%). Fossil fuel power capacity addition increased fast over 2005-19, with coal power capacity more than tripling, that of gas doubling while that of diesel increased by roughly 50%. If coal and gas represented the largest share of installed capacity at the national level (and most of western Indonesia) in 2019, diesel represented the largest share of power capacity in the eastern part of the country as well as the island of Kalimantan (see Figure 1.6). This is mostly explained by the pervasiveness of diesel generators on these islands to make up for a still limited access to the grid.

More fossil fuel-based capacity is likely to come on board in the coming years, to satisfy growing electricity demand. Of the 56.6 GW of additional capacity planned for development between 2019-28, most would be sourced from coal (around half) and gas (22%) while only a third would either come from large hydro power plants (17%) or non-large hydro renewables (13%) (PLN, 2019[13]). Were all planned coal plants to be operational by 2028, their emission trajectory would completely deviate off a 2°C pathway as early as 2022 and their emissions' level would double by 2028 (IESR, 2021[11]).

Figure 1.5. Installed power capacity per fuel type, 2005 & 19

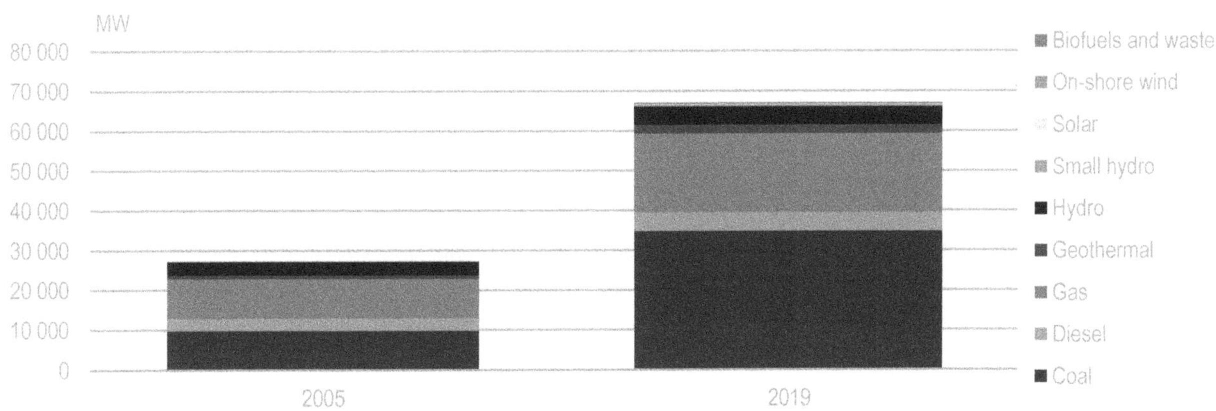

Source: OECD based on MEMR and PLN Statistics.

StatLink https://stat.link/caqytp

Figure 1.6. Installed power capacity by fuel type and island, 2019

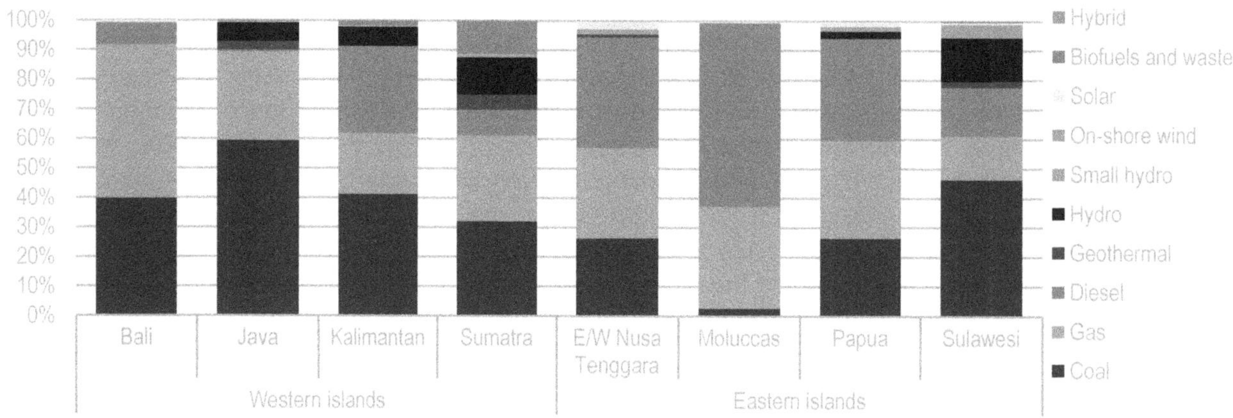

Note: E/W=East & West. Java and Bali have an integrated grid network, thus data for Bali do not necessarily refer to power capacity physically located in Bali (e.g. Bali has no coal or gas plants but uses the installed power capacity of coal and gas plants on Java island).
Source: OECD based on MEMR and PLN statistics.

StatLink https://stat.link/sifvk1

Given plans to continue expanding fossil fuel capacity, Indonesia faces high risks of locking in emissions and stranding assets. Despite some efforts to modernise the existing (albeit relatively young) fleet, most coal-fired power plants continue to use and invest in inefficient sub-critical technology. Carbon capture, use and storage (CCUS) also remains at a very early phase of adoption with no commercial CCUS project developed to date (Oxford Business Group, 2018[4]; IEA, 2020[14]). As a result, Indonesia's power generation system is one of the world's most carbon intensive and accounts for a large share of the energy sector's GHG emissions. Coal-fired power plants are also a major source of air pollution in the country and considered a direct cause of numerous non-communicable diseases (Sanchez and Luan, 2018[15]; OECD, 2019[1]). In the face of these issues, Indonesia urgently needs to limit coal capacity to the absolute minimum, ratchet up standards for existing coal plants and accelerate the decommissioning of such plants (well before a 30-year lifetime) in order to attain emission reduction targets under the Paris Agreements and improve air quality (IESR, 2021[11]). Revising plans to add coal capacity is also important to reduce the risk of stranding assets; indeed, under a Paris Agreement compliant scenario, Indonesia's coal power owners risk losing close to USD 35 billion in stranded coal assets (Carbon Tracker, 2018[16]).

Renewables deployment continues lagging behind

Despite a timid increase over the last decade and a half, Indonesia's renewable power potential remains largely untapped (see Figure 1.7). Indonesia boasts remarkable renewable energy power potential – from 18 GW for tidal energy to 208 GW for solar, and its geothermal and hydropower potential ranks among the largest in the world. While this potential is technical in nature and not all of it might be economically viable, Indonesia has hitherto only exploited a negligible share of it. Indeed, as of 2019, Indonesia has utilised less than 2% of its total renewable energy potential, resulting in non-large hydro renewable power representing 3.5% of total installed capacity and less than 5% of total 2018 electricity generation. Power storage solutions are also at an early phase of deployment, despite the role they can play in supporting increased variable renewable integration as well as Indonesia's considerable storage potential (e.g. through pumped-storage hydro or green hydrogen).

Figure 1.7. Renewable technical potential and actual utilisation rate, 2019

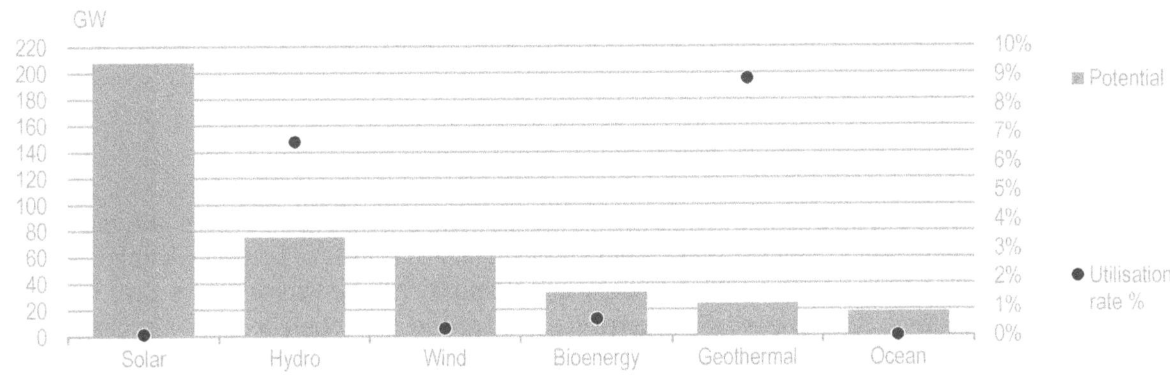

Note: GW=Giga watts.
Source: OECD based on MEMR and PLN statistics.

StatLink https://stat.link/2ye5rq

Figure 1.8. Renewable energy installed capacity and targets, 2019 & 25

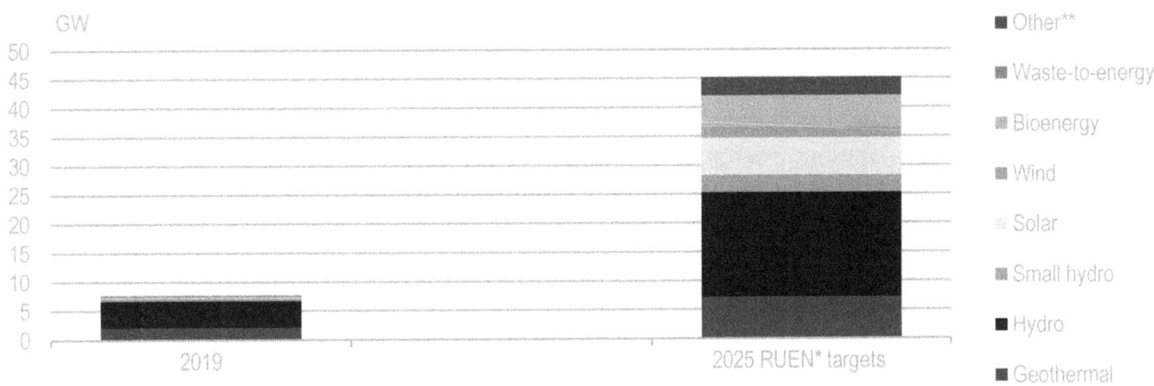

Note: *RUEN (Rencana Umum Energi Nasional or General Plan for National Energy) defines Indonesia's objectives for energy development over 2025-50, including for renewable energy; ** "Other" includes diesel mixed with biofuels and ocean energy (tidal, thermal energy).
Sources: OECD based on MEMR and PLN statistics as well as Presidential Regulation No. 22/2017 Concerning General Planning for National Energy.

StatLink https://stat.link/owqplx

As mentioned before, renewable power capacity increased since 2005, but at a relatively slow pace. There has been roughly 2 GW of (non-hydro) renewable capacity added in 2005-19 (see Figure 1.5), which compares with 8 GW in Thailand or 5.5 GW in Viet Nam over the same period (IRENA, 2021[17]). Geothermal capacity largely led this increase (nearly 1 GW), driven by the development (or extension) of large-scale projects, among the largest in the world, mostly on Sumatra and Java islands. Mini and micro hydro (i.e. less than 10 MW) installed capacity remains relatively small (around 326 MW) but increased exponentially (although from a low level) since 2005, with numerous projects springing up across Indonesia (mainly in Java, Sumatra and Sulawesi). More recently, variable renewable energy deployment has started to pick up, albeit marginally. In 2018, two utility-scale on-shore wind projects started operation (72 MW Tolo power and 75 MW Sidrap wind farms in the South Sulawesi province). Similarly, four 7 MW utility-scale solar projects in Lombok and Sulawesi started operation in 2018. The country is also developing a 145 MW floating solar project (the largest in Southeast Asia) in West Java, whose construction phase began in early 2021 (IEEFA, 2020[18]). While these are encouraging developments, more efforts will be required to attain targets defined in the RUEN by 2025 (Figure 1.8; **see Chapter 2**).

Clean energy investment trends

Coal continues to represent the bulk of power investment

Fossil fuels dominate Indonesia's power investment, which has been on the rise over the last years. Power generation has led the increase in power investment although, in 2019, 80% of power generation spending went to coal power plants; in other words, for every dollar spent on renewables, more than three were spent on coal. Public and State-owned Enterprise (SOE) finance has been a considerable source of funding for fossil fuels, much more so than for renewables over 2016-19. Private finance, by contrast, provided around half of renewable power plant funding over the same period (**see Chapter 6**). These trends are not in line with Indonesia's ambitions under the Paris Agreement. They also greatly contrast with global trends in renewable power generation investment, which has largely outpaced trends in fossil fuel in numerous countries over the last few years (IEA, 2020[19]). Equally, while a handful of traditional fossil fuel corporations are increasingly showing interest in developing renewable projects (some having already started), most are yet to commit to carbon neutrality, here again, contrasting with global trends (Financial Times, 2020[20]; IESR, 2021[11]).

Network investment has been on the rise over the last decade, albeit at a slower rate than for power generation. SOE finance represented the main source of funding for such investment, as private actors are limited to investing in that segment of the power market. Despite the increase, around 50% more spending on networks would be needed over the medium term under the *International Energy Agency* (IEA)'s Sustainable Development Scenario to connect the expanding power fleet, particularly renewables as these are usually faster to build out than network infrastructure (IEA, 2020[19]). Hence, allowing more private investment will be key to develop Indonesia's power network infrastructure (**see Chapter 7**).

More renewable energy investment is needed to help meet growing demand and achieve targets

Based on official data, renewable energy investment has been sluggish over the last decade. To achieve the renewable power target by 2025 (excluding large hydro), around USD 44.2 billion[2] of cumulated power generation investment would be needed (IESR, 2019[21]). Yet, levels of investment in renewable energy (excluding large hydro) achieved over the last years have been far below that level (see Figure 1.9), largely due to an unconducive and fast-changing regulatory framework for renewable energy investment (**see Chapters 3 and 5**).

Geothermal dominates the market for dispatchable renewable technology, with a market potential estimated at USD 21 billion over 2020-25 (UK Foreign & Commonwealth Office, 2018[22]). Over the last two decades, the sector has successfully attracted a significant number of large foreign developers as well as engineering, procurement and construction contractors (in large part from Japan and Southeast Asia) thanks to some regulatory improvements (CPI, 2015[23]). Alongside well-established and large local independent power producers (IPPs), these foreign investors have participated in the development and acquisition of some of the world's largest geothermal projects (e.g. 330 MW Sarulla project in South Sumatra and 227 MW Wayang Windu project in West Java). By contrast, investment in mini-micro hydro as well as biomass projects have largely been driven by small local IPPs, which, however, have suffered from low creditworthiness and capacity issues (**see Chapter 4**).

Figure 1.9. Annual clean energy investment flows, 2011-19

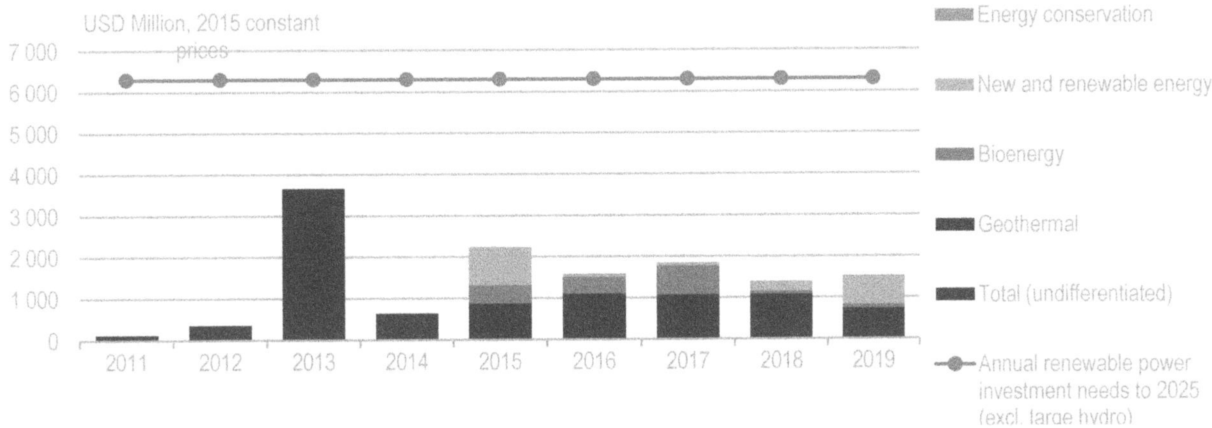

Note: "New and renewable energy" includes all renewables (aside from geothermal, bioenergy and large hydro). Investment needs were estimated for the period 2015-25 based on (IESR, 2019[21]). Only data for 2017-19 include investment in energy conservation (which excludes public street lighting).
Source: OECD calculations based on MEMR annual performance reports from 2011-19.

StatLink https://stat.link/dfkvq6

In comparison, Indonesia's utility-scale solar and wind sectors remain at an earlier phase of development. Current market size for utility-scale solar and wind is relatively small and still dominated by a few large foreign IPPs (mostly from Southeast Asia and Australia). Over 2020-25, both technologies have a market potential estimated at USD 769.3 million for solar PV (of which USD 675.5 million was for utility scale solar PV) and USD 1.5 billion for on-shore wind (UK Foreign & Commonwealth Office, 2018[22]). To service the small but increasing variable renewables market, Indonesia has started to develop a small local manufacturing base mainly focused on assembling imported components for solar and wind technologies. In the case of solar, however, panels assembled locally are relatively more expensive than those sold by leading Chinese manufacturers, in part due to local content rules (**see Chapter 4**; (IEEFA, 2019[24]; IESR, 2019[25])).

While the investment gap remains large, renewables are increasingly becoming cost competitive

Most renewable technologies can already be developed and operated at lower costs than gas, diesel and even coal technologies, as shown in (IESR, 2019[26]). This is also shored up by tariffs in power purchase agreement (PPA) contracts signed in 2018-21, as shown in Table 1.2. While this is encouraging, investment costs[3] of some of these technologies remain high by international comparison. For instance, investment costs for utility-scale solar (1158 USD/kW in 2019) and on-shore wind (1400-2000 USD/kW in 2018) are higher than in leading Asian markets such as India (618 USD/kW for solar PV in 2019) or China (1170 USD/kW for on-shore wind in 2018). Persisting regulatory bottlenecks prevent Indonesia from achieving the outstanding investment cost reductions observed globally for solar PV (between 66-85% in major markets over 2010-19) and on-shore wind (between 25-66% in major markets over the last three decades) (IRENA, 2019[27]; IRENA, 2020[28]). This, in turn, constrains renewable technologies' competitiveness compared to fossil fuel technologies. According to IESR, achieving a 20% reduction in investment costs of utility-scale solar, on-shore wind and geothermal could lower their Levelised Cost of Electricity (LCOE) by 15.3%, 16.5% and 19.2% respectively (IESR, 2019[25]).

Table 1.2. PPA tariffs of selected technologies, 2018-21

	Capacity range (MW)	Price ranges (USD cents/kW)	
		Min.	Max.
Coal mine mouth	>100-150	5.17	5.54
	>150-300	-	4.86
Coal	>10-50	6.92	9.05
	>50-100	7.02	7.10
	>100-300	-	4.09
Gas	>10	6.15	6.19
Geothermal	>10-50	9.4	11.35
	>50-100	8.1	13
	>100	4.94	9.47
Biomass	<10	6.68	11.61
Mini hydro	<10	6.51	10.52
Solar	>10	5.71	10
Wind	>10-50	-	12.51
	>50-100	-	10.48

Note: Tariff set out in PPAs can be higher than project's actual levelised cost of electricity. kW=Kilo Watt.
Source: MEMR and PLN.

The domestic market for energy efficiency has ample room for expansion

Investment in energy efficiency projects has not yet taken off and remains much lower than that of renewables. For instance, investment grade audits (IGAs) conducted in a small sample of manufacturers and buildings in 2016-18, indicated an energy efficiency investment potential for those end-users at around IDR 290 billion (USD 20 million). However, only a tenth of that was actually invested over the same period (MEMR, 2020[29]). The industry and commercial building sectors are the largest recipients of energy efficiency spending; in 2020, according to official data, these represented 80% and 19.5% of total energy efficiency spending respectively while public building accounted for the remainder.

Indonesia's energy efficiency businesses continue to face significant challenges. The majority of energy efficiency project developers (including energy services companies or ESCOs) in Indonesia are small engineering firms providing energy audits and other services (APEC, 2017[30]). Few have the capacity to undertake IGAs, resulting in a limited number of IGAs being conducted annually, with some of them being hardly bankable due to considerable quality issues (e.g. in projecting cash flows from energy savings) (MEMR, 2020[29]). The few existing ESCOs in the market also face significant hurdles in accessing debt finance, with stringent collateral requirements from commercial banks (which do not accept cash flows from energy savings as collateral) being a key barrier (**see Chapter 6**). Overall, subsidised electricity tariffs and low compliance levels with energy management regulation (**see Chapter 3**) tend to constrain demand for energy efficiency and limit market expansion opportunities. Indeed, in the commercial building sector, electricity makes up to 15% of operation costs meaning that savings in the range of 10-35% are generally perceived as insignificant to implement projects (APEC, 2017[30]).

References

APEC (2017), *Energy Efficiency Finance in Indonesia Current State Barriers and Potential Next Steps*, https://apec.org/Publications/2017/10/Energy-Efficiency-Finance-in-Indonesia-Current-State-Barriers-and-Potential-Next-Steps (accessed on 8 April 2020). [30]

BPS (2021), *Economic and trade*, Badan Pusat Statistik (National Statistics Agency), https://www.bps.go.id/ (accessed on 2 March 2021). [5]

Carbon Tracker (2018), *Economic and financial risks of coal power in Indonesia*, https://carbontracker.org/reports/economic-and-financial-risks-of-coal-power-in-indonesia-vietnam-and-the-philippines/ (accessed on 15 April 2020). [16]

CPI (2015), *Using Private Finance to Accelerate Geothermal Deployment: Sarulla Geothermal Power Plant, Indonesia*, http://www.climatepolicyinitiative.org (accessed on 16 April 2020). [23]

DEN (2019), *Indonesia Energy Outlook 2019*. [7]

Financial Times (2020), *US oil producers begin to follow Europe with emissions pledges*, https://www.ft.com/content/612e7440-2cc9-425f-8759-631a8194e2d1 (accessed on 3 March 2021). [20]

IEA (2020), *Attracting private investment to fund sustainable recoveries: The case of Indonesia's power sector*, IEA, Paris, https://www.iea.org/reports/attracting-private-investment-to-fund-sustainable-recoveries-the-case-of-indonesias-power-sector (accessed on 19 January 2021). [19]

IEA (2020), *World Energy Investment 2020*, International Energy Agency, Paris, https://dx.doi.org/10.1787/6f552938-en. [14]

IEA (2017), *Energy Efficiency 2017*, International Energy Agency, Paris, https://dx.doi.org/10.1787/9789264284234-en. [10]

IEA (2016), *Energy Technology Perspectives 2016*, OECD Publishing, Paris, https://dx.doi.org/10.1787/energy_tech-2016-en. [12]

IEEFA (2020), *Indonesia begins construction of 145MW Cirata floating solar project*, Institute for Energy Economics & Financial Analysis, https://ieefa.org/indonesia-begins-construction-of-145mw-cirata-floating-solar-project/ (accessed on 16 April 2021). [18]

IEEFA (2019), *Indonesia's solar policies – designed to fail?*, http://ieefa.org/ieefa-report-indonesias-solar-policies-designed-to-fail/ (accessed on 6 March 2019). [24]

IEEFA (n.d.), *Indonesia moves forward with plans for 145MW floating solar project*, https://ieefa.org/indonesia-moves-forward-with-plans-for-145mw-floating-solar-project/ (accessed on 20 March 2020). [31]

IESR (2021), *Indonesia Energy Transition Outlook 2021 - Tracking Progress of Energy Transition in Indonesia*, https://iesr.or.id/pustaka/indonesia-energy-transition-outlook-2021 (accessed on 2 March 2021). [11]

IESR (2019), *Kebutuhan Investasi Energi di Indonesia (English translation: Energy investment needs in Indonesia)*, http://iesr.or.id/pustaka/kebutuhan-investasi-energi-indonesia/ (accessed on 3 April 2020). [21]

IESR (2019), *Levelized Cost of Electricity in Indonesia - Understanding The Levelized Cost of Electricity Generation*, http://www.iesr.or.id (accessed on 6 April 2020). [25]

IESR (2019), *Levelized Cost of Electricity in Indonesia - Understanding The Levelized Cost of Electricity Generation*, http://www.iesr.or.id (accessed on 6 April 2020). [26]

IRENA (2021), *Data & Statistics*, https://www.irena.org/Statistics (accessed on 15 April 2021). [17]

IRENA (2020), "Renewable Power Generation Costs in 2019", */publications/2020/Jun/Renewable-Power-Costs-in-2019*, http:///publications/2020/Jun/Renewable-Power-Costs-in-2019 (accessed on 2 March 2021). [28]

IRENA (2019), *Renewable Power Generation Costs in 2018*, http:///publications/2019/May/Renewable-power-generation-costs-in-2018 (accessed on 16 December 2020). [27]

MEMR (2020), *Data & Information of Energy Conservation 2019, 3rd Edition*, Directorate of Energy Conservation, Ministry of Energy and Mineral Resources, http://www.ebtke.esdm.go.id (accessed on 15 December 2020). [29]

MEMR (2017), "Rencana Umum Energi Nasional (RUEN, General National Energy Plan)". [8]

Ministry of Environment and Forestry (2019), *Laporan Inventarisasi Gas Rumah Kaca (GRK) dan Monitoring, Pelaporan, Verifikasi (MPV) Tahun 2018 (Greenhouse Inventory and Monitoring, Reporting, Verification (MRV) report 2018).* [9]

OECD (2021), *Clean Energy Finance and Investment Mobilisation*, http://www.oecd.org/cefim/ (accessed on 5 March 2021). [32]

OECD (2021), *Economic Surveys of Indonesia 2020 - Upcoming.* [34]

OECD (2021), *OECD Economic Surveys: Indonesia 2021*, OECD Publishing, Paris, https://dx.doi.org/10.1787/fd7e6249-en. [3]

OECD (2020), *OECD Investment Policy Reviews: Indonesia 2020*, OECD Investment Policy Reviews, OECD Publishing, Paris, https://dx.doi.org/10.1787/b56512da-en. [2]

OECD (2020), *OECD Tourism Trends and Policies 2020*, OECD Publishing, Paris, https://dx.doi.org/10.1787/6b47b985-en. [6]

OECD (2019), *OECD Green Growth Policy Review of Indonesia 2019*, OECD Environmental Performance Reviews, OECD Publishing, Paris, https://dx.doi.org/10.1787/1eee39bc-en. [1]

OECD (2015), *Policy Guidance for Investment in Clean Energy Infrastructure: Expanding Access to Clean Energy for Green Growth and Development*, OECD Publishing, Paris, https://dx.doi.org/10.1787/9789264212664-en. [33]

Oxford Business Group (2018), *The Report: Indonesia 2018*, https://oxfordbusinessgroup.com/indonesia-2018 (accessed on 17 February 2020). [4]

PLN (2019), *Rencana Usaha Penyediaan Tenaga Listrik (RUPTL) PT. PLN 2019 - 2028 (PT PLN Power Supply Business Plan 2019-2028)*, PT Perusahaan Listrik Negara (Persero) , Jakarta, https://gatrik.esdm.go.id//assets/uploads/download_index/files/5b16d-kepmen-esdm-no.-39-k-20-mem-2019-tentang-pengesahan-ruptl-pt-pln-2019-2028.pdf (accessed on 16 December 2020). [13]

Sanchez, L. and B. Luan (2018), *The Health Cost of Coal in Indonesia*, IISD, http://www.iisd.org/gsi (accessed on 11 February 2021). [15]

UK Foreign & Commonwealth Office (2018), "Indonesia Renewable Energy Business Opportunities". [22]

Notes

[1] The "10 New Balis" refers to government plans to promote 10 new tourist destinations in Indonesia includes: Borobudur Temple (Central Java); Belitung (Sumatra); Mount Bromo (East Java); Labuan Bajo (East Nusa Tenggara); Lake Toba (North Sumatra); Thousand Islands (Jakarta); Mandalika (West Nusa Tenggara); Wakatobi (Southeast Sulawesi); Tanjung Lesung (Banten); and Morotai (North Maluku).

[2] Including large hydro, total investment needs stand at USD 72.5 billion (or USD 7.25 billion per year).

[3] Investment costs are typically made up of equipment cost (usually above 50%), installation and logistic cost as well as pre-development cost (e.g. cost related to permitting process, land acquisition).

2 Planning and public governance

This chapter examines governance for clean energy finance and investment governance and power planning in Indonesia. It provides an overview of Indonesia's institutional framework for clean energy and electricity market structure, as well as identifies areas to improve coordination across institutions, at all levels of government, to ensure effective and consistent goals and policies. The chapter also highlights progress and opportunities to improve the country's clean energy finance and investment-related targets, strategies and power planning mechanisms with a view to sending credible, ambitious and long-term signals to investors.

Indonesia has committed to ambitious clean energy and emission reduction targets, which will necessitate strong policy action in order to mobilise the substantial amount of finance and investment needed to realise these goals. Considering the number of policy areas and government institutions (including at the sub-national level) involved in that effort, good public governance as well as effective coordination mechanisms will be essential enabling factors. Equally, defining a long-term pathway to realise a clean energy transition, with clear targets and milestones, backed by strong political commitment as well as transparent monitoring and evaluation to track progress, will be critical to build market confidence and give investors early signals of future market development.

Assessment and recommendations

Strengthening of the National Energy Council's co-ordination role is needed

The National Energy Council (DEN) is the main body responsible for cross-sector energy issues and is responsible for overseeing the implementation of national energy targets outlined in the RUEN (National Energy General Plan) across different line ministries. DEN also plays a vital role to guide and assist regional governments to establish regional energy general plans (RUED) and supports provinces interested in developing clean energy. In practice, few of DEN's recommendations reach the implementation phase due to challenges in internal co-ordination and implementation, despite DEN's prominent role under the President of Indonesia and being chaired by the Minister of Energy and Mineral Resources. In addition, from 2009 to 2020, regular coordination meetings to discuss and overcome energy issues were limited and not able to be conducted consistently. Over this period, only four of the required 22 plenary meetings were held while only 28 of the 72 minimum required member meetings took place. The operationalisation of DEN according to its original mandate as stated in the 2007 Energy Law and Presidential Regulation No. 26/2008 would strengthen its role and improve the implementation of its recommendations.

Strengthening co-ordination between government institutions is crucial to enhance and streamline the regulatory environment

Progress on clean energy development is currently hindered, in part, by the large number of ministries involved in energy policy, with sub-optimum coordination. This includes the Ministry of Energy and Mineral Resources, the Ministry of Industry, the Ministry of Public Works and Housing, the Ministry of Finance, the Ministry of Trade, the Ministry of Transport, the National Development Planning Agency, the Ministry of Research and Technology; and the Agency for Assessment and Application of Technology. Regional and local governments are also responsible for developing energy efficiency and renewable energy regulations, as are sub-national governments. Co-ordinating policy and improving clarity in the roles and responsibilities of these actors would help to create a more cohesive and conducive environment to accelerate clean energy development. The national government should work closely with regional governments to insure they have the skills and resources necessary to deliver the clean energy transition.

Economic dynamics impact energy and should be better reflected in energy planning and target setting

A high economic growth assumption in the 2011 Masterplan for Acceleration and Expansion of Indonesia's Economic Development (MP3EI) was used in the RUEN model for setting the 23% renewable energy target for 2025. The 35 GW expansion programme announced in 2015 for completion by 2019 also used this high assumption. Yet, economic growth has been substantially less than forecasted and energy demand growth even lower, as digitalisation, a shift towards less energy-intensive services and behaviour changes have all slowed down energy demand since 2015 (MEMR, 2020[11]). As a result, in 2018 the government revised the 35 GW programme's target commercial operation date to 2024. It recently revised the target again to 2028 to reflect the global economic recession. These repeated changes highlight the need to better account for economic dynamics within Indonesia's energy plans and target setting.

Aligning energy planning with One Map tools could improve clean energy investment

RUEN is referenced by the National Power Utility (PLN) in its annual electricity business plan (RUPTL), though RUPTL uses lower short-term economic growth assumptions, creating inconsistencies with lower PLN outlooks compared to RUEN targets. Both RUEN and RUPTL's overestimation of energy demand also creates uncertainty on the timing for new capacity additions, which negatively impacts the return potential for projects and discourages investments. Renewable energy project locations stated in RUPTL, likewise do not align with project developers preferred sites to meet the potential market demand, limiting integration of potential renewable electricity without expansion of the transmission network. The government has developed the Indonesia One Map tool gathering spatial information from various ministries, including renewable energy potential and electricity infrastructure that can be layered with other elements such as demographic data, transportation and communication infrastructure, and forestry and mining areas. The One Map tool is an opportunity to align RUEN and RUPTL models to improve outlooks and information on renewable energy potential, making energy planning more consistent and robust to increase investor confidence.

Data transparency and accessibility is a key for enhancing financial project support

Clean energy projects have characteristics such as geographic location, energy resource type and intermittency of electricity production, which many financial institutions are unfamiliar with. This creates challenges to assess and manage risks associated with the projects. To overcome these challenges, financial institutions require transparent data that can be used to compare information provided by project developers in their feasibility studies and that ideally can be assessed by an independent verifier. The government is expected to provide some data currently held by various government institutions, such as topography data, rainfall levels, catchment area status and potential for renewable energy resources. In spite of OJK's efforts to report financial institutions' data needs, there is still a considerable lack of easily accessible data.

Energy efficiency and promotion of renewable energy can support green economic recovery

The 2020-24 Medium-term National Development Planning (RPJMN) adopted a low-carbon development initiative (LCDI), which will allow more sustainable activities to help achieve Indonesia's climate change target. While the 2020-24 RPJMN referred to RUEN and has more stringent aspects that need to be applied by all ministries and government bodies, there is no clear indication of how investment can meet the LCDI objectives. With abundant renewable energy resources and significant energy savings potential across the economy, as well as the LCDI that can guide green recovery measures, there is great opportunity for Indonesia to invest in clean energy as a way to bolster economic recovery while reducing emissions. Further efforts are needed if this potential is to be realised, as Indonesia has only reached a 9.15% share of renewables in Total Primary Energy Supply (TPES) in 2019, which is far behind the 23% target set in the RUEN for 2025 (DEN, 2020[2]). Unlocking access to low-cost finance is also critical if the targets are to be met.

Clean energy development needs clear, long-term signals from the government that reflect opportunities for investors

Changes in clean energy planning and governance can negatively impact investor confidence and project development. In recent years, abrupt changes such as the 2018 revocation of the 2016 energy service company (ESCO) regulation have complicated clean energy finance and investment, especially given the often long-term nature of those projects. Impending measures such as the revision of Government Regulation on Energy Conservation and the New and Renewable Energy Law currently under preparation should help to create a more coherent framework for energy efficiency and renewable energy governance since it would allow the ESCO business model and feed-in-tariff (FiT) scheme to improve clean energy investment. Ensuring the intent of those measures is reflected across national energy planning and policy implementation will be critical to encouraging and enabling the market to seize clean energy opportunities by providing long-term signals to investors.

Box 2.1. Main policy recommendations on planning and public governance

- Strengthen DEN's co-ordination role in order to ensure effective implementation of its policy recommendations can speed up Indonesia's clean energy transition. Importantly, ensuring that DEN can be operationalised according to its original designation stated in the 2007 Energy Law and Presidential Regulation No. 26/2008 can improve the implementation of its recommendations and thereby help achieve the country's clean energy targets.
- Facilitate capacity building and technical assistance for local governments and universities to carry out energy transition programs as well as provide incentives for effective implementation of energy efficiency and renewable energy projects at the local and regional levels. Share good practices and success stories across different provincial and municipal governments, and where relevant provide support to help replicate success from one province or municipality to another.
- Conduct a transparent and integrated assessment of the economic and behavioural assumptions behind energy outlooks used to set policy targets and energy plans. This includes ensuring there is appropriate planning capacity (e.g. within the Ministry of Energy and Mineral Resources, or MEMR) to address evolving needs and opportunities in a more complex and dynamic energy system, particularly as demand forecasting increasingly will need to account for the links between network changes and expansion, decentralised energy production and energy efficiency uptake.
- Consider revising the RUEN to reflect changes in Indonesia's economic situation and in the costs and performance of clean energy technologies. These adjustments then will be referred by the annual RUPTL revision process using the One Map tool to improve the outlook for clean energy development, market demand, and electricity or other infrastructure.
- Consult with stakeholders, including from the financial sector, to help build consensus and investor confidence in the clean energy targets, increasing the attractiveness of those projects and facilitating access to finance.
- Prioritise the development of a transparent and accessible database that links clean energy data with financial aspects of clean energy projects to minimise perceived risk. Encourage independent entities to provide project data and support overall enhancement of clean energy project feasibility studies, which will contribute to more viable business and financial plans.

- Identify priority clean energy technologies and communicate as part of the energy planning process. This will help signal investment opportunities and identify required support mechanism to help achieve Indonesia's affordability, economic development, and environmental sustainability goals. Setting priorities for clean energy technology development can also be used as a benchmark to track progress over time and make necessary adjustments to energy planning and governance to ensure the long-term success of those targets.

Policy coherence, co-ordination, and monitoring

Clean energy policy, finance and investment governance is split across multiple institutions

Indonesia's institutional framework for clean energy policy, finance and investment is fragmented across numerous institutions see Figure 2.1). The Ministry of Energy and Mineral Resources (MEMR) is the main institution responsible for developing and implementing Indonesia's energy policy, including renewable energy and energy conservation, and the monitoring of energy use through the online energy management reporting system. The clean energy sector falls under the purview of the Directorate-General (DG) of New and Renewable Energy and Energy Conservation (NREEC). MEMR is also responsible for regulating the power sector through the DG of Electricity. Additionally, MEMR has a number of agencies exerting key responsibilities over, for example, clean energy Research and Development (R&D) and innovation (the Agency for R&D); the mapping of geological resources, volcanology and disaster mitigation (the Geological Agency); and the continuous development of MEMR's staff and human resources in the field of energy (through the HR Development Agency) (**see Chapter 7** for more details on R&D and training and capacity building).

In addition to MEMR, the Ministry of Finance (MoF) and Financial Services Authority (Otoritas Jasa Keuangan, OJK) also hold important responsibilities over clean energy finance and investment. The MoF approves tax and price incentives as well as guarantees that may be provided to support power projects (**see Chapter 5** for a detailed discussion on Indonesia's clean energy incentive schemes). MoF's Directorate of Government Support Management and Infrastructure Financing is responsible for reviewing and approving guarantee requests. MoF also recommends the maximum level of electricity subsidies to PLN in the national budget and reviews loan arrangements entered into by PLN (including eventual government guarantees of PLN's loans) (PwC, 2017[3]). As the financial market supervisor and regulator, OJK has played a key role in mainstreaming sustainable finance in the country through a number of policies and measures, including in the field of clean energy (**see Chapter 6**).

At the heart of overall investment promotion, facilitation and regulation is the Indonesian Investment Coordinating Board (Badan Koordinasi Penanaman Modal, or BKPM), which has played an instrumental role in establishing a business-friendly environment in the country in recent decades, co-ordinating across the entities that influence investment policies or their implementation (OECD, 2020[4]) . In recent years, its focus has been to simplify licensing, facilitate investment projects and improve conditions to attract investments (**see Chapter 5**). This is a challenging task, however, given the number of ministries and public agencies – including the Coordinating Ministry for Maritime and Investment Affairs (CMMIA), the Coordinating Ministry for Economic Affairs (CMEA), and the President's Staff Office – involved in clean energy investment promotion and facilitation, not excluding the provincial, district and municipal governments that also play a role.

Figure 2.1. Indonesia's clean energy finance and investment institutional setting

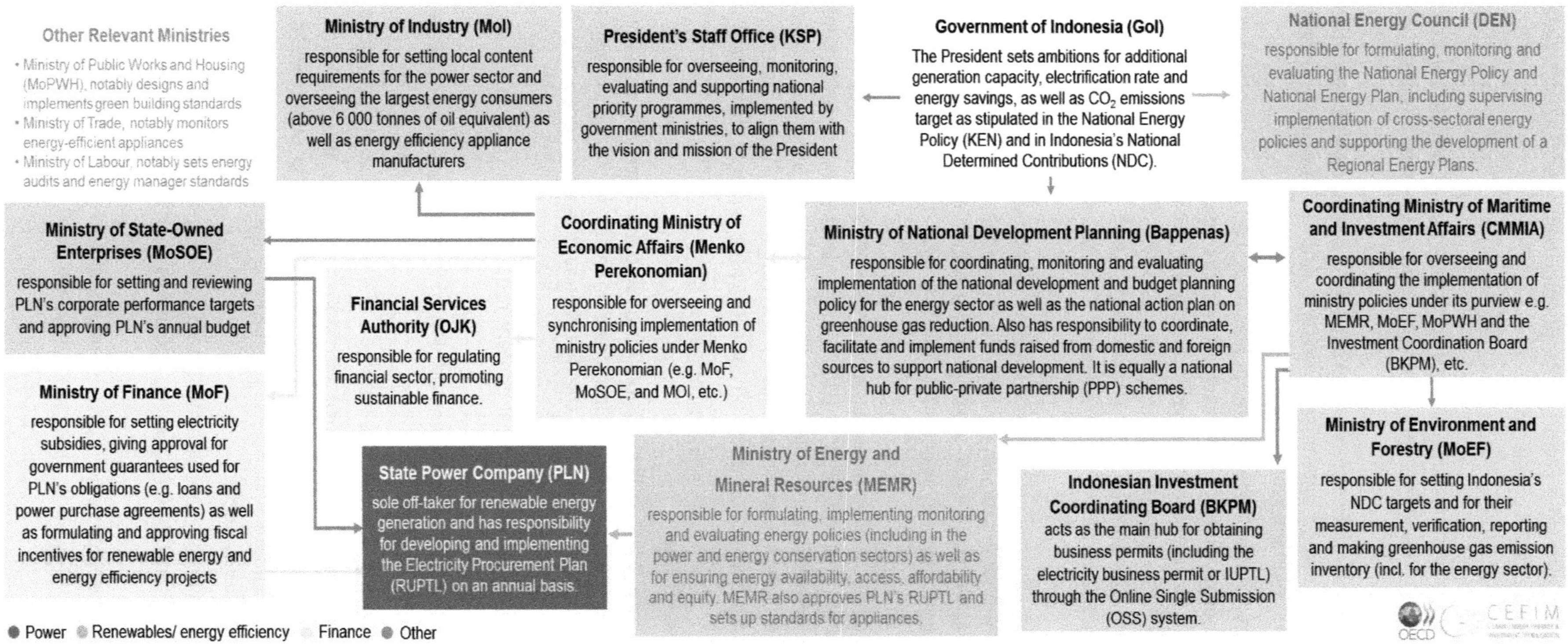

Source: OECD, 2020.

Other government institutions also hold important responsibilities over matters related to clean energy finance and investment (see Table 2.1), including:

- **Co-ordination bodies:**
  - The Co-ordinating Ministry of Maritime and Investment Affairs (CMMIA) co-ordinates line ministries responsible for energy, transport, environment, and investment issues and provides policy implementation support.
  - The Co-ordinating Ministry of Economic Affairs (CMEA) co-ordinates line ministries responsible for finance, industry, state-owned enterprises, research and technology, and spatial planning issues and provides policy implementation support.
  - The National Energy Council (Dewan Energi Nasional, DEN) is a co-ordination body responsible for co-ordinating energy-related cross-sectoral matters and monitoring progress towards clean energy targets. It brings together ministries indirectly involved in the energy sector, namely MEMR, MoF, the Ministry of Environment and Forestry (MoEF), the Ministry of National Development Planning (Bappenas), the Ministry of Transport (MoT), and the Ministry of Industry (MoI). DEN is chaired by the President and Vice President. The Minister of MEMR serves as Executive Chairperson.
  - The President's Staff Office is an ad-hoc institution responsible for monitoring the implementation of all the President's priority programmes by line ministries; such as (in clean energy) increasing the capacity of installed renewable energy in the national energy mix; the implementation of minimum energy performance standards (MEPS); and the mandatory labelling of electrical appliances.
  - The Ministry of National Development Planning or Bappenas (Badan Perencanaan Pembangunan Nasional) establishes the national medium- and long-term development plans, manages international development funding sources as well as monitors progress towards targets set out in Indonesia's National Determined Contribution (NDC) under the Paris Agreement. Bappenas is also responsible for facilitating cooperation on infrastructure projects between the government and private investors.
- **Line ministries and institution:**
  - The Ministry of Finance (MoF) is responsible for setting the electricity subsidy, gives the approval for government guarantees for PLN's obligations in loans and power purchase agreements (PPAs) as well as formulating and approving the fiscal incentives for renewable energy and energy efficiency projects
  - The Ministry of Industry (MoI) sets local content requirements (LCRs) for a range of renewable technologies.
  - The Ministry of Public Works and Housing (MoPWH) is responsible for establishing green building codes and setting green building standards.
  - The Ministry of Trade (MoTrd) monitors the trade of energy efficient appliances.
  - The Ministry of State-owned Enterprise (MoSOE) oversees the business and management performance of the national state-owned power utility (PT PLN or simply PLN).
  - The Ministry of Environment and Forestry (MoEF) is responsible for governing environmental issues related to the energy sector.
  - The Indonesian Investment Coordinating Board (BKPM) is Indonesia's investment promotion agency, notably responsible for granting business permits to clean energy projects (**see Chapters 4 and 5**).
  - The Financial Services Authority (OJK) is responsible for formulating the financial industry regulation and the sustainable finance policy as well as monitoring and evaluating its implementation.

Lack of an effective co-ordination body is a challenge

According to the 2007 Energy Law, DEN has the strongest position to oversee the implementation of the national energy policy (Kebijakan Energi Nasional, or KEN) which is the guideline for the country to achieve some of the energy targets including to reach 23% of renewable energy share by 2025 in the TPES. DEN is the sole co-ordination platform for cross-sectoral energy issues and is led by the President with daily activities chaired by the Minister of Energy and Mineral Resources. The government is represented by eight ministries (AUP-Anggota Unsur Pemerintah) (see Table 2.1) and eight members representing other stakeholders (AUPK-Anggota Unsur Pemangku Kepentingan) are chosen by parliament.

DEN addresses energy issues through its plenary meetings which are supposed to be conducted at least twice a year and led by the President, as well as member meetings led by the Minister of Energy and Mineral Resources every two months. These meetings are expected to establish policy recommendations that need to be implemented by the ministries and stakeholders that are then subsequently monitored and evaluated by DEN. While, ministries need to report to DEN on the progress of implementing the policy recommendations, they also need to report to other existing co-ordination bodies i.e. CMMIA, CMEA, Bappenas, and the President's Staff Office.

The multiplicity of these co-ordination bodies has had unintended consequences, however, sometimes resulting in implementation of overlapping policy measures. For example, the CMMIA, the President's Staff Office, and Bappenas have all included the rural electrification programme (consisting of the development of renewable power plants in remote areas and small islands) in their broader policy programmes, but all have done so with different levels of detail as well as inconsistencies in the type of technology and size of project to be developed under the programme. Setting up a single online reporting mechanism could thus help address this issue, through enhancing co-ordination across programmes and facilitating the monitoring of their implementation.

Overall, the lack of an effective co-ordination body for clean-energy-related issues has made the co-ordination process a challenge. Despite its co-ordination role, DEN has been perceived to be ineffective and lacked the authority to ensure acceptance and application of its recommendations by other line ministries. For example, DEN has faced significant challenges in getting different line ministries to agree on Indonesia's electric vehicle programme on a range of issues under its co-ordination, e.g. on local content requirements, incentives, safety, and environment aspects[1], before it was ultimately approved by the President in 2019. Acting on this issue, parliament recently recommended the government amend current regulations to strengthen DEN's role and functions, although it remains to be seen how this will be followed through[2].

Table 2.1. Co-ordination structure of line ministries

Member Ministry of DEN	Ministry under CMMIA	Ministry under CMEA
Ministry of National Development Planning (Bappenas)	Ministry of Energy and Mineral Resources	Ministry of Finance
Ministry of Energy and Mineral Resources	Ministry of Transport	Ministry of Industry
Ministry of Finance	Ministry of Environment and Forestry	Ministry of Agriculture
Ministry of Environment and Forestry	Ministry of Public Works and Housing	Ministry of Trade
Ministry of Industry	Ministry of Tourism and Creative Economy	Ministry of Labour
Ministry of Transport	Ministry of Marine and Fishery	Ministry of State-owned Enterprise
Ministry of Agriculture	Indonesian Investment Coordinating Board	Ministry of Agrarian and Spatial Planning
Ministry of Research and Technology		Ministry of Research and Technology

Source: DEN regulation, CMMIA regulation, CMEA regulation

Indonesia has provided long-term goal setting to promote clean energy investment

Setting a long-term strategy to achieve a clean energy transition is important to send the right market signals and help drive up investment. To be credible, clean energy targets should be ambitious but also realistic, well-budgeted, and time-bound. Ambitious objectives should be accompanied with quantified intermediate milestones that can help investors get a sense of how (fast) clean energy markets are expected to develop (OECD, 2015[5]).

Indonesia's policy-planning mechanism for clean energy finance and investment is complex and articulated over different time horizons. MEMR is the main body responsible for defining Indonesia's clean energy strategy while Bappenas is responsible for mainstreaming that strategy into the country's overarching medium- and long-term development plan – that sets the course for the country's development in all policy areas – as well as climate strategy. Ensuring that these different policies and plans are consistent, coherent, well-articulated, with clear, time-bound and measurable objectives is important in order to scale up clean energy investment that can meet the low-carbon development and climate change targets.

Clean energy plays an important role in Indonesia's climate strategy

Indonesia defined long-term carbon emission reduction objectives as part of its Nationally Determined Contribution (NDC) under the 2015 Paris Agreement to address climate change and contribute to the global mitigation effort. Under its NDC, Indonesia committed to lowering carbon emissions by 29% (or around 834 million tons CO2 equivalent) and up to 38% (or about 1 081 million tons CO2 equivalent) with international assistance by 2030 compared to the 2010 baseline. Additionally, the target shows that Indonesia relies heavily on the forestry sector to reduce emissions by 60%; whereas the energy sector also plays a pivotal role in national carbon reduction efforts, accounting for around 38% of targeted emission reduction under its unconditional NDC (see Table 2.2). However, the impact of the current COVID pandemic could affect the trajectory and achievement of emissions; hence, this should be reflected in NDC targets.

Emission reduction in the energy sector will be achieved through the implementation of various programmes as defined in the 2012 National Action Plan for Greenhouse Gas Reduction (RAN-GRK) and the 2019 Roadmap of NDC Implementation on Mitigation Action, such as the development of renewable and energy efficiency projects. Interestingly, although the energy sector is the second major contributor to reduce emissions after the forestry sector, the government estimates that around USD 236 billion will be absorbed by the energy and transport sectors or around 95% of total USD 247 billion investment needed to achieve the country's NDC by 2030[3]. This requires further evaluation from the government to recalculate the investment needs as the cost of clean energy technology has significantly declined over the last decade.

Table 2.2. Indonesia's NDC targets

No	Sector	GHG Emission Level 2010*	GHG Emission Level 2030 (MTon CO2e)			GHG Emission Reduction				Annual Average Growth BaU (2010-2030)	Average Growth 2000-2012*
		MTon CO2e	BaU	CM1	CM2	(MTon CO2e)		% of Total BaU			
						CM1	CM2	CM1	CM2		
1	Energy*	453.2	1,669	1,355	1,271	314	398	11%	14%	6.7%	4.50%
2	Waste	88	296	285	270	11	26	0.38%	1%	6.3%	4.00%
3	IPPU	36	69.6	66.85	66.35	2.75	3.25	0.10%	0.11%	3.4%	0.10%
4	Agriculture	110.5	119.66	110.39	115.86	9	4	0.32%	0.13%	0.4%	1.30%
5	Forestry**	647	714	217	64	497	650	17.2%	23%	0.5%	2.70%
	Total	**1,334**	**2,869**	**2,034**	**1,787**	**834**	**1,081**	**29%**	**38%**	**3.9%**	**3.20%**

Note: * including fugitive
** including peat fire
CM1 = Counter Measure (unconditional mitigation scenario)
CM2 = Counter Measure (conditional mitigation scenario)
Source: NDC Indonesia

Indonesia's clean energy goals are laudable but could prove challenging to achieve

In the energy sector, the 2007 Energy Law is the primary reference for Indonesia's long-term energy policy and targets. The law notably mandated the issuance of Indonesia's National Energy Policy (Kebijakan Energi Nasional, KEN) in 2014 to provide an overarching policy framework for the energy sector. KEN devises a high-level strategy for Indonesia to achieve energy security and energy independence based on energy management principles such as accessibility, affordability, and sustainability. To reach those objectives, KEN defines a range of high-level targets to be achieved over the 2025 and 2050 horizons (see Table 2.3), including a 23% renewable energy share in Total Primary Energy Supply (TPES) by 2025 as well as a 1% annual reduction in energy intensity until 2025. While KEN is embedded in Government Regulation No. 79/2014, it is not legally binding.

Table 2.3. KEN's selected targets

	2025	2050
TPES	400 MTOE	1000 MTOE
Total installed capacity	115 GW	430 GW
Renewable Energy in TPES	23%	31%
Energy intensity reduction	1% per year	-

Note: TPES=Total Primary Energy Supply. MTOE=Million Tonnes of Oil Equivalent. GW=Giga Watts.
Source: Government Regulation no. 79 of 2014 on the National Energy Policy.

To complement the commitment to establish more efficient energy use, Government Regulation No. 70/2009, which notably governs how the country should implement energy conservation activities to reduce energy consumption by, for example, setting the standard and labelling programme. It also establishes the obligation for large energy consumers (above 6 000 TOE per year) to report their energy consumption and energy management actions. To promote its implementation, the government provides incentives and assistance to stakeholders. In reality, the implementation of these regulations face obstacles including the electricity oversupply which discourages energy efficiency activities as the government prioritises programs to increase electricity consumption.

Alongside the commitment to achieve KEN objectives, the government enacted the National Energy General Plan (Rencana Umum Energi Nasional or RUEN) in 2017, which defines more detailed, annual targets, as well as programmes to be implemented by line ministries. RUEN notably breaks down KEN's 2025 installed power capacity target into annual technology sub-targets for each province, based on estimates of their renewable resource potential (**see Chapter 1** for more details on Indonesia's renewable potential). It also sets out a number of programmes and measures to achieve targets, including: renewable energy resource management, incentive and price scheme design, capacity building, and research and development, as well as areas for international cooperation. However, it is not clear how these programmes align with Indonesia's NDC and RAN-GRK. Additionally, RUEN does not provide estimates of investment needs to realise targets, let alone a strategy to mobilise domestic and foreign sources of finance and investment. In this regard, the Institute for Essential Services Reform (IESR) and Institute for Energy Economics (IIEE) (2019)[4] estimated that USD 72.3 billion (or 44.2 billion excluding large hydropower i.e. above 10 MW) will be needed to reach RUEN's renewable energy targets by 2025, far below what has been realised to date (**see Chapter 1**) (IESR, 2019[6]).

RUEN's targets could be ambitious, as it is based on optimistic underlying assumptions. There are a number of assumptions used in the RUEN model to estimate future energy demand, of which two are of particular importance: economic growth projections ranging from 4.8% in 2015 to 8.0% in 2025 – derived from the 2011 Masterplan for Acceleration and Expansion of Indonesia's Economic Development (MP3EI)[5] document – and population growth projections ranging from 1.3% in 2015 to 0.8% in 2025. However, economic growth assumptions underlying RUEN's targets turned out to be greatly over-estimated; for instance, the MP3EI projected an annual GDP growth average of 6.54% over 2015-19, while actual economic growth only averaged 5.03% over that period based on Indonesia's Statistical Agency (BPS, 2020)[6], mechanically inflating targets (including installed power capacity for both renewables and fossil fuels by 2025)[7].

Local governments need to play a greater role in implementing clean energy targets

While the 2007 Energy Law obligates local governments (province and regency) to establish Regional Energy General Plans (RUEDs) referring to RUEN, close to half of the country's local governments have yet to do so. As of 2021, for instance, 19 provinces (out of 34 in total) have enacted a RUED while the plans of the remaining provinces are still being developed[8].

There is also a mismatch between RUEN's provincial-level targets and provinces' actual level of ambition. For example, the Papua province, which abounds with renewable sources (albeit with a low population) is yet to prepare a RUED while South Kalimantan continues to prioritise coal projects in its RUEDs, despite this being inconsistent with RUEN plans. Equally, many provinces' RUED targets differ from those stated in RUEN; for example, South Sumatera's RUED plans for the construction of 50 MW of solar PV projects by 2025, while RUEN plans for 296 MW over the same period (based on the province's potential and demand projections). Notwithstanding these challenges, some provinces have been particularly ambitious under their RUEDs, with the Bali province being a case in point, as it is committed to 100% renewable electricity by 2050.

Most of the difficulties faced by local governments in developing robust RUEDs, are attributable to a lack of capacity as well as limited understanding about clean energy. Many local governments, for example, lack the financial and human resources to undertake the modelling and research work needed to develop RUEDs. Local governments also lack the authority to set a sufficiently attractive renewable power price as set out at the national level. Adding to the challenges, there is a very long bureaucratic process to obtain local parliaments' final approval of RUEDs.

Indonesia's new mid-term plan could help revive support for clean energy

The Ministry of National Development Planning (Bappenas) is responsible for establishing the Medium-term National Development Plan (Rencana Pembangunan Jangka Menengah Nasional or RPJMN), which sets the course for Indonesia's development over a five-year horizon (tallying with presidential mandates) through a range of multi-sectorial objectives and targets. The RPJMN is designed through a series of bottom-up and top-down consultations, and allocates state budget to different line ministries and agencies. These institutions and local governments then use the RPJMN as a reference to develop and implement their own plans and policies, e.g. the annual Government Work Plan (or Rencana Kerja Pemerintah) and Medium-Term Regional Development Plan.

The recently adopted 2020-24 RPJMN has made the low-carbon development initiative (LCDI) and the green economy the cornerstone of its development strategy. This is a welcome step for clean energy given the plan recognises the importance of renewable and energy efficiency for Indonesia's economic development and reiterates the government's commitment to achieve RUEN and NDC targets. The RPJMN represents a great opportunity to demonstrate that clean energy and the green economy can help support Indonesia's economic growth, particularly as it recovers from the impact of the COVID-19 crisis.

Institutional framework for electricity market

Electricity Law No. 30/2009 is the main legal basis for Indonesia's electricity market. The law notably allocates roles and responsibilities to different government institutions and other market players as well as defines the electricity permitting, tariff-setting and planning processes (see next section for more details on electricity planning). The law also states that Indonesia's State Electricity Company (PLN) shall maintain a dominant position in all segments of the power market, making it a *de facto* (vertically-integrated) monopoly (see Figure 2.2).

Figure 2.2. Indonesia's electricity market structure

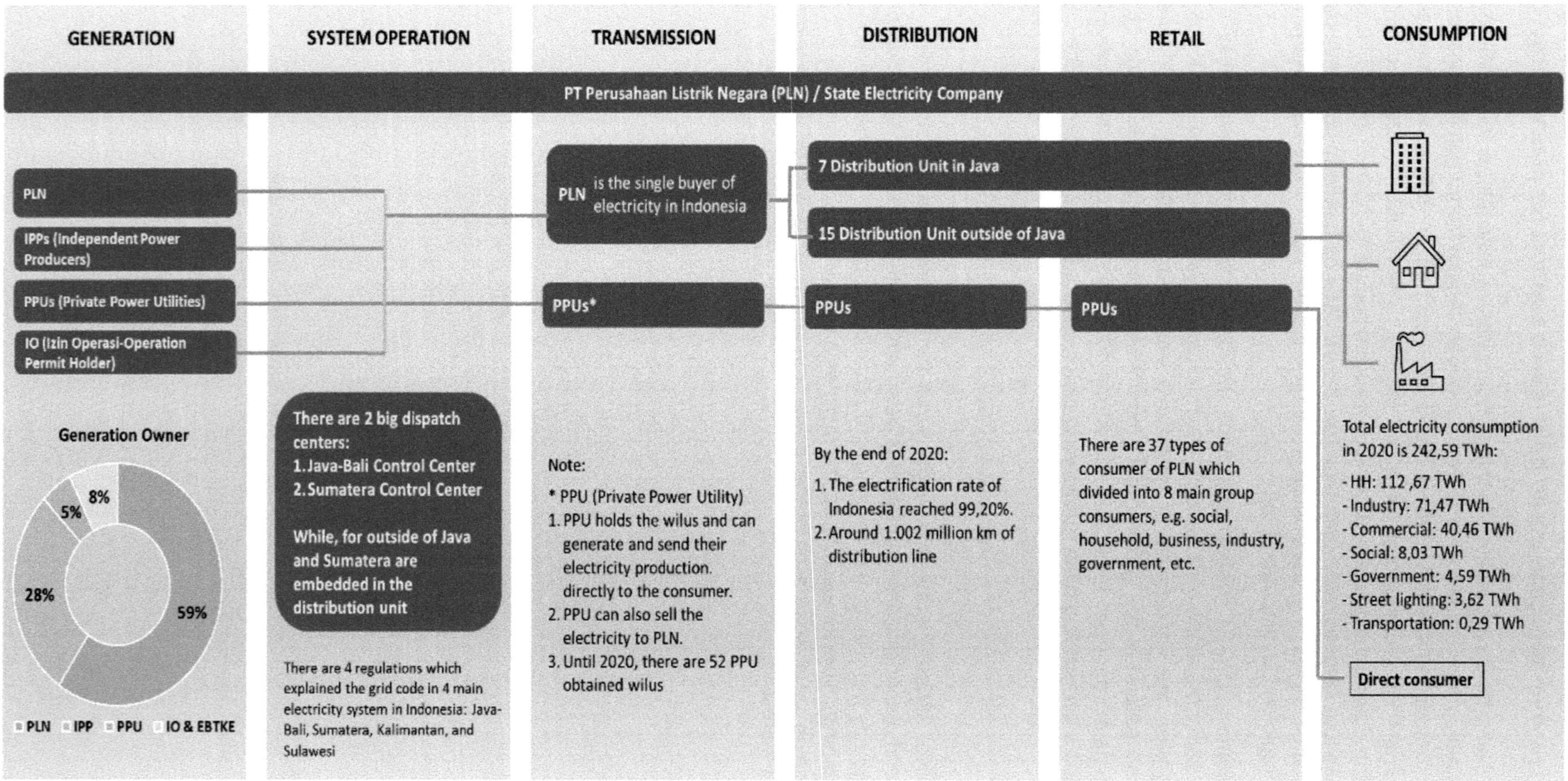

Source: OECD, 2020

There have been attempts to unbundle PLN and liberalise Indonesia's power market through the enactment of Electricity Law No. 20/2002. However, the law was later rescinded by the Constitutional Court of Indonesia on grounds that it was contrary to the constitution, which states that electricity provision should remain the responsibility of the state. Consequently, the government issued a number of government decrees (and close to 40 implementing regulations summarised in Table 2.4) to guarantee fair-competition and well-functioning of the market, although implementation has proved challenging in practice (**see Chapter 4**). Despite PLN's dominant role in power generation (owning two-thirds of generation assets), the government has been encouraging increased participation by Independent Power Producers (IPPs) and electricity business area (Wilayah Usaha Ketenagalistrikan) permit holders in the market over the last five years, in a bid to re-allocate PLN's limited resources to generation and transmission infrastructure. As a result, the share of IPPs in total power generation rose from 21% of total installed capacity in 2015 to 26% in 2019 (MEMR, 2020[7]).

In addition, to ensure that the implementation and management of the electricity market is carried out in a more transparent and fair manner, there are some suggestions of establishing an independent renewable energy regulatory body which is also expected to accelerate the utilisation of clean energy. The Indonesia Renewable Energy Society (Masyarakat Energi Terbarukan Indonesia, or METI) proposed this idea to parliament, which is currently drafting the New and Renewable Energy Law[9]. In a recent study, meanwhile, the Asian Development Bank (ADB) emphasised that such a regulatory body could be formed through the stipulation of government regulation or presidential regulation in a similar manner to the establishment of the SKK Migas (the Upstream Oil and Gas Special Regulatory Taskforce) or the BPTJ (the Indonesia Road Toll Regulatory Agency)[10]. If Indonesia intends to consider and assess this suggestion, there are some lessons that can be learnt from other countries, such as SEDA (Sustainable Energy Development Authority) in Malaysia, ERC (Energy Regulatory Commission) in the Philippines, EMRA (Electricity Market Regulatory Authority) in Turkey or ANRE (the National Electricity Regulatory Authority) in Morocco.

Table 2.4. Indonesia's key electricity regulation

Law	Government Regulation	Minister Regulation
No. 30/2009 about Electricity	No. 14/2012 about Electricity Business Activity in conjunction with No. 23/2014 about the Changes of GR No.14/2012	No. 28/2012 about the Submission Requirement to Get Electricity Business Area amended by No. 07/2016 about the Changes of MR No. 28/2012
		No.10/2017 about Power Purchase Agreement Principles
		No. 24/2017 about Electricity Production Cost Stipulation Mechanism
		No. 50/2017 about RE Sources Utilisation for Electricity Supply updated by No. 47/2018 and No. 04/2020
		No. 03 /2020 about Electricity Price provided by PLN
	No. 42/2012 about the Interstate Power Trading	No. 26/2012 about the Mechanism to Require the Electricity Trading and Interconnection Permit
	No. 62/2012 about Electricity Support Services Business	No. 2/2018 about the Obligation to Apply the National Indonesia Standard on Electricity Sector

Source: MEMR, 2020

Unlike in the generation segment, PLN has been the sole developer of the country's transmission and distribution infrastructure. Although regulation allows private developers to build transmission and distribution lines, there are some requirements, such as obtaining an electricity business area permit, establishing a feasibility study, providing adequate funding and obtaining power wheeling approval from the Energy Minister, which the process and the practice have been a deterrent for developers to invest in the electricity downstream business. Until the end of 2019, 52 private power utilities (PPUs) have obtained the electricity business area permit, allowing it to provide electricity directly to its customers.

In line with the generation plan, PLN submitted its commitment to the government to build a transmission and distribution line which is stated in the Electricity Business Plan (RUPTL). This is very important since it can help PLN to reach more of the market thus lowering its oversupply capacity in some areas of the country. Hence, the government asked PLN to invest more in transmission and distribution lines[11]. Despite some delays in its development, by December 2020, PLN had built around 61 960 circuit kilometres (ckm) of transmission lines spread across 28 electricity systems, as well as two big dispatch centres, i.e. the Java-Bali Dispatch Centre and the Sumatera Dispatch Centre (other dispatch centres being embedded in each PLN distribution units). Concerning distribution lines, PLN has built around 1 005 080 ckm, which helped increase the country's electrification rate to 99.20% (see Figure 2.3; **see Chapter 1**).

Figure 2.3. Indonesia's electrification rate in 2020

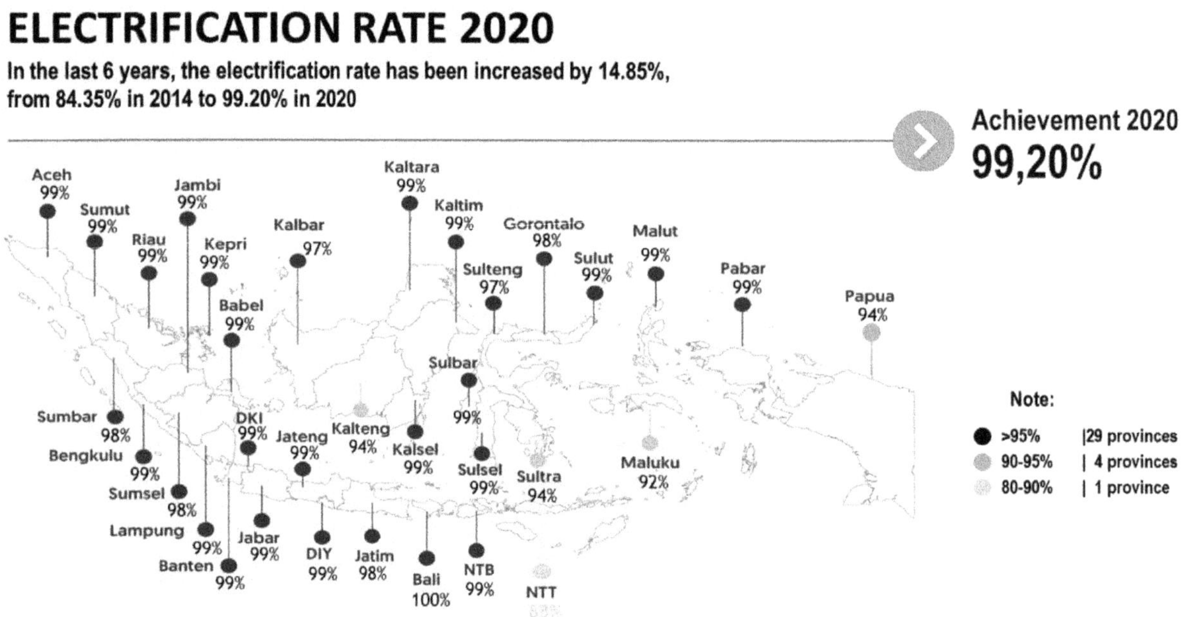

Source: MEMR, 2021

Electricity planning

Electricity planning is set out in a number of planning documents (see Figure 2.4):

- The National Electricity General Plan (Rencana Umum Ketenagalistrikan Nasional, or RUKN) constitutes the backbone of Indonesia's electricity planning. Referring to KEN, the plan notably makes forecasts for power supply and demand as well as plans investment and utilisation of renewable energy resources over a 20-year horizon. MEMR's DG of Electricity is tasked to develop and update RUKN on a regular basis with the current RUKN covering the years 2019-2038.
- The Regional Electricity General Plan (Rencana Umum Ketenagalistrikan Daerah or RUKD) is prepared by local governments in reference to the RUKN to guide how the electricity infrastructure

will be developed based on regional conditions. Although it is mandated by Electricity Law, until the end of 2020, no provinces had established RUKD using 2019 RUKN. However, there were some provinces which established RUKD using 2008 RUKN, i.e. East Kalimantan, Central Java, and West Nusa Tenggara.

- The Electricity Business Plan (Rencana Umum Penyediaan Tenaga Listrik or RUPTL) is a ten-year electricity development plan developed by PLN on a regular basis, in reference to RUKN, KEN and RUEN. The RUPTL is a very important document for all investors in the Indonesian power sector as it contains detailed and up-to-date demand forecasts, future expansion plans, electricity production forecasts, and fuel requirements, etc. It also allocates project development to PLN and IPPs, as well as defines the procurement route for IPPs to build power plants. All projects should be listed in the RUPTL prior to procurement.

Figure 2.4. Power and energy planning

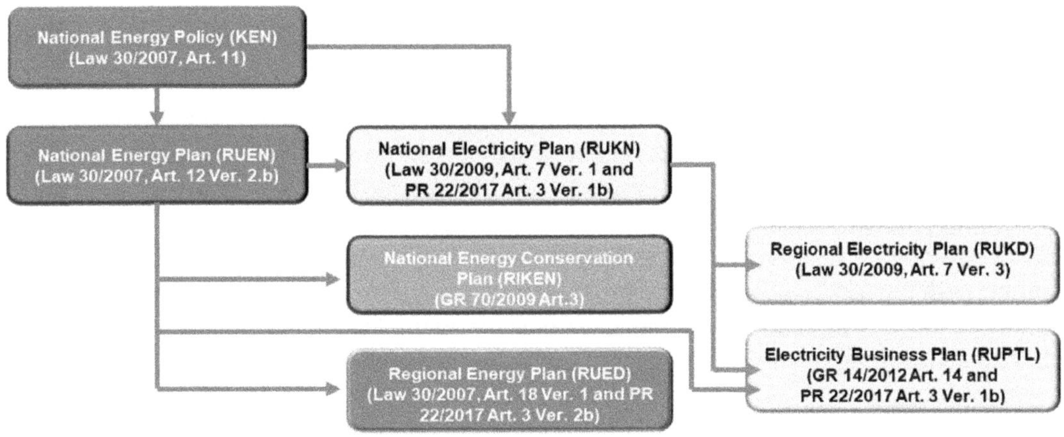

Source: 2007 Energy Law, 2009 Electricity Law

In addition to these plans, in 2015 President Joko Widodo launched the 35 GW programme to accelerate the achievement of the 100% electrification ratio and RUEN's targets. Some of the capacity of the 35 GW programme is to continue the FTP-2 project that was not implemented after 2015 due to the changes of demand projections. Furthermore, the 35 GW programme is to be integrated into the RUPTL. However, the plan is confronting similar challenges as faced by previous Fast Track Programmes (FTPs) causing some delays in project delivery (see Box 2.2).

Box 2.2. Acceleration programmes to electrifying the country

To address the electricity shortage and lowering fuels import that caused a heavy subsidy on fossil fuels in the state budget, in 2006, Indonesia launched the 1st Fast Track Programme (FTP-1) targeted to build around 10 000 MW of coal-fired power plants by 2010. Referring to Presidential Regulation No. 71/2006, of the 40 different locations of coal-fired power plants, 10 of them are located in Java (with a total capacity of 7 430 MW) and 30 locations outside Java (total capacity 2 121 MW).

In 2009, the government revised the regulation and changed some objectives, e.g. the completion date from 2010 to 2014, the location from 40 to 37, and the total capacity from 9 551 MW to 9 935 MW. However, until March 2011, only 9.5% of the 9 935 MW installation target had been reached. Later, the government's evaluation found that some obstacles were hindering the project completion, such as land clearance, the developer's financial capability, and mismatched power plant technical specifications[12]. Furthermore, these factors forced the government to amend the FTP-1 regulations several times to revise the project list, with the last changes stipulated by Presidential Regulation No. 193/2014 that postponed the completion of FTP-1 until 2016.

Despite the low achievement of the FTP-1 target, in 2010, Indonesia confidently launched the 2nd FTP (FTP-2), which highlighted a major contribution of renewable energy power plants from hydro 1 753 MW and geothermal 4 925 MW or 66% of total 10 047 MW target generation capacity, while the rest consisted of coal-fired power plants 3 025 MW and gas power plants 344 MW[13]. To ensure the delivery of the FTP-2, the government introduced a MEMR regulation, but these regulations have been revised several times, with the last regulation enacted in 2014 to add more coal-fired power plants, making the total target reached 17 428 MW that needs to be built by 2019. As of December 2020, only 2 170 MW of FTP-2 projects were commercially operated.

Table 2.5. Target achievement of Indonesia's electricity development programmes

	Timeframe	Target delayed	Total capacity target	Achievement as December 2020	Identified obstacles
FTP-1	2007-2010	2016*	9.935 MW	9.722 MW	Land clearance, developer's financial capability, technical issues
FTP-2	2010-2014	2019	10.047 MW 17.428 MW**	2.170 MW	Land clearance, increasing coal price, technical issues
35 GW Program	2015-2019	2028***	35.000 MW	9.730 MW	Land clearance, lower economic growth, slowing demand

Note: * revised by President Regulation 193/2014
** to add around 7400 MW coal-fired power plant stated in MEMR Regulation 21/2013
*** due to the Covid-19 pandemic caused slowing demand, the government revised the target completion
Source: RUPTL 2019-2028

Those electricity development programmes show an acute problem in providing a land area for the project. Although Presidential Regulation No. 71/2006 – as well as other regulations afterwards – stated that land procurement should be cleared within a maximum of 120 days, in reality, this is not happening. Hence, Indonesia needs to ensure that there will be a thorough solution to overcome the land clearance issue. The experience of the State Asset Management Agency (Lembaga Manajemen Aset Negara or LMAN) to provide land for the toll-road project (**see Chapter 4**) will be a good reference should the government decide to accelerate the clean energy project.

Differences across energy and power plans affect the clean energy investment climate

The three main energy and electricity planning documents (RUEN, RUKN, and RUPTL) use different models and assumptions to determine installed generation capacity needs leading to significant discrepancies across these documents (see Table 2.6). Slower economic and energy demand growth have also caused delays in the build-out of planned generation capacity under the RUPTL, which could further widen the gap between planned and installed capacity. These numerous inconsistencies, in turn, create confusion among investors and ultimately affect the clean energy investment climate. More co-ordination across government institutions is needed to align plans, targets and underlying projection assumptions.

Table 2.6. Differences in Indonesia's energy & electricity plans

	Institution	Timeframe	Investment needs	Planned renewable installed capacity by 2025	Economic growth assumptions	Other assumptions
RUEN	DEN (energy, national coverage)	2015-2050	USD 72 billion*	45 GW of 135 GW total installed capacity	4.8 – 8.0% (2015-2025) Source: 2011 MP3EI	Population growth, number of households
RUKN	DG Electricity (national coverage	2019-2038	USD 179 billion**	28 GW of 118 GW total installed capacity	5.0 – 5.6% (2019-2025) Source: 2019 Bappenas Moderate Economic Growth Scenario	Population growth, inflation rate, electrification rate
RUPTL	PLN (PLN business area coverage)	2019-2028	USD 55 billion***	24 GW of 118 GW total installed capacity	5.5 – 6.5% (2019-2025) Source: 2019 Bappenas High Economic Growth Scenario	Population growth, inflation rate, potential demand

Note: *estimation number from IESR and IIEE study 2019 to build renewable energy power plant as targeted in RUEN until 2025
**estimation to cover electricity infrastructure (generation, transmission, and distribution) until 2025
***PLN estimation to cover electricity infrastructure until 2028
Source: IESR & IIEE (2019), RUKN (2019), RUPTL (2019)

A more transparent and sound RUPTL is needed to boost investment

As mentioned above, PLN is responsible for submitting their plan which includes the involvement of IPPs to get the approval from the government before they start to build power plants. However, there have been concerns over the transparency and fairness of the allocation process since it uses a bottom up process based on the input from PLN regional offices that sometimes neglect the input from potential project developers backed with a proper pre-feasibility study as a requirement to be considered in the preparation of RUPTL.

According to Electricity Law No. 30/2009 and Presidential Regulation No. 4/2016 – later revised by Presidential Regulation No. 14/2017 – PLN shall be given priority to develop power infrastructure under the following conditions:

- PLN has adequate equity or can access cheap funding.
- The project has a low-construction risk.
- The project has secured fuel supply.
- The project is a peaker power plant.
- The project is an isolated system.

Equally, PLN shall work with, or allow private companies (IPPs and PPUs / IO (Izin Operasi-Operation Permit Holders) to develop electricity infrastructure under the following conditions:

- The project requires a large investment.
- The project has a high-construction risk, especially if it requires land clearance.

- The project has a high-risk of not securing fuel supply.
- The project is a renewable energy project.
- The project includes the expansion of existing IPPs.
- IPPs/PPUs build their project in a specific area.

Despite these requirements, in practice, PLN can arbitrarily allocate the development of projects, with some projects being categorised as "unallocated" – meaning they can be undertaken either by PLN or IPPs. However, there have been inconsistencies in terms of projects being planned across RUPTLs (e.g. with projects being modified, if not erased, from one RUPTL version to another).

One Map Policy and Indonesia One Data could support a more coherent electricity planning

To address institutional co-ordination issues over spatial planning, the government established the One Map Policy through President Regulation No. 9/2016. The One Map Policy consists of a single online repository called the Geoportal One Map – which launched in 2018 – to archive and centralise various infrastructure and other sectorial spatial plans (established and managed by different line ministries) and hence, help solve Indonesia's long-lasting issues of overlapping spatial plans and land rights (see (OECD, 2019[8]) for more details on Indonesia's spatial planning issues). To complement the One Map Policy, the government enacted President Regulation No. 39/2019 on Indonesia One Data that requested data holders (ministries and other government institutions) to provide dynamic data based on the format and definition guided by this regulation.

This repository will allow multiple users to overlay existing infrastructure and sectoral plans. In the energy sector, the Geoportal One Map (also called Energi dan Sumber Daya Mineral / ESDM One Map) will notably include data on renewable resource potential mining areas, transmission lines, and power plant locations. In addition, MEMR is still preparing to publish the ESDM One Data which will consist of dynamic data including daily electricity production, electricity and energy price, energy export and import value, etc. Thus, the ESDM One Map and One Data provides a great opportunity for Indonesia to further integrate energy models by better linking them and verifying adequacy with actual renewable resource potential, transmission infrastructure as well as energy demand.

It would be an important step for Indonesia if the PLN electricity system planning could be integrated with the ESDM One Map and ESDM One Data to make it more transparent and reliable, which could lead to better investment decisions by stakeholders. Currently, electricity planning lacks a linkage between the potential energy resources and the market demand towards the generation, transmission and distribution lines development plan. One example of this is the Mahakam (East Kalimantan) electricity system whereby the available supply of around 200 MW could not be delivered to the new market demand since the development of transmission and distribution lines are left behind. Other examples can also be seen in the Papua region where big hydro potential around 1 000 MW exists, but there is no demand nor any plans to build transmission and distribution lines.

With the available datasets on the ESDM One Map and ESDM One Data, the government and PLN could use it to monitor and evaluate the implementation of electricity planning and progress of the project. This has occurred for example when the government and PLN assessed the price proposals from geothermal project developers. Some of the price components include availability of supporting infrastructure close to the project location, and resource potential in areas that lack supporting infrastructure or where low potential resources could lead to higher price requirements for the developer. The government and PLN evaluated this claim using the infrastructure availability data resource potential available on the ESDM One Map and ESDM One. This allowed for the agreed geothermal price to fairly reflect the real conditions of the project.

Referring to the situation mentioned above, Indonesia could usefully draw from Australia's experience in developing the Australia Renewable Energy Mapping Infrastructure (AREMI) (see Box 2.3). Similar to the One Map, the AREMI centralises a comprehensive set of clean energy-related data and plans, such as real-time power plant performance, market demand potential, network infrastructure gap and renewable resource potential. Through integrating multiple energy data, the AREMI map greatly helped investors to identify clean energy investment opportunities and thereby helped avoid risks of stranded assets.

Box 2.3. Australian Renewable Energy Mapping Infrastructure (AREMI), supporting the clean energy investment decision

During the first decade of the 2000s, effective energy efficiency and renewable energy programs reduced the overall demand for centralised fossil fuel generated energy. Major investments had been made into the electricity grid based on projected ongoing growth in energy demand and in particular to enable supply at times of peak demand in rural areas. In 2014, the Australian Renewable Energy Agency (ARENA) funded a project to build an online national renewable energy mapping platform to inform investors and other stakeholders about potential Renewable Energy (RE) resources, existing electricity infrastructures and real-time electricity system performance, as well as spatial map and demographic demand information on other infrastructures.

The objective of this project – the Australian Renewable Energy Mapping Infrastructure (AREMI) – was to establish a one stop shop for renewable energy mapping data which furthermore could support the investment decision on what kind of electricity infrastructure needed to be built in a specific area, e.g. either a power plant with certain capacity and type of technology or transmission/distribution lines with certain lengths and capacity. While this map could assist the government to promote and monitor the electricity projects in various regions, it was also expected to reduce the time and costs of project preparation, and to support the analytical work by stakeholders.

In the beginning, the Australian Government appointed National Information and Communication Technology Australia (NICTA) to develop the system with support from Geoscience Australia, the Bureau of Meteorology, and the Commonwealth Scientific and Industrial Research Organisation (CSIRO). In mid-2016, Data61, under CSIRO, took over the project and continued to expand the AREMI maps that until recently had collected around 1 100 datasets consisting of electricity and renewable infrastructure, environmental data, topography, and population from various data custodians.

A further report from Data61, stated that according to the evaluation conducted by the Centre for International Economics (CIE), AREMI was attributed to generate a benefit of around AUD 11.7 million of a total AUD 47.5 million net benefit made by investors. The CIE also found the utilisation of AREMI created a benefit-cost ratio of more than 5:1 which means for every dollar spent, AUD 5 in new economic value is generated for the Australian economy in terms of time saved, improved decision making, and higher valued activities[14].

Clean energy technology development and demand behaviour will reshape Indonesia's energy landscape

Fast-changing renewable technology development and cost-decline globally will greatly influence renewable generation planning in Indonesia. Worldwide, the cost of renewable technologies has plummeted over the last decade, for example, the cost of solar photovoltaics (PV) dropped by 82% between 2010 and 2019 eventually leading to a substantial increase in the share of renewables in electricity generation (IRENA, 2020). Yet, Indonesia's electricity sector continues to rely heavily on coal (63%) with renewables only playing a minor role (11.5%) (**see Chapter 1** for more details on Indonesia's power system fuels). Some coal-fired power plants have been in operation for over 30 years, which recently led the government to plan for the gradual replacement of around 1.6 GW of coal-fired power plants with solar PV (Jakarta Post, 2020)[15].

Like other countries, Indonesia is experiencing a changing behaviour in energy consumption driven by digitalisation. It is supported by a large share of millennials and generation Z (age 8-39 years), around 53.81% of the total population of 270.2 million people (BPS, 2021)[16], while the rate of Internet penetration in the country is 73% as reported in Digital 2021 Indonesia by We Are Social and Hootsuite[17]. Millennials are more familiar with Internet-based economic activities (digitalisation) and they also prefer to use more efficient energy technology, such as ride-sharing services (i.e. GoJek and Grab), and live near cities. In addition, the IEA *Digitalisation and Energy* report (2017) stated how digitalisation is reshaping the energy sector and this furthermore should encourage Indonesia to remodel its energy supply and demand projection.

References

Bridle, R. et al. (2018), *Missing the 23 Per Cent Target: Roadblocks to the development of renewable energy in Indonesia GSI REPORT*, http://www.iisd.org/gsi (accessed on 15 January 2019). [10]

DEN (2020), *Buku Bauran Energi Nasional*, Dewan Energi Nasional, https://den.go.id/index.php/publikasi/index/BauranEnergi. [13]

DEN (2020), *Buku Bauran Energi Nasional 2020 (National Energy Mix Book 2019)*, Dewan Energi Nasional, Jakarta, https://den.go.id/index.php/publikasi/index/BauranEnergi (accessed on 19 April 2021). [2]

IESR (2019), *Kebutuhan Investasi Energi di Indonesia (English translation: Energy investment needs in Indonesia)*, http://iesr.or.id/pustaka/kebutuhan-investasi-energi-indonesia/ (accessed on 3 April 2020). [6]

Kennedy, S. (2020), *Research: land use challenges for Indonesia's transition to renewable energy*, The Conversation, https://theconversation.com/research-land-use-challenges-for-indonesias-transition-to-renewable-energy-131767 (accessed on 6 November 2020). [12]

MEMR (2020), *Handbook of Energy & Economy Statistics of Indonesia 2019*, Ministry of Energy and Mineral Resources, Jakarta. [1]

MEMR (2020), *Statistik Ketenagalistrikan 2019 (Electricity Statistics 2019)*, Ministry of Energy and Mineral Resources, Jakarta, https://gatrik.esdm.go.id/assets/uploads/download_index/files/c4053-statistik-2019-highres.pdf (accessed on 19 April 2021). [7]

OECD (2020), *OECD Investment Policy Reviews: Indonesia 2020*, OECD Investment Policy Reviews, OECD Publishing, Paris, https://dx.doi.org/10.1787/b56512da-en. [4]

OECD (2019), *OECD Green Growth Policy Review of Indonesia 2019*, OECD Environmental Performance Reviews, OECD Publishing, Paris, https://dx.doi.org/10.1787/1eee39bc-en. [8]

OECD (2015), *Overcoming Barriers to International Investment in Clean Energy*, Green Finance and Investment, OECD Publishing, Paris, https://dx.doi.org/10.1787/9789264227064-en. [11]

OECD (2015), *Policy Guidance for Investment in Clean Energy Infrastructure: Expanding Access to Clean Energy for Green Growth and Development*, OECD Publishing, Paris, https://dx.doi.org/10.1787/9789264212664-en. [5]

PWC (2019), *As many as 21 PPAs for new and renewable energy power plants planned to be signed this year*, https://www.pwc.com/id/en/media-centre/infrastructure-news/april-2019/planned-to-be-signed-this-year.html (accessed on 9 November 2020). [9]

PwC (2017), *Power in Indonesia - Investment and Taxation Guide*, http://www.pwc.com/id (accessed on 11 January 2019). [3]

Notes

[1] https://www.thejakartapost.com/news/2019/07/29/division-among-ministers-may-delay-issuance-of-ev-regulation.html.

[2] http://www.dpr.go.id/berita/detail/id/25269/t/Peran+DEN+Belum+Optimal.

[3] Dian Lestari, Head of Center for Climate Finance and Multilateral Policy, "Green Finance Facility to Support Clean Energy Projects in Indonesia", Online FGD Developing a Green Finance Facility, October 2020.

[4] https://iesr.or.id/en/pustaka/kebutuhan-investasi-energi-indonesia.

[5] MP3EI is a development planning document stipulated by Presidential Regulation Number 32 of 2011 in the early presidency of Susilo Bambang Yudhoyono. It contained various government development programmes in six economics corridors—big islands based, e.g., Java, Sumatera, Kalimantan, Sulawesi, Papua-Maluku, and Bali-Nusa Tenggara—to accelerate the development across the country to achieve a developed country status by 2025 through some indicators, e.g., income per capita, economic growth, and GDP value. Source: https://www.bappenas.go.id/id/berita-dan-siaran-pers/kegiatan-utama/master-plan-percepatan-dan-perluasan-pembangunan-ekonomi-indonesia-mp3ei-2011-2025/.

[6] https://www.bps.go.id/indicator/11/104/1/-ser, i-2010-laju-pertumbuhan-pdb-seri-2010.html.

[7] President Regulation No. 22/2017 about National General Energy Policy (RUEN).

[8] https://den.go.id/index.php/publikasi/index/pembinaanrued.

[9] https://www.cnbcindonesia.com/news/20200917152103-4-187563/ruu-ebt-ada-usul-badan-pengelola-energi-terbarukan-dibentuk.

[10] https://www.adb.org/sites/default/files/publication/668226/better-regulation-future-indonesia-electricity-sector.pdf.

[11] https://www.reuters.com/article/indonesia-electricity-idAFL4N2AY2AO.

[12] https://www.esdm.go.id/id/media-center/arsip-berita/direktorat-jenderal-ketenagalistrikan-review-program-10000-mw-tahap-i.

[13] https://inilah.com/news/1957390/program-listrik-10-ribu-mw-pakai-energi-terbarukan.

[14] AREMI decommissioning letter

[15] https://www.thejakartapost.com/news/2020/11/30/ministry-mulls-retiring-giant-suralaya-coal-plant-replacing-it-with-solar-farm.html.

[16] https://www.bps.go.id/website/materi_ind/materiBrsInd-20210121151046.pdf

[17] https://datareportal.com/reports/digital-2021-indonesia

3 Regulatory framework

This chapter examines clean energy policies and regulations in Indonesia. It analyses Indonesia's evolving policy environment for energy efficiency and renewable energy development, as well as how regulatory conditions and reforms have been shaping the market landscape for clean energy investment. The chapter reviews the role of expanding energy performance standards and labelling schemes, as well as the need for clearer regulatory conditions for energy service companies. It also considers the impact of recent and expected regulations on renewable electricity generation, and identifies opportunities to align with international best practice and facilitate the development of renewable energy capacity.

Indonesia's energy policy environment has transformed greatly since 2007, when Energy Law No. 30/2007[1] set forth the legal foundation and institutional structure for energy management. Since then, the government has implemented a number of regulatory changes to encourage and promote energy efficiency and renewable energy development, in line with the vision set forth in the country's National Energy Policy (KEN), adopted by parliament under Government Regulation No. 79/2014[2], and Indonesia's National Energy Plan (RUEN), set forth in Presidential Regulation No. 22/2017[3] (**see Chapter 2**).

These actions, complemented by a number of energy efficiency and renewable energy policies and regulations, are steps in the right direction, affirming Indonesia's resolve to turn its clean energy ambitions into legal commitments using market rules and regulations. Strengthening these reforms, for example through measures to facilitate business development in the new Omnibus Law (**see Chapter 4**), will help to ensure Indonesia's regulatory framework addresses remaining policy gaps and market barriers in order to enable a vibrant and robust investment environment for clean energy development.

Assessment and recommendations

A clear and assertive regulatory framework is central to achieving Indonesia's clean energy transition

The government is to be commended for signalling from the highest political offices that clean energy is an important part of Indonesia's future. The evolution of regulations in support of energy efficiency and renewable energy over the last decade is a positive step towards those ambitions, and developments such as the country's first energy performance standards alongside the expected presidential regulation on renewable energy are important milestones denoting Indonesia's commitment to accelerate clean energy deployment. Still, Indonesia has had many revisions in rules and regulations that govern renewable energy and energy efficiency, some of which have caused uncertainty for project developers and investors. Achieving wide-spread uptake of clean energy solutions will thus require further evolution in Indonesia's regulatory environment (as well as improved co-ordination [**see Chapter 2**]), building upon what has worked and addressing shortcomings in existing policies.

Expanding policy strength and coverage is vital to energy efficiency development

Regulations have helped create some demand for energy-efficient products and services in recent years, but there are still important gaps in policies, including low public awareness about minimum energy performance standards (MEPS) and energy labels (CLASP, 2020[1]; MEMR, 2020[2]). Air conditioner (AC) and lighting energy performance standards have not been updated regularly to ensure they keep up with market trends and product availability. Work on MEPs for ten new appliance categories is encouraging, but further effort is needed to expand and strengthen overall energy efficiency regulations. Indonesia can pull from international knowledge, such as the International Energy Agency's collaborative platform on Energy Efficient End-use Equipment[4], and work with partners such as the United for Efficiency[5] and ASEAN SHINE[6] initiatives to increase its energy efficiency policy strength and coverage.

Enforcement, monitoring and evaluation of energy efficiency policy needs to improve

Progress in developing and implementing new energy efficiency regulations is important. Improvement in the number of products in the market officially tested is equally positive, though emerging data, for example on AC equipment, show that policy is not always keeping up with market developments, with MEPS below least available efficiency levels. Addressing these gaps requires strengthening of monitoring and evaluation of regulations, not only to ensure compliance but also to improve data on product availability and market preferences (e.g. trends in equipment size and features, which influence energy consumption). Indonesia can pull from international experiences and best practices with monitoring, verification and enforcement of energy efficiency policy, such as the International Energy Agency's policy pathway on improving compliance within equipment energy efficiency programmes (IEA, 2010[3]), to improve its regulatory capacity and ensure compliance in product testing and industry reporting.

The energy service market remains an untapped resource for efficiency deployment

The 2018 revocation of the Ministry of Energy and Mineral Resources (MEMR) regulation on energy conservation services leaves the market without standard documents for energy performance contracting, limiting the market to mostly small engineering firms operating on a business-to-business basis. To tap into the enormous potential for energy service models that have been successful in other countries, clear regulation, including standard documentation, is needed to address repayment conditions (e.g. minimum charges for energy service companies [ESCOs] if energy savings are not as expected), security of payment and contract terms between parties. The government can also support development of an energy services market, for instance by providing technical support and supporting pilot projects to help the market recognise monetised energy savings, which has been a critical factor in enabling wide-spread and bankable ESCO markets in other countries.

Electricity market development requires a clearer regulatory framework

Recent growth in renewable power generation capacity is encouraging, though there remain barriers to scale up development. This includes issues with electricity market practices in which power purchase agreements (PPAs) may not be negotiated in a transparent manner with the state electricity company, Perusahaan Listrik Negara (PLN). Lack of clear and consistent application of procurement not only creates the impression of unfair and/or risky investment conditions but also reduces competition in the market, which is critical to achieve cost-competitive electricity market development. In other countries, the terms and conditions of a tender that have relevance for PPA pricing are typically made public, at least to pre-qualified bidders, to encourage competition focused on price, experience and the financial stability of developers. Indonesia should look to address these types of barriers in regulations governing independent power producers (IPPs) and PLN's purchase of power to create clear and credible market conditions.

New and impending measures will strengthen renewable electricity development, so long as policy implementation is carried out consistently and transparently

New measures such as the Omnibus Law (**see Chapter 4**) and forthcoming presidential regulation are expected to provide a clearer policy framework and improved business environment for renewable electricity. Development of a presidential regulation rather than ministerial decree also is a clear signal that the government is serious about the clean energy transition. Ensuring these measures achieve their intended effect will require a clear, consistent and fair regulatory environment – essential conditions to unlock wide-spread private sector engagement. In particular, it is vital to address perceived and real risks for renewable project developers, avoiding unclear operational conditions or abrupt changes in rules that discourage investment while also creating a regulatory environment that encourages competition and provides opportunities to achieve cost reductions.

Indonesia's renewable electricity market has major potential, if properly facilitated

Regulatory changes addressing IPPs and electricity tariffs in recent years have not necessarily helped to facilitate renewable electricity development. Large untapped market potential, for instance through corporate sourcing of renewables, is still hindered by a number of barriers, such as lack of implementing regulation on power-wheeling and current net-metering policy, which are not in line with good practice in other countries. These issues can make it uneconomical to invest in self-generation or challenging to procure off-site generation, thus hindering development of a vibrant market for renewable electricity. To tap into the significant potential for renewables procurement in Indonesia, current regulations and pricing practices need to be reviewed, ensuring transparent and fair application of settlement for self-generation and facilitating contractual agreements between businesses, PLN and IPPs.

Box 3.1. Main policy recommendations on clean energy regulatory framework

- Strengthen and expand energy performance standards and labelling in Indonesia, building upon past experience and forthcoming new standards to remove inefficient products from the market and improve the availability and certainty of demand for more efficient ones.
- Streamline and standardise PPAs to address concerns about project bankability and ensure transparent negotiations, thus avoiding perceived risks or perception of unfair treatment. Critically, avoid policy changes that affect the economic value of a PPA once it is signed and ensure regulation integrates economic incentives to limit disruption, including establishing clear rules on compensation when curtailment or disruption occurs.
- Ensure reforms such as the Omnibus Law and expected presidential regulation on renewable electricity are translated into consistent and transparent operational rules and regulations. In particular, ensure there is clear and fair competition in forthcoming auctions as well as a streamlined application of feed-in-tariffs (FiTs), so that investors have a clear, predictable understanding of the terms and conditions that apply to renewable energy projects (e.g. on how auction winners are chosen).
- Address the regulatory gap in the energy services market holding back development of those opportunities, ensuring there are transparent conditions for energy service contracting. This includes establishing standard documentation that accounts for basic terms of service, such as contract terms between parties, security of payment and repayment conditions (e.g. minimum charges for ESCOs if energy savings are not as expected).
- Ensure fair and non-discriminatory settlement of self-generation and review current regulations to address barriers in the net-metering scheme limiting uptake of corporate sourcing of renewables. As part of this review, also address the regulatory gap for power wheeling arrangements, facilitating businesses that would seek procurement of off-site renewable electricity production.
- Take a leading role in enabling uptake of energy efficiency, building upon existing initiatives such as the on-going street lighting replacement programme, and instruct government institutions and state-owned enterprises to identify and implement energy efficiency measures, for example creating a recognition scheme to encourage public servants to find opportunities with short pay-back periods.
- Review public procurement practices to facilitate and empower public spending on energy efficiency and review support for public private partnerships (PPPs), which currently are more suited to large infrastructure projects and are difficult to apply to energy efficiency projects given their typically smaller investment cost. Also consider possible exceptions or conditions in which local authorities and public entities can engage in energy savings contracts that are longer than one year, which would help in development of local energy efficiency markets.
- Build upon positive development in enforcement of industry energy management reporting, work with businesses to bring forward success stories and potentially expand upon the National Energy Efficiency Awards (PEEN) to provide a reward structure for those improving energy intensity. Equally penalise businesses that fail to comply with energy reporting and management requirements.

Energy efficiency policies and regulations

Indonesia has initiated several programmes and policies on energy conservation and efficiency over the last decade and since its National Master Plan for Energy Conservation (RIKEN) in 1995. Notable measures include implementation of several regulations for energy management and energy performance standards, such as Ministry of Industry (MoI) Regulation No. 51/2015[7] on mandatory minimum energy standards for heavy industry users (pulp and paper, textiles, cement and ceramics). The government has also initiated several awareness raising initiatives to increase uptake of energy efficiency as well as capacity building programmes (**see Chapter 7**).

These measures reflect Indonesia's commitment to reduce overall national energy intensity, though they can lack incentives or clear implementing guidelines in terms of enforcement of energy efficiency policy. The RUEN minimum 1% annual energy intensity improvement target (for total of 17% energy savings by 2025), is encouraging, but these targets are unlikely to be met. The 1% intensity improvement also is less ambitious than calls to put the world on a path to three percent annual efficiency improvement by the Energy Efficiency Global Alliance[8]. To meet those recommended improvements, Indonesia's energy intensity targets would need to be in the order of 2% or 3% per year, alongside increased coverage and enforcement of energy efficiency regulations to send a strong market signal for energy efficiency development. This would also give greater incentive to asset owners or managers, particularly in sectors with often long-lived assets such as industry and buildings, by encouraging them to prioritise actions and investment that will meet policy requirements.

Energy efficiency regulations are improving, but coverage should be expanded

Government Regulation No. 70/2009[9] set requirements on energy conservation for companies with annual energy consumption exceeding 6 000 tonnes of oil equivalent, representing around 60% of Indonesia's industry energy consumption (IEA, 2018[4]). It requires those users to appoint an energy manager, develop an energy conservation plan, perform an energy audit and report annual energy consumption to the government. MEMR later enacted its Regulation No. 14/2012[10] to implement the 2009 Government Regulation, establishing provisions for energy preservation and management for these targeted energy users by establishing requirements to: develop short, medium and long-term energy conservation programmes; conduct regular energy audits (at least once every three years); implement the recommendation of those audits; and submit reports to the government each year on the status of energy conservation and energy audit implementation.

MEMR has also worked with the MoI and the National Standardisation Agency (Badan Standardisasi Nasional) through the support of the United Nations Industrial Development Organisation and the Global Environment Facility to support adoption of energy management and system optimisation standards for industry, based on the International Organisation for Standardisation (ISO) 50001 energy management system, which was used in over 100 countries across more than 42 000 sites in 2019 (ISO, 2020[5]). The resulting Indonesian National Standard (Standar Nasional Indonesia, or SNI) ISO 50015/2014[11] established the general principles and guidelines for measurement and verification of energy performance of an organisation or its components, and by 2019, 76 sites in Indonesia were ISO-50001 certified.

Indonesia has also taken steps over the last decade to establish building standards and mainstream energy efficiency into building codes. The first SNI on Energy Conservation in Building Envelopes[12] established in 2011 set code references for energy conservation and energy audit procedures for all new non-residential buildings and those undergoing substantial renovations. While the code is voluntary, it did create needed standards for building envelopes, air-conditioning systems, lighting and energy audit procedures, all of which are critical steps for moving towards mandatory building energy codes. In effect, the Ministry of Public Works and Housing (MPWH) issued a 2015 decree[13] requiring buildings with more than 500 square metres to meet minimum energy performance requirements, with obligations for implementation and certification as well as related incentives for green buildings (**see Chapter 5)**. Unfortunately, the decree does not impose any sections for non-compliance, although it did provide an important framework for the development of green building codes at the sub-national level (Hakim, 2015[6]).

By 2017, 412 of 508 local jurisdictions had a form of building regulation in place, including growing use of international certification programmes such as the EDGE certification[14], which was used to certify 339 green buildings in Jakarta in 2018 (Rahman, 2019[7]). The Green Building Council of Indonesia has also been supporting introduction of its Greenship Rating Tools[15]. In practice, though, application of local building energy codes and standards is rather weak, and only three cities (Jakarta, Bandung, and Surabaya) had implemented the 2015 MPWH decree on green buildings as of 2019.

Bandung has local green building codes with mandatory energy efficiency requirements for large buildings and some additional energy performance requirements for small buildings (Pahnael, Soekiman and Wimala, 2020[8]). Jakarta also passed Regulation No. 38/2012[16] on mandatory energy efficiency requirements and energy use consumption standards for large buildings. Importantly, Jakarta's regulation legalised the planning, construction, utilisation, maintenance, and deconstruction of buildings, focusing on energy efficiency, water efficiency, indoor air quality, waste and soil treatment, and construction activities. It also prevents and restricts buildings that fail to meet these standards from receiving building permits – a vital regulatory measure that other cities could adopt to improve compliance with energy performance regulations.

For end-use equipment, Indonesia established its first energy efficiency labelling programme under MEMR Regulation No. 6/2011[17] to provide information on compact fluorescent lamp (CFL) energy performance. The initial programme covered voluntary labels for CFLs, and then for AC equipment, refrigerators, and freezers. In 2014, first mandatory labelling requirements and MEPS were developed for CFLs[18] and then later for single split, wall-mounted residential ACs (inverter and non-inverter types) in 2015[19]. These mandatory energy labels use Indonesia's one-to-four-star rating scheme, developed in 2016, which shows product energy performance alongside the star rating, with four stars reserved for top-performing products.

The government is pursuing plans to increase the coverage of MEPS for ten other end-use equipment such as electric fans, televisions, rice cookers, refrigerators, and electric motors. This is an important step, as increased MEPS will help to address critical gaps in policy coverage, such as the lack of mandatory performance standards for electric motor systems, which account for around 60% of electricity use in industry (IEA, 2018[4]). In fact, an estimated 35% of the installed motor stock in Indonesia operates at an International Energy (IE) efficiency class of IE0, leaving large room for energy savings. If currently planned MEPS for electric motors set the threshold as the IE2 level (as in China), industrial electricity use by 2030 could be cut by more than 2 terawatt-hours (TWh), or nearly four times the electricity generated by solar and wind power in Indonesia in 2019 (IEA, 2017[9]; IEA, 2020[10]).

The planned expansion of MEPS in Indonesia is a critical step forward, given that energy efficiency policy covers only around 18% of total final energy use in Indonesia, without taking into account actual compliance and enforcement of energy efficiency regulations (Figure 3.1). Policy coverage is highest in industry, thanks to the 2009 Government Regulation and 2012 MEMR requirements for large energy users, though compliance is not comprehensive. Energy codes for large commercial buildings similarly mean there is solid policy coverage of non-residential building energy use, though, again, this does not reflect actual uptake of energy efficiency measures, as codes are mostly voluntary. On the residential side, lack of building energy codes and limited MEPS for appliances and end-use equipment mean there is very low policy coverage (IEA, 2018[4]).Transport similarly lacks energy performance standards, particularly for the rapidly expanding fleet of passenger vehicles.

Figure 3.1. Mandatory policy coverage of energy consuming sectors in Indonesia, 2018

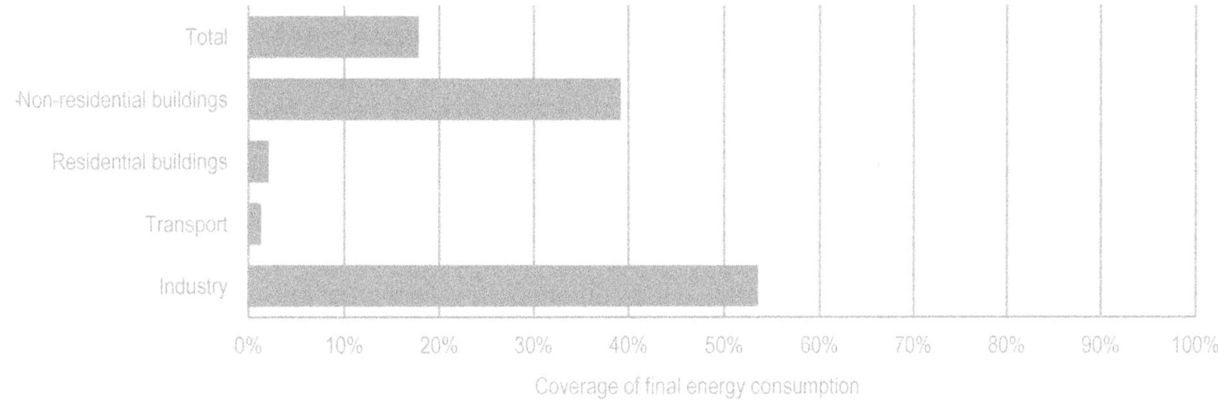

Source: (IEA, 2019[11]), *Energy Efficiency 2019.*

StatLink https://stat.link/ivftpj

Better monitoring, verification and enforcement will increase energy efficiency uptake

Roll-out of Indonesia's energy efficiency regulations, standards and labelling regimes has come with a number of limitations in compliance, enforcement and policy effectiveness, though this has been improving in recent years. For example, MEPS such as the CFL and AC regulations require products on the market to be tested in a government-approved facility before obtaining commercialisation permits. Yet, only 18 of 35 companies were complying with CFL testing in 2016, covering just 27% of the 280 million CFL sales that year (IEA, 2017[9]).

The government has taken this lack of compliance seriously, for instance revoking permits in recent years and telling producers to withdraw products that do not comply with regulations. The result has been an increase in product compliance. For instance, 32 companies were compliant with CFL MEPS and labelling requirements as of 2019.

Similar compliance issues could be seen in industry energy management reporting. Of the 346 industries covered by MEMR energy audit reporting requirements in 2018, only 44 submitted their results, underscoring missed opportunities for energy savings, as the companies that did submit their reporting alleged total energy savings of 1.1 TWh that year (MEMR, 2019[12]). The government has since increased its monitoring and compliance, and by 2019, 148 companies were reporting their energy management activities. This number can still be increased further, in line with the growing number of companies that comply with ISO 50001 (up from 26 companies in 2017 to 106 in 2019). In early 2020, MEMR also expressed its intention to increase significantly energy audits and surveys, and it upgraded its Energy Management Online Reporting System (IESR, 2021[13]).

Another challenge faced by the government on energy efficiency policy is poor market data on available efficiency levels. For example, 2015 AC MEPS were designed with a minimum energy efficiency rating (EER) of 2.5. However, improved data through AC registration and other market statistics showed that the least efficient imported AC was already a 2.53 EER, while the least efficient locally produced AC was above a 2.65 EER. In fact, as much as 80% of available ACs in the Indonesian market already met the highest rating (four stars) in 2015, illustrating the gap between policy and market trends (Letschert et al., 2017[14]).

Positively, an update of AC MEPS was announced under MEMR Regulation No. 57/2017[20], targeting the minimum EER values of 2.64 by August 2018 and 2.92 after July 2020. These EERs are still close to the lower end of available efficiency levels in the market (IEA, 2018[4]), but the new regulation sets an essential requirement for testing procedures to be carried out by a certified agency, which should help to improve market data on available performance levels. SNI 8476/2018[21] also added testing requirements for liquid-chilling packages with a vapour compression system and cooling capacity of 350 kilowatts or more.

Indonesia has enacted a number of other policies to support the effective implementation of its energy efficiency regulations. For instance, the 2015[22] and 2016[23] MoI Regulations designated accredited institutions and testing laboratories to implement and monitor SNI for ACs, refrigerators and washing machines. MEMR Regulation No. 01/2016[24] also provided guidelines and procedures on the actual testing and certification of products, implementing Presidential Regulation No. 79/2010 concerning Ratification of the Association of Southeast Asian Nations (ASEAN) agreement regarding harmonization of procedures for the regulation of electrical and electronic equipment[25].

Additional standards have been implemented to support effective validation of energy performance in the market. SNI ISO 50006/2014[26] provided general principles and guidelines on how to establish, use and maintain energy performance indicators and energy baselines as part of the process of measuring energy performance, while SNI ISO 50002/2014[27] applied ISO standards and specified the principles of carrying out energy audits, including requirements for common processes during the audits, and deliverables for the energy audits. These measures are important milestones to ensure the operative application of Indonesia's growing energy efficiency regulations.

As Indonesia looks to expand its energy efficiency regulations, it can look to other countries' experiences in ensuring better monitoring, verification and enforcement of standards and labelling programmes. For example, Australia has shown good practice in monitoring through a mandatory product registration database coupled with market sales data to provide very detailed tracking of the market (Energy Rating, 2016[15]). In India, the Bureau of Energy Efficiency created an independent agency for monitoring and evaluation[28], similar to the national independent market surveillance programme established by the Government of the United Kingdom with ring-fenced funding (OPSS, 2019[16]). Likewise, the European Union's Anti-Circumvention of Standards for Better Market Survey project was set up in recent years to address gaming of test procedures (AntiCSS, 2019[17]).

Indonesia should also accelerate the update of its existing standards and labelling schemes to close the gap between policy and market-available energy efficiency potential (e.g. taking advantage of the big cost declines in light-emitting diode [LED] technology). In addition, the government can complement its growing energy performance standards with supportive elements such as financial incentives, technical assistance and awareness raising programmes to create a "push and pull" approach that is common in other countries, helping to drive out least efficient products and encouraging adoption of the most efficient ones (**see Chapter 5**).

Expanding awareness raising efforts will encourage energy efficiency implementation

Indonesia has a number of awareness building programmes that aim to promote energy efficiency uptake and compliance. The PEEN energy efficiency awards[29] was initiated by MEMR's Directorate-General of New, Renewable Energy and Energy Conservation in 2012 to improve energy efficiency in the building and industry sectors. Aligned with the ASEAN Energy Award, PEEN promotes energy efficiency in building and industry by: recognising institutions that have successfully implemented energy efficiency measures; improving participation and awareness of stakeholders in implementing energy efficiency and energy conservation; introducing best practices for energy management systems; and providing incentives to central and local governments that have implemented energy efficiency measures. In 2019, there were 120 participants in the PEEN awards, a tenfold increase since the 2012 kick-off (MEMR, 2020[18]).

MEMR also has three programmes in place to improve awareness of the importance of energy efficiency, targeting different groups of audiences. These include:

- *Kampanye Potong 10%* (the 10% [Energy] Cut Campaign), a nation-wide programme kicked off in 2016 targeting stakeholders in the energy sector. There are no incentives to participate, although MEMR encourages energy consumers to participate and benefit from reduced energy bills.
- *Konservasi Energi Goes to Campus* (Energy Conservation Goes to Campus), a programme introducing university students to the basic principles of energy efficiency, the ISO 50001 standard and job opportunities for energy auditors and energy managers.
- A street lighting initiative kicked-off in 2016 to replace conventional halogen lamps with LED lighting in 93 cities as part of a public campaign for energy efficiency using state budget each year. As of late 2018, around 15 000 units had been installed, saving 6.7 gigawatt-hours of electricity each year (MEMR, 2019[12]).

Similar initiatives include the Ministry of Environment's *Adiwiyata Award* targeting about 500 junior and senior high schools that implement an environmental approach, including energy efficiency, in their school activities. MEMR and the Ministry of Home Affairs have also collaborated in recent years to encourage energy efficiency in buildings owned by provincial and regional governments, targeting implementation in 18 provinces in 2020. Similarly, MEMR has cooperated with the Muslim clerks and other Islamic associations to promote energy efficiency, as well as with the Dharma Wanita housewives association and sub-district government in the greater Jakarta area.

More recent communications such as MEMR's annual editions tracking *Data & Information of Energy Conservation*[30] help to demonstrate progress on energy efficiency policy implementation and initiatives. This information is critical to an effective energy efficiency policy regime, and the government could consider tracking additional indicators such as the evolution in shares of star-rated appliances in the market. This would inform the public on policy progress, while equally increasing capacity to identify gaps and opportunities in the market.

The government should continue to build upon its awareness raising initiatives, as these are important elements of an interactive process to engage citizens, business and related energy stakeholders through communication and empowerment strategies that have proven effective in other countries. For example, France has a media campaign to promote residential building energy retrofits, pointing to non-profit organisations that provide free and independent advice to help homeowners choose appropriate energy efficiency solutions (IEA, 2019[19]). The media campaign also uses renovations in schools to communicate the value of sustainable buildings with teachers, children and parents (IEA-UNEP, 2018[20]). These efforts have complemented policies aiming to improve the energy performance of existing buildings in France, helping to create a growing public acceptance of the need to invest in building energy efficiency measures.

Energy services market development can grow with a clearer regulatory framework

The energy services market, which has played an important role in delivering energy performance improvements in other major economies like China, India, the United States and Europe, remains quite nascent in Indonesia, with limited development of ESCOs and energy performance contracting models. These contractual arrangements, typically using a guaranteed or shared savings approach, can help overcome critical barriers to energy efficiency investment, such as lack of technical capacity or adequate financing for upfront capital expenses.

To date, Indonesia's experience with the ESCO market has been mixed, and the regulatory environment can make it challenging for third-party actors to step into the energy services space. MEMR Regulation No. 14/2016[31] on the implementation of energy conservation services put forward the policy framework for ESCOs, including standards on the operation of energy conservation service companies to ensure they are independent, reliable, transparent, competitive and efficient, notably with provisions for use of guaranteed and shared savings.

While these types of standards are generally good practice in other countries with robust ESCO markets, the MEMR regulation itself unfortunately did not drive noticeable ESCO market development in Indonesia. This was due in part to other related concerns or market issues, such as lack of sufficient capital or collateral for many ESCOs to meet banks' requests for a guarantee. Other barriers such as underdeveloped capacity to finance and perform investment grade audits also can impede market growth, as most energy service contracting to date in Indonesia has been with smaller engineering firms.

Ultimately, the MEMR regulation was revoked in 2018 to leave energy service contracting to a business-to-business model, thus leaving ESCOs without a proper regulatory environment common in other countries with robust ESCO markets. By default, Energy Law No. 70/2009 provides an overall policy context for ESCOs. However, this does not provide sufficient provisions or guidelines to unlock the potential for energy service agreements or energy performance contracting on a large scale.

The result is that Indonesia's ESCO market remains small: the Indonesia ESCO association, APKENINDO, estimates there were around 25 companies listed as ESCOs in 2018 (Tumiwa et al., 2019[21]). In comparison, there are about 50 ESCOs operating in Viet Nam, 125 enlisted by the Bureau of Energy Efficiency in India, and 205 registered in neighbouring Malaysia (Anh, 2020[22]; BEE, 2019[23]; STEC, 2020[24]).

In principle, government regulations on energy audits and energy management systems should help to grow demand for energy services in coming years. To a certain extent, the energy services market may also naturally be driven by the growing number of firms looking to achieve energy savings (e.g. those with ISO 50001 energy management requirements). Yet, the business-to-business model in practice may only work for smaller firms like engineering services, as the lack of regulatory conditions (e.g. standard contract documents, transparent accounting rules and procedures for arbitration) leave risks for overall growth of the ESCO market in Indonesia.

The government also faces its own challenges in spaces where the public sector could lead by example, for instance, by driving energy service market development through public procurement or PPPs. Regulatory conditions have made this engagement challenging, notably because of limitations to government institutions entering multi-year contracts. Presidential Regulation No. 38/2015[32] on PPPs to provide public infrastructure (including energy conservation) set to make the PPP process more efficient and bankable (Hermawan, Hermawan and Bahar, 2015[25]). Yet, PPPs for energy efficiency are still uncommon, in part because the process requires extensive co-ordination of many stakeholders and also because government contracting agencies often lack the skills and experience to prepare PPPs.

The government does have a PPP Joint Office to support capacity building with central and local governments and to facilitate government contracting agencies in preparing PPP projects. However, the number of energy efficiency PPPs across the country has still remained limited. In turn, the lack of energy efficiency PPPs contributes to banks and other market actors being unfamiliar with these types of projects and their risks, thus limiting overall appetite to provide finance to ESCOs for these types of projects.

There are ways to address these barriers and enable use of market-based solutions for public procurement of energy efficiency, ranging from pilot programmes to demonstrate the potential for energy efficiency PPPs to creation of standardised documents for those projects. For example, the government can develop institutional guidelines and standard PPP documents, such as the Australian government's Best Practice Guide (AEPCA, 2000[26]) to support government institutions (as well as businesses and facility owners/managers) in using energy performance contracting. This would complement existing Bappenas Regulations No. 04/2015 and No. 02/2020, providing the overall standards for PPP planning and implementation in Indonesia, as well as the toolkit on preparing preliminary study documents that Bappenas produced for street lighting PPPs. Indonesia could also look at potential solutions to address limitations to multi-year contracting, for instance by allowing municipal energy budgets to "freeze" throughout the term of the service agreement, which in turn would help address some of the bank concerns over financing those projects.

Addressing regulatory barriers for public procurement of energy services and solutions will help create a sizeable demand for energy efficiency services, where well-establish ESCO markets in places such as the United States, Europe, India and China all developed largely as the result of the public sector. Insights can also be taken from global experience addressing barriers to energy service market development. For example, the Czech Republic reformed public procurement procedures to facilitate ESCO contracts in the public sector, allowing multi-year contracts and retention of savings for energy efficiency projects (Hofer, Limaye and Singh, 2016[27]). Other countries such as Singapore, Thailand and Turkey developed ESCO accreditation schemes to increase confidence of both public and private actors looking to engage in energy performance contracts, while in India, the creation of the publicly-owned Energy Efficiency Services Limited company was used to apply standard offers for contracts between public agencies and ESCOs.

Electricity market design and renewable energy policies and regulations

Electricity Law No. 30/2009[33] established that PLN would remain the main provider of electricity generation, while also maintaining control of the national transmission network and remaining the sole provider of overall transmission and distribution networks, except in some specific locations or industrial zones. As such, Indonesia remains a traditional vertically integrated market in which IPP electricity generation is sold to the single buyer, PLN. There is no independent regulator, and MEMR's Directorate General of Electricity is the only institution with mandate to regulate PLN and the electricity sector (**see Chapter 2**).

Regulatory conditions have improved but still complicate electricity market progress

While PLN is granted first priority in electricity generation, transmission and distribution, other electricity supply businesses can still operate under the Electricity Law, provided they have the appropriate licence (an "IUPTL"). Government Regulation No. 14/2012[34] established the formal rules on obtaining licences for electricity supply businesses, and the subsequent MEMR Regulation No. 35/2013[35] set the procedures to obtain permits. MEMR Regulation No. 12/2016[36] amended this with additional provisions for private companies to sell electricity to the public or directly to customers, so long as they obtain an electricity business area (Wilayah Usaha) licence as per MEMR Regulation No. 28/2012, later amended by MEMR Regulation No. 07/2016[37].

The Electricity Law and MEMR regulations stipulate that electricity businesses carry out activities in an integrated way, though this does not include all types of electricity activities. Specifically, the Constitutional Court ruled in its Decision No. 111/PUU-XIII/2015[38] that unbundling (notably vertical unbundling by directly supplying electricity to consumers) is unconstitutional. This decision in effect means that the power sector allows either disaggregated businesses, with PLN as the off-taker, or private power companies that operate within Wilayah Usaha (e.g. direct electricity generation and use for industrial zones). As such, a business license is needed to sell renewable electricity directly to another entity. It also complicates eventual wheeling of power, for instance for corporate sourcing of off-site renewables, as any wheeling arrangements need to be agreed with PLN, as per MEMR Regulation No. 01/2015[39].

Intrinsically, PLN's role as the single buyer and single retailer electricity market greatly influences electricity market development in Indonesia. Its electricity supply business plan (RUPTL) sets forth development plans with the expected role of IPPs, and as such, it is a critical document for project developers, laying forth the path for procurement of and investment in power generation and electricity grids (Figure 3.2). In principle, developers can propose projects that are not in the RUPTL, or conversely propose to change planned projects (MEMR, 2017[28]). However, in practice, PLN is the counterpart of any PPA governing the sale of electricity from IPPs. This creates a convoluted operating environment in which other market actors can manoeuvre.

Figure 3.2. Planned electricity capacity additions by type of developer in the 2019-28 RUPTL

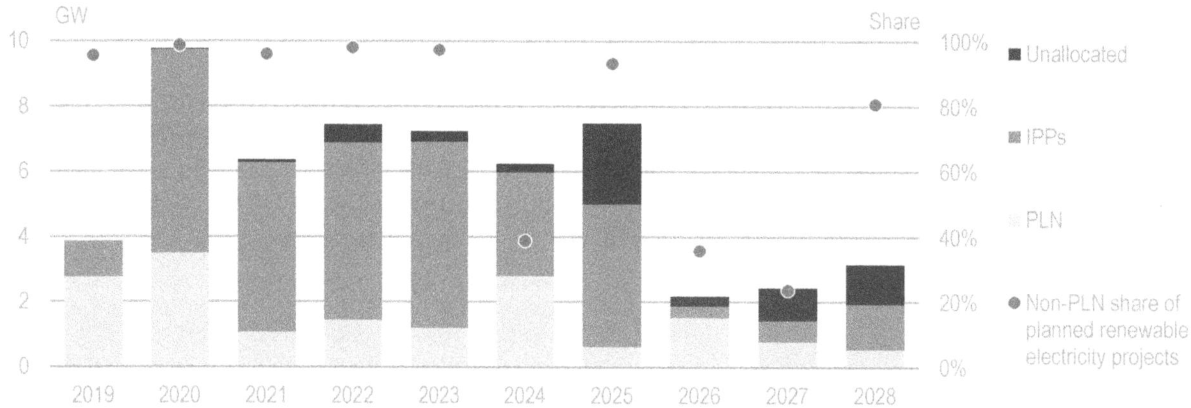

Notes: GW = gigawatt. PLN is currently revising the 2019-28 RUPTL, which may (or may not) affect current planned capacity additions.
Source: Adapted from (PLN, 2019[29]), *PT PLN Power Supply Business Plan 2019-28.*

StatLink https://stat.link/z4oavh

Legally, procurement by PLN can be done through three tracks, as regulated in MEMR Regulation No. 01/2006[40] (later amended by MEMR Regulation No. 04/2007) on the procurement of electricity; PLN Director Regulation No. 0022P/DIR/2018[41] (amended by No.1720P/DIR/2018 and No.0062P/DIR/2020) on Electricity Purchasing from Renewable Energy Sources; and by Government Regulation No. 14/2012[42] (with amendments in Government Regulation No. 21/2014) regulating electricity supply business activities. These three tracks are (PLN, 2017[30]):

1. Direct appointment, wherein an IPP is directly appointed by PLN without reviewing or competitively selecting other projects. This includes unsolicited proposals, which must be listed in the next RUPTL, as a first step after being accepted, before proceeding to PLN's assessment.

2. Direct selection, in which more than two IPPs submit a project proposal for selection by PLN. The selection process can be tied to a capacity quota (offered by PLN, where the direct selection is based on RUPTL), and PLN performs its due diligence per MEMR Regulation No. 10/2017[43] on the technical and financial capabilities of the IPPs.

3. Competitive tender, which has not been used successfully, despite the legal possibility. A large-scale solar auction was organised in 2013 when MEMR announced a reverse auction for 140 megawatts (MW) of solar photovoltaic (PV). However, the auction was cancelled as the practice of foreign investors using only imported components was deemed unconstitutional (Burke et al., 2019[31]).

In practice, direct appointment is the easiest procurement route with PLN. IPPs that signed PPAs through the direct selection process have not always reached financial close, though this can be due to low quality of feasibility study documents (**see Chapter 6**). The direct selection process from pre-qualification to contract arrangement can also be long, taking up to 150 days (PwC, 2018[32]). MEMR Regulation No. 03/2015[44] would have shortened the process time to 45 days (PLN, 2017[30]), but it was revoked under MEMR Regulation No. 03/17.

In theory, Presidential Regulation No.16/2018[45] on public procurement of goods and services (revoking and replacing Presidential Regulation No. 54/2010[46]) simplified and optimised the procurement process. However, the regulation does not officially apply to state-owned enterprises like PLN. Even if it did, the rules do not oblige disclosure of the basis for using a non-competitive procedure, but instead only to indicate the type of procedure (IDFI, 2018[33]). This is different from best practice in countries where there are clear and transparent regulations for electricity procurement, whether it is through direct selection processes or competitive tenders.

The process for IPP grid connection and operations, while regulated, similarly lacks transparency. MEMR Regulation No. 01/2015[47] set forth the conditions for joint use of the electric power network, and in principal, there is no discrimination in connection to the grid for IPPs, as long as they meet reliability, security and economic considerations. Notably, Regulation No. 01/2015 Article 6 states that power wheeling should follow applicable costs by the transmission licence holder. However, with no detailed implementing regulation on how applicable costs should be understood, the methodology of applicable costs can be different from area to area, thereby creating uncertainty in determining grid and network usage costs, which may deter project development.

Lack of transparency and consistency for electricity market development can create the impression that procurement through PLN is unpredictable and risky (**see Chapter 4**). This not only limits potential investment in the electricity market but also dissuades a competitive environment that has been critical to cost-effective development in other countries.

Indonesia should look to address these barriers, considering international experiences, such as market reform in Morocco that established an independent agency to organise tendering of renewable energy projects. Morocco succeeded in creating a level playing field between the utility and private investors by performing tenders outside the incumbent utility. These types of practices in other countries and their lessons learned can help Indonesia to apply regulatory conditions that lead to clear and fair competition across all actors and investors.

Complex regulations and perceived risks have limited renewable electricity deployment

MEMR Regulation No. 50/2017[48] on the utilisation of new and renewable energy required most renewable electricity projects to be procured through direct selection with capacity quotas. PLN subsequently implemented Decree No. 0022P/DIR/2018 (and then PLN Director Reg No.0062P/DIR/2020) regarding the purchase of renewable energy, and in order to participate, IPPs must pre-qualify based on certain criteria in order be integrated in the final list (the “DPT”) of qualified IPPs (Hadiputranto, 2019[34]). Criteria are administrative (e.g. having fulfilled tax obligations), technical (e.g. experience in developing IPPs and being able to meet local content requirements issued by the Ministry of Industry) and financial (e.g. demonstrated credit rating or sound financial statement (PwC, 2018[32]).

These changes made the renewable electricity procurement process more transparent, but perhaps not simpler. For example, a direct selection process by PLN was organised in 2017 with a capacity quota of 168 MW, but as of 2019, results still had not been announced (Burke et al., 2019[31]). Part of this is due to local content requirements factored into the selection process, limiting opportunities to achieve cost reductions and creating a possible issue for international IPPs who would compete in the process.

Similarly, MEMR Regulation No. 10/2017 expanded mandatory provisions (e.g. for commissioning and commercial operation dates, dispute resolution and termination of PPAs) for dispatchable electricity projects (PwC, 2018[32]). This helped to provide greater consistency with standards already applied for thermal, geothermal and hydroelectric PPAs. Yet, officially, the regulation only applied to geothermal, hydropower and biomass plants, but not to intermittent renewable energy projects such as solar and wind (regardless of size), mini-hydro (below 10 MW), biogas and waste-to-energy power plants. Moreover, previous specific regulations, such as PPAs for solar PV projects under MEMR Regulation No. 19/2016[49], were revoked in MEMR Regulation No. 9/2018[50]. The result, despite its intent, is an uncertain regulatory environment for project developers concerning those types of renewable electricity projects.

MEMR Regulation No. 49/2017[51] integrated additional provisions to MEMR Regulation No. 10/2017, mandating that build-own-operate-transfer (BOOT) schemes for PPAs have concession periods no longer than 30 years. The regulation also required all PPAs (including renewable electricity) to apply the BOOT scheme, effectively transferring IPP facilities to PLN at the end of the agreement and implying that PPA renewals will not be possible. This may not be a concern for all project developers (e.g. 30 years would not be an issue for typical renewable electricity discounted cash flow analysis), and most projects already effectively constitute BOOT arrangements with PLN. However, the requirement can create issues for some renewable electricity projects, such as biomass power plants, where the power assets are sometimes inseparable from other IPP assets (e.g. land to produce the biofuel feedstock).

MEMR Regulation No. 10/2018[52] further amended MEMR Regulation No. 10/2017, creating concerns of risk allocation between IPPs and PLN. Previous regulations distinguished several types of risks, including natural force majeure (NFM) and government force majeure (GFM), which was differentiated for "change in laws and policies" and "unjustified government action or inaction" such as unjustified license revocation. Those force majeure risks were traditionally borne by PLN, but MEMR Regulation No. 10/2017 integrated a provision that released both parties in the case a GFM caused the IPP to stop operating, thus shifting the de facto risk to IPPs. The 2018 amendment then removed the mention of GFM altogether, leaving it up to the PPA parties to negotiate risk allocation on a business-to-business basis. The amendment also released PLN from making a deemed dispatch payment when NFM events prevent PLN from taking power, instead allowing compensation by extending PPAs by the length of time lost by the disaster and any associated repairs. This can be problematic for IPPs with regular debt service payments from project cash flow (PwC, 2018[32]). It also poses a risk to asset owners since they would still have debt to service in the event of force majeure, thus influencing the bankability of PPAs.

MEMR Regulation No. 04/2020[53] again amended the 2017 regulation, notably enacting three changes to the procurement of renewable electricity projects. The first re-established the possibility for PLN to use direct appointment of renewable IPPs, and the second removed the requirement for those projects to be developed exclusively under the BOOT scheme. The third requires PLN to prioritise electricity from renewable IPPs based on a must-run regime, without restriction on the generation capacity of those IPPs. These are all positive developments, more closely in line with international practice.

A presidential regulation on renewable electricity is also expected in 2021, and this should help to facilitate further renewable electricity projects. For example, it is expected that MEMR will provide renewable energy quotas, that the Ministry of Spatial Planning will provide assistance with land permitting issues, that MoI will relax some of its local content requirements, and that the Investment Coordinating Board, BKPM, will implement an integrated permitting process to monitor and ease permit issuance with central and local governments. At the same time, future implementing regulations will need to ensure that the overall procurement process is clear and consistent across all renewable electricity projects. The government should work to ensure that recent positive policy changes are part of a more predictable and transparent process. This has been a critical element in making large-scale and wide-spread renewable electricity development attractive in other countries.

Rules on renewable electricity tariffs should be aligned with global market practice

MEMR Regulation No. 31/2009 was the basis for renewable energy pricing in Indonesia, stipulating a single flat FiT for renewable electricity purchases by PLN. Subsequent changes by MEMR and PLN raised the FiT successively in an attempt to attract renewable electricity project development, but the FiT was revoked by MEMR Regulation No. 04/2012 and then by MEMR Regulation No. 07/2018. An entirely new price ceiling system was introduced under MEMR Regulation No. 50/2017 (later revised by MEMR Regulations No. 53/2018 and 04/2020). As such, tariffs for renewable electricity projects are determined relative to PLN's average costs of electricity provision (Biaya Pokok Penyediaan, or BPP) at the national and local level.

In essence, BPP represents the cost to PLN of procuring power from different systems listed in a BPP decree, which is reviewed annually. The BPP must include considerations of fuel price, operation and maintenance depreciation, incurred costs for generating power and an annual adjustment. Present year BPPs are based on the BPP realised in the previous year and should take into account the principles of effective, efficient and accountable processes. MEMR has the right to set the formula for calculating the BPP, as spelled out in MEMR Regulation No. 24/2017 on the mechanism for determining the generation cost for PLN, though the actual calculation of the listed BPP is still not very clear. By contrast, the use of the listed BPPs is straightforward: where local BPP is above national BPP, tariffs for solar PV, wind, biomass, biogas and ocean power shall not exceed 85% of local cost (for municipal waste, geothermal and hydropower, it is 100%); where the local BPP is below national BPP, IPPs and PLN can mutually agree on the tariff, the most likely being 100% of local BPP.

This approach to remuneration is not typical practice used globally (Figure 3.3), and may create barriers to creating price reductions that benefit consumers and attract further investment. FiT and feed-in-premium (FiP) schemes have been the most common method used to determine renewable electricity tariffs, though the number of countries using these has decreased slightly in recent years as the use of auction schemes has increased. In the growing market for auction schemes, price caps can be implemented, but they are more commonly related to a calculation of an acceptable rate of return, rather than the current generation cost of a system. International experiences also show that the price of renewables reduces significantly once a country obtains a certain scale of deployment. Thus, by tying the price of renewables to BPP, Indonesia may be creating a barrier to achieving price reductions that attract further investment.

Figure 3.3. Countries with FiT/FiP, auctions and certificate remuneration schemes

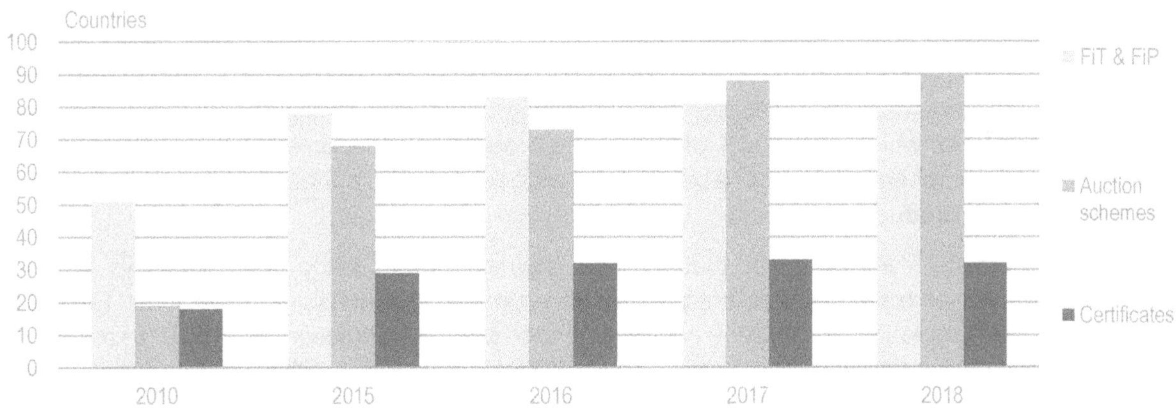

Source: (IEA, 2018[35]), *Renewables 2018: Analysis and Forecasts to 2023.*

StatLink https://stat.link/9i6qph

The change in regulation to use of BPPs was widely criticised by renewable energy proponents, who noted that the tariff structure is both challenging and risky for developers. In particular, continued use of subsidies for consumer electricity prices (**see Chapter 5**) indirectly encourages use of cheap coal, which decreases BPPs in many regions, thereby creating an uneven playing field for renewable electricity generation (Bridle et al., 2018[36]). In fact, a study by the Global Subsidies Initiative found that if coal subsidies (e.g. through credit support and domestic market obligations) were removed, the price of electricity from coal-fired power generation would rise by as much as USD 0.05 per kilowatt-hour (kWh), making renewable electricity projects more attractive under the current BPP scheme (Attwood et al., 2017[37]). Thus, while the government's goal understandably is to reduce BPPs across the country in order to ensure affordable electricity, the continued use of fossil fuel subsidies does not create a level playing field to achieve those ambitions in a cost-effective and competitive manner.

It remains to be seen whether future regulatory measures such as the presidential regulation on renewable electricity will address the BPP pricing scheme and resulting concerns for renewable project bankability. One key expectation for the forthcoming Regulation is that it will introduce auctions for larger scale renewable projects and reintroduce a FiT for smaller projects. The threshold is expected to be 10 MW, and a locational component is anticipated in the pricing structure, though it is not clear if there will be a locational component for both auctions and the FiT. It is also envisaged that remuneration of the FiT will use two levels, with a higher FiT in the beginning of the PPA and lower one towards the end of the agreement.

Such a layered payment is not necessarily common in other remuneration mechanisms around the world, but it should not be a disadvantage in the FiT design. The most important element is the transparency of pricing and the balance between level of pricing and other factors such as ease of permitting, perception of regulatory stability and related contractual elements (e.g. arbitrage clauses). If designed and implemented carefully, the presidential regulation on renewables can be a facilitator of higher levels of renewable investment in Indonesia, addressing some of the issues in current regulations that can act as barriers in attracting investors for renewable electricity projects.

Net-metering regulations should change to mirror solar ambitions

RUEN set a target of installing around 6.5 GW of solar projects, including distributed rooftop solar, and the government has tried to encourage development of solar capacity through its "One Million Solar Rooftops" initiative, which achieved more than 2 300 customers by mid-2020, with a total capacity reaching 11.5 MW (MEMR, 2020[38]). Yet, recent changes in the regulatory framework have not mirrored these ambitions. Notably, MEMR Regulation No. 49/2018[54] on the utilisation of solar rooftop changed net-metering arrangements with PLN. Under the regulation, customers are required to submit a formal application to benefit from the net-metering scheme, under which any electricity exported to the grid is counted at 65% of the applicable PLN tariff. In practice, this means that if rooftop PV produces and exports 600 kWh, then the customer will be credited only 390 kWh (600x65%). The justification for this 65% benchmark is to pay for the cost of grid infrastructure supporting the generating asset. Yet, as the calculation clearly favours on-site consumption (in which case 100% of the on-site production is deducted from the consumer's final bill), the net-metering scheme does not necessarily provide real incentive for potential exporters of on-site renewable electricity production.

This practice contrasts historical policy that credited "savings" from rooftop solar electricity production, meaning every kWh of electricity was credited up to a year in the consumer's balance. Forthcoming changes to MEMR Regulation No. 16/2019 (which amended MEMR Regulation No. 49/2018) are expected to raise the export calculation from 65% to 75%, and to 90% for consumers with battery capacity. However, these tariff rules are still not in line with net-metering schemes globally. Depending on the sophistication of the market, in some countries exported power is paid at a FiT rate, while in others it is settled at the hourly spot price. In Denmark, for example, any power exported from rooftop solar is settled at the hourly market price, and grid tariffs are calculated separately. India uses different settlement structures, depending on the state and business model. In general, if net metering is used, the net between consumption and self-production is settled at the applied tariff (i.e. the tariff would be 100% if compared to Indonesia). In the case of gross metering, exported generation is settled at a FiT, which typically is below the tariff applied to consumption.

The lack of transparency about the value of exported solar in Indonesia, by integrating grid tariffs into the settlement of exported power, has likely created a barrier for investment, in addition to making it difficult to benchmark the pricing of grid services from PLN. This is true not only for small rooftop solar installations (e.g. on residential buildings), but also for the growing number of businesses and industry looking to procure renewable electricity through corporate sourcing of renewables (**see Chapter 5**). While captive power plants within Wilayah Usaha may work for some consumers, a large number of corporate customers looking to source renewable electricity require a grid connection. Settling the net-metering export price at a reduced rate can thus be seen as a disadvantage for on-site renewables (for example compared to investing in energy conservation measures to achieve the equivalent of on-site power generation).

Aligning renewable and energy efficiency policies will influence future system flexibility

There is no official alignment of renewable electricity and energy efficiency regulations in Indonesia, though KEN and RUEN both oblige Indonesia's planning authorities to include energy conservation in electricity planning. As a result, energy modelling for RUEN and the 2019-28 RUPTL include energy efficiency targets in their electricity supply scenarios. This is important, as integration of energy efficiency with renewable electricity will be key to decreasing the burden of peak loads on power needs.

In practice, Indonesia does have some experience in combining efficiency and renewable energy as part of its development plans, for instance to achieve 100% electrification across the archipelago. The Energy Saving Solar Lights (Lampu Tenaga Surya Hemat Energi) programme launched in 2017 was part of a pre-electrification programme in areas of low energy access. Each household under the programme was given four LED lamps, together with a 20 watt-peak solar PV module and lithium battery that can last for 60 hours. While relatively small in size (the programme aimed to reach 175 782 homes in 15 provinces by 2018) and scale (in terms of electricity supply), the programme did underscore the importance of integrating renewable energy with energy-efficient end-use equipment to ensure secure and reliable energy access. In fact, had incandescent lamps of equivalent light output been used, the households would have needed six to eight more solar PV modules of the same watt-peak power (IEA, 2018[4]).

A similar initiative called TaLis (for Tabung Listrik, or Electric Tube) was launched by the University of Indonesia in 2018 to provide lightweight, portable batteries with 630 watt-hours of electricity for underserved and rural areas. Given the relatively small capacity of those batteries, use of energy-efficient lighting and equipment plays a central role in how often households need to recharge.

As renewable electricity shares increase in Indonesia's power generation mix, integrated planning of renewable energy and energy efficiency policy will be critical to transcending eventual supply and demand silos, which presents both challenges and opportunities at higher levels of renewable electricity penetration (IEA, 2020[39]). For instance, electricity savings in one area can mitigate need for additional power generation capacity, potentially allowing construction of power plants elsewhere in areas or regions that do not have limited or insecure access to electricity. Combination of digital, real-time information with electric power systems can also provide benefits with increasing decentralisation of electricity supply.

Integrated planning and policy can take advantage of emerging opportunities such as peer-to-peer electricity trading models that can address balancing and congestion issues in the electricity system, while enabling higher system flexibility and providing ancillary services (IRENA, 2020[40]). Currently, there are no smart grid or demand-side management (DSM) policies in place in Indonesia, although PLN's RUPTL does have plans to develop smart grid and DSM pilots in the Java-Bali area (PLN, 2019[29]). PLN also kicked off several smart grid programmes in 2020, such as work on advanced metering infrastructure, digital substations and a smart community pilot project in Karawang outside Jakarta.

Indonesia should consider opportunities to align energy efficiency and renewable energy policies and regulations, which will help to improve energy system flexibility and costs in the future. Improvements in energy performance and demand-side response will also enable higher use of distributed electricity generation. Ensuring that happens in an integrated way will require a portfolio of policies that incentivise participation and reward flexibility (e.g. through price signals in a dynamic electricity tariff scheme), which may require modifications to existing regulations (e.g. in the current net-metering scheme).

References

AEPCA (2000), *A Best Practice Guide to Energy Performance Contracts: reducing operating costs through guaranteed outcomes*, Canberra, https://www.eec.org.au/uploads/images/NEEC/Information%20Tools%20and%20Resources/Best%20Practice%20guide%20to%20EPC.pdf (accessed on 15 December 2020). [26]

Anh, T. (2020), "ESCO Vietnam has potential but faces challenges", *Vietnam Investment Review*, https://www.vir.com.vn/esco-vietnam-has-potential-but-faces-challenges-80370.html (accessed on 15 December 2020). [22]

AntiCSS (2019), *Anti-circumvention of standards for better market surveillance*, https://www.anti-circumvention.eu/about-project/project-introduction (accessed on 17 December 2020). [17]

Attwood, C. et al. (2017), *Financial Supports for Coal and Renewables in Indonesia*, Global Subsidies Initiative, International Institute for Sustainable Development, https://www.iisd.org/system/files/publications/financial-supports-coal-renewables-indonesia.pdf (accessed on 16 December 2020). [37]

BEE (2019), *Programmes: ESCOs*, Bureau of Energy Efficiency, https://beeindia.gov.in/content/escos-0#:~:text=Currently%2C%20127%20ESCOs%20are%20empaneled,tapped%20by%20ESCOs%20so%20far. (accessed on 15 December 2020). [23]

Bridle, R. et al. (2018), *Missing the 23 Per Cent Target: Roadblocks to the development of renewable energy in Indonesia*, Global Subsidies Initiative, International Institute for Sustainable Development (IISD), https://www.iisd.org/sites/default/files/publications/roadblocks-indonesia-renewable-energy.pdf (accessed on 15 December 2020). [36]

Burke, P. et al. (2019), *Overcoming barriers to solar and wind energy adoption in two Asian giants: India and Indonesia.* [31]

CLASP (2020), *Indonesia Residential End Use Survey*, Collaborative Labeling and Appliance Standards Program (CLASP), Washington, D.C., https://clasp.ngo/publications/indonesia-residential-end-use-survey (accessed on 15 December 2020). [1]

Energy Rating (2016), *Whitegoods Efficiency Trends 1993-2014*, Equipment Energy Efficiency (E3) programme, Australian Government, https://www.energyrating.gov.au/document/whitegoods-efficiency-trends-1993-2014 (accessed on 17 December 2020). [15]

Hadiputranto, H. (2019), *PLN re-opens prequalification process for Indonesian renewable projects*, Global Business Guide Indonesia, http://www.gbgindonesia.com/en/main/legal_updates/pln_re_opens_prequalification_process_for_indonesian_renewable_projects.php (accessed on 15 December 2020). [34]

Hakim, H. (2015), "Kementerian PUPR Dorong Pemda Gencarkan Bangunan Hijau (The PUPR Ministry Encourages Local Governments to Increase Green Buildings)", *Bisnis Indonesia*, https://ekonomi.bisnis.com/read/20150507/47/430566/kementerian-pupr-dorong-pemda-gencarkan-bangunan-hijau (accessed on 15 December 2020). [6]

Hermawan, J., I. Hermawan and J. Bahar (2015), “New PPP Regulations: PR No. 38/2015”, *Mondaq*, https://www.mondaq.com/government-contracts-procurement-ppp/456354/new-ppp-regulations-pr-no-382015 (accessed on 15 December 2020). [25]

Hofer, K., D. Limaye and J. Singh (2016), *Fostering the Development of ESCO markets for energy efficiency*, Live Wire 2016/54, World Bank Group, https://openknowledge.worldbank.org/handle/10986/23949 (accessed on 15 December 2020). [27]

IDFI (2018), *Recommendations for the Public Procurement System of the Republic of Indonesia*, Institute for Development of Freedom of Information, https://openupcontracting.org/assets/2019/04/Indonesia-Brief-on-Public-Procurement.pdf (accessed on 15 December 2020). [33]

IEA (2020), *Data & Statistics*, Electricity Information, International Energy Agency, https://www.iea.org/data-and-statistics?country=INDONESIA&fuel=Electricity%20and%20heat&indicator=ElecGenByFuel (accessed on 15 December 2020). [10]

IEA (2020), *Power systems in transition: Challenges and opportunities ahead for electricity security*, OECD Publishing, Paris, https://dx.doi.org/10.1787/4ad57c0e-en. [39]

IEA (2019), *Energy Efficiency 2019*, International Energy Agency, Paris, https://dx.doi.org/10.1787/ef14df7a-en. [11]

IEA (2019), *Perspectives for the Clean Energy Transition: The Critical Role of Buildings*, International Energy Acency, Paris, https://webstore.iea.org/perspectives-for-the-clean-energy-transition (accessed on 16 December 2020). [19]

IEA (2018), *Energy Efficiency 2018: Analysis and outlooks to 2040*, International Energy Agency, Paris, https://dx.doi.org/10.1787/9789264024304-en. [4]

IEA (2018), *Renewables 2018: Analysis and Forecasts to 2023*, International Energy Agency, Paris, https://dx.doi.org/10.1787/re_mar-2018-en. [35]

IEA (2017), *Energy Efficiency 2017*, International Energy Agency, Paris, https://dx.doi.org/10.1787/9789264284234-en. [9]

IEA (2010), *Policy Pathway: Monitoring, Verification and Enforcement*, International Energy AGency, Paris, https://www.iea.org/reports/policy-pathway-monitoring-verification-and-enforcement-2010 (accessed on 15 December 2020). [3]

IEA-UNEP (2018), *2018 Global Status Report: Towards a zero-emission, efficient and resilient buildings and construction sector*, International Energy Agency, United Nations Environment Programme, https://webstore.iea.org/2018-global-status-report (accessed on 17 December 2020). [20]

IESR (2021), *Indonesia Energy Transition Outlook 2021 - Tracking Progress of Energy Transition in Indonesia*, https://iesr.or.id/pustaka/indonesia-energy-transition-outlook-2021 (accessed on 2 March 2021). [13]

IRENA (2020), *Peer-to-peer electricity trading: innovation landscape brief*, International Renewable Energy Agency, Abu Dhabi, https://www.irena.org/-/media/Files/IRENA/Agency/Publication/2020/Jul/IRENA_Peer-to-peer_trading_2020.pdf?la=en&hash=D3E25A5BBA6FAC15B9C193F64CA3C8CBFE3F6F41 (accessed on 15 December 2020). [40]

ISO (2020), *ISO survey of management system standard certifications*, International Organisation for Standardisation, https://isotc.iso.org/livelink/livelink?func=ll&objId=18808772&objAction=browse&viewType=1 (accessed on 15 December 2020). [5]

Letschert, V. et al. (2017), *Baseline Evaluation and Policy Implications for Air Conditioners in Indonesia*, Lawrence Berkeley National Laboratory, https://eta.lbl.gov/publications/baseline-evaluation-policy (accessed on 15 December 2020). [14]

MEMR (2020), *Data & Information of Energy Conservation 2019, 3rd Edition*, Directorate of Energy Conservation, Ministry of Energy and Mineral Resources, http://www.ebtke.esdm.go.id (accessed on 15 December 2020). [18]

MEMR (2020), *More Competitive Price, Key to Indonesia's One Million Rooftop Solar Systems*, Ministry of Energy and Mineral Resources, https://www.esdm.go.id/en/media-center/news-archives/harga-makin-kompetitif-pemerintah-optimis-wujudkan-satu-juta-surya-atap (accessed on 16 December 2020). [38]

MEMR (2020), *Penerapan SKEM Label Hemat Energi Pada Masa 'Normal Baru' (Application of Energy Saving Label SKEM in the 'New Normal' Period)*, Directorate of Energy Conservation, Ministry of Energy and Mineral Resources, https://www.esdm.go.id/id/berita-unit/direktorat-jenderal-ebtke/penerapan-skem-label-hemat-energi-pada-masa-normal-baru (accessed on 15 December 2020). [2]

MEMR (2019), *Data & Information of Energy Conservation 2018, 2nd Edition*, Directorate of Energy Conservation, Ministry of Energy and Mineral Resources, https://drive.esdm.go.id//wl/?id=cwFohj0AaWgwlWQMNr5Yu68d8ptxTg4o (accessed on 15 December 2020). [12]

MEMR (2017), *Investment Opportunity of Renewable Power Generation in Indonesia*, Directorate General of New, Renewable Energy and Energy Conservation; Ministry of Energy and Mineral Resources, https://fr.slideshare.net/AbdurrahmanArum/investment-opportunity-renewable-power-generation-in-indonesia-2017 (accessed on 15 December 2020). [28]

OPSS (2019), *Regulations: ecodesign of energy-consuming products*, Office for Product Safety & Standards, United Kingdom, https://www.gov.uk/guidance/placing-energy-related-products-on-the-uk-market (accessed on 17 December 2020). [16]

Pahnael, J., A. Soekiman and M. Wimala (2020), "Penerapan Kebijakan Insentif Green Building di Kota Bandung (Implementation of Green Building Incentive Policies in Bandung City)", *Jurnal Infrastruktur*, Vol. 6/1, pp. 1-13, http://dx.doi.org/10.35814/infrastruktur.v6i1.1315. [8]

PLN (2019), *Rencana Usaha Penyediaan Tenaga Listrik (RUPTL) PT. PLN 2019 - 2028 (PT PLN Power Supply Business Plan 2019-2028)*, PT Perusahaan Listrik Negara (Persero) , Jakarta, https://gatrik.esdm.go.id//assets/uploads/download_index/files/5b16d-kepmen-esdm-no.-39-k-20-mem-2019-tentang-pengesahan-ruptl-pt-pln-2019-2028.pdf (accessed on 16 December 2020). [29]

PLN (2017), *General Terms in IPP Business in PLN*, PT Perusahaan Listrik Negara (Persero) , Jakarta, https://web.pln.co.id/statics/uploads/2017/05/Buku-IPP.pdf (accessed on 16 December 2020). [30]

PwC (2018), *Power In Indonesia - Investment and Taxation Guide*, http://www.pwc.com/id (accessed on 19 July 2019). [32]

Rahman, R. (2019), "Poor customer awareness holds back green building projects - Business - The Jakarta Post", *The Jakarta Post*, https://www.thejakartapost.com/news/2019/02/20/poor-customer-awareness-holds-back-green-building-projects.html (accessed on 15 December 2020). [7]

STEC (2020), *List of Registered Energy Service Company (ESCO)*, Suruhanjaya Tenaga Energy Commission, https://www.st.gov.my/web/consumer/esco (accessed on 15 December 2020). [24]

Tumiwa, F. et al. (2019), *Industrial Energy Accelerator: Indonesia Diagnostic*, Industrial Energy Accelerator, https://www.industrialenergyaccelerator.org/wp-content/uploads/FINAL-Indonesia-Diagnostic_WEB.pdf (accessed on 15 December 2020). [21]

Notes

[1] Energy Law No. 30/2007

[2] Government Regulation No. 79/2014

[3] Presidential Regulation No. 22/2017

[4] For more information, visit: https://www.iea-4e.org/.

[5] https://united4efficiency.org/

[6] http://www.aseanshine.org/

[7] Ministry of Industry Regulation No. 51/2015 specifies limits on the amount of energy used to produce one tonne of product for: pulp and paper (514/M-IND/Kep/12/2015), textiles (515/M-IND/Kep/12/2015), cement (512/M-IND/Kep/12/2015) and ceramics (513/M-IND/Kep/12/2015)

[8] For more information, see https://eeglobalalliance.org/three-percent-club.

[9] Government Regulation No. 70/2009

[10] MEMR Regulation No. 14/2012

[11] SNI ISO 50015/2014

[12] National Energy Efficiency Standard for Buildings and its standards for: building envelopes (SNI 03-6389/2011); air-conditioning systems (SNI 03-6390/2011); lighting systems (SNI 03-6197/2011) and energy audit procedures (SNI 03-6196/2011)

[13] MPWH Regulation No. 02/PRT/M/2015

[14] For more information, see https://edgebuildings.com/.

[15] For more information, visit: http://gbcindonesia.org/EN/download/doc_details/22-choosing-the-right-green-building-materials?tmpl=component

[16] Governor Regulation of DKI Jakarta No. 38/2012

[17] MEMR Regulation No. 06/2011

[18] MEMR Regulation No. 18/2014

[19] MEMR Regulation No. 07/2015

[20] MEMR Regulation No. 57/2017

[21] SNI 8476/2018

[22] MoI Regulation No. 13/2015

[23] MoI Regulation No. 13/2016

[24] MEMR Regulation No. 01/2016

[25] https://asean.org/?static_post=agreement-on-the-asean-harmonized-electrical-and-electronic-equipment-eee-regulatory-regime-kuala-lumpur-9-december-2005

[26] SNI ISO 50006/2014

[27] SNI ISO 50002/2014

[28] For more information, visit: https://beeindia.gov.in/content/iame.

[29] National Energy Efficiency Award

[30] https://drive.esdm.go.id//wl/?id=cwFohj0AaWgwlWQMNr5Yu68d8ptxTg4o

[31] MEMR Regulation No. 14/2016

[32] Presidential Regulation No. 38/2015

[33] Electricity Law No. 30/2009

[34] Government Regulation No. 14/2012

[35] MEMR Regulation No. 13/2013

[36] MEMR Regulation No. 12/2016

[37] MEMR Regulation No. 07/2016

[38] Decision No. 111/PUU-XIII/2015

[39] MEMR Regulation No. 01/2015

[40] MEMR Regulation No. 01/2006

[41] Decree No. 0022P/DIR/2018

[42] Government Regulation No. 14/2012

[43] MEMR Regulation No. 10/2017

[44] MEMR Regulation No. 03/2015

[45] Presidential Regulation No. 16/2018

[46] Presidential Regulation No. 54/2010

[47] MEMR Regulation No. 01/2015

[48] MEMR Regulation No. 50/2017

[49] MEMR Regulation No. 19/2016

[50] MEMR Regulation No. 9/2018

[51] MEMR Regulation No. 49/2017

[52] MEMR Regulation No. 10/2018

[53] MEMR Regulation No. 04/2020

[54] MEMR Regulation No. 48/2018

4 Investment and competition policy

This chapter reviews Indonesia's investment and competition framework in the context of clean energy. It examines the country's efforts to level the playing field between the national power utility and independent power producers, as well as to create a fair, efficient and transparent procurement process for renewables. It assesses Indonesia's foreign direct investment regime, highlighting possible avenues to make it more attractive to foreign investors in the clean energy sector. The chapter also explores other important avenues to improve the framework for clean energy investment, including how to facilitate land access and acquisition and reduce the costs of clean energy equipment (local content requirements) as well as how to better harness public-private partnerships for clean energy.

In light of its clean energy investment needs and limited public resources, Indonesia will need to attract increasing amount of private investments, including from foreign sources, if it is to realise its clean energy goals by 2025. Luckily, Indonesia's tremendous clean energy potential makes it a naturally attractive destination for Foreign Direct Investment (FDI) for clean energy, which is confirmed by the upward trends observed in the share of renewables in FDI (albeit from a low level) over the last decade. However, FDI in clean energy is still far from where it could be and continues to be dwarfed by FDI in fossil fuels.

Reversing this trend will necessitate a strong investment and competition framework that can level the playing field between foreign and domestic, state-owned and private investments as well as allow for a transparent, clear and predictable investment process. At the same time, Indonesia urgently needs to continue greening its economy and enable corporate access to clean energy or it faces the risk of missing out on investment opportunities from global investors who are increasingly aware and committed to sustainability. Aware of these challenges, Indonesia has already taken a number of actions to reverse these trends. Most notably, Indonesia passed the Omnibus Law on Job Creation in October 2020, which is expected to usher in far-reaching improvements in Indonesia's investment and competition framework, although its impact will ultimately depend on follow-on regulations.

Assessment and recommendations

There is a need to improve the transparency and fairness of PLN's (the state electricity company) power procurement process

PLN's dominant position in power procurement is a challenge for many independent power producers (IPPs), particularly under Ministry of Energy and Mineral Resources (MEMR) Regulation No. 50 of 2017 on the utilisation of renewable energy, which makes procurement complex, long and opaque. This is particularly the case for direct selection under PLN, which has led to few pre-qualifications over the last two years, with long delays in the process. Similarly, getting projects listed in the Electricity Business Plan (RUPTL) has been particularly challenging for developers, given the lack of legal basis for developers' partnerships with PLN's subsidiaries (a way to avoid listing in the RUPTL), resulting in few financial institutions willing to provide financing for those projects. The implementation of Ministerial Regulation No. 04/2020 as well as on-going preparations of a Renewable Energy Law should help to improve the transparency and competition aspects of the procurement process, although subsequent implementation and consistency of those regulations will be critical to scale up private investment for renewable energy.

Indonesia's FDI regime for clean energy remains restrictive although reforms are under way

Indonesia has taken positive steps to improve the attractiveness of its FDI regime for clean energy. Most notably through the replacement of the 2016 "negative" investment list regulation with Presidential Regulation No. 10/2021 on Investment Business Lines (often called the "positive" investment list) in a bid to liberalise the country's FDI regime. The list notably allows foreign investment (up to 100%) in a large number of power business fields, including 1-10 MW projects that used to be restricted to 49% foreign ownership. Such effort is particularly important as the level of FDI inflows in Indonesia (including in clean energy) lags behind that of many neighbouring countries. Nevertheless, Indonesia continues to impose limits on employment of foreign personnel at key management positions as well as minimum capital requirements (IDR 10 billion – around USD 700,000) that are 200 times higher than what is required from domestic companies. As a result, Indonesia's FDI regime tends to create higher entry barriers for foreign clean energy developers that have an important role to play in clean energy deployment, especially in eastern and smaller islands (where projects are often below 10 MW), given capacity issues of smaller local developers.

Local content requirements (LCRs) remain high and weigh on project investment cost

LCRs can be a key roadblock for renewable IPPs. Indonesia applies LCRs to the power sector, including some renewable energy technologies (solar, geothermal and hydro power) in a bid to grow the country's manufacturing base and thereby contribute to wider industrial development and job creation goals. For solar photovoltaics (PV), minimum LCRs have been increased from 40% in 2012 to 60% in 2019. Given the typical small size of local manufacturers and lack of competitiveness in the market, these requirements mean developers can struggle to get projects off the ground. Higher prices of locally produced and assembled components also means that LCRs can significantly weigh on project investment costs. While Indonesia's goals to promote industrial expansion and job creation are laudable, global evidence shows that LCRs for wind and solar have overall had mixed (if not negative) effects on industrial development, job and value creation. Consequently, the gradual removal of LCRs, in tandem with support measures to increase local manufacturers' capacity and competitiveness, can reduce renewable electricity costs while supporting intended job creation and industrial expansion.

Indonesia is making efforts to improve land access

Land acquisition remains one of the longest lead items in renewable power project development, due to lack of clarity in Indonesia's land registry and borders. Inconsistent and often overlapping sectoral spatial plans, alongside fragmented land administration, add to this lack of clarity and risks overlap across multiple project land rights. Indonesia has made commendable efforts to clarify land tenure and spatial plans, for instance under its ONE Map Policy and by creating a legal framework (e.g. the 2012 Land Acquisition Law). Further measures on land acquisition (e.g. Presidential Regulation No. 04/2016 on the Acceleration of Power Development and Presidential Regulation No. 38/2015 on PPPs) have also facilitated this process. The Omnibus Law should also help streamline and facilitate land access, although it remains to be seen how this will be ultimately implemented.

More can be done to harness public-private partnerships (PPPs) for clean energy

Indonesia has created a comprehensive legal framework for PPPs, including specific measures allowing government contracting agencies to use PPPs for clean energy projects. In recent years, Indonesia has taken steps to reverse this and implemented a number of clean energy projects. In the energy efficiency sector, there are three on-going street lighting projects being conducted under PPP arrangement (e.g. the Surakarta Street Lighting project). In the power sector, some waste-to-energy PPP projects are being conducted in five municipalities, which could prove particularly useful to achieve ambitions such as the presidential target to have 12 municipal waste-to-energy power plants in operation by 2022. Yet, in spite of these efforts, the use of PPP contractual arrangements for clean energy remain overall very limited. To harness the considerable potential for PPPs, effort is needed to address barriers such as limited capacity of government contracting agencies to implement such arrangements and restrictions for government institutions to enter into multi-year contracts.

Box 4.1. Main policy recommendations on investment and competition

- Gradually move towards a competitive auction system for the procurement of renewable power across all technologies, build upon past and international experiences in holding competitive tenders for geothermal projects. Consider embedding such procurement requirements in the Renewable Energy Law (now under preparation), which would shelter developers from possible regulatory changes due to political cycles. Develop clear implementing regulations and guidelines for PLN in order to guarantee transparency, predictability and competition in the procurement process
- Building on current reforms, consider conducting regular and comprehensive clean-energy-sector assessments of the FDI regime to ensure alignment with and support of clean energy objectives. In particular, consider evaluating current limits for foreign equity for projects below 1 MW and other FDI restrictions such as minimum capital requirements and restrictions on foreign personnel, which remain higher than that of the OECD as well as Thailand and Viet Nam. In the process, Indonesia should ensure current rules are justified (particularly in light of domestic firms' capacity and resources) and do not impinge on clean energy and energy affordability objectives, involving relevant stakeholders and ensuring their input is thoughtfully considered.
- Evaluate LCRs and ensure current regulations reduce project costs, as this will contribute to growth in sector employment, including demand for manufactured equipment. To promote local manufacturing capacity and competitiveness, provide support to the local industry through targeted research and development programmes, knowledge and technology transfer as well as training and capacity building activities.
- Accelerate efforts under the One Map Policy to reduce land access uncertainties and reduce market barriers, which weigh on clean energy project costs. As is already the case for PPP projects, endeavour to secure tracts of land prior to project tenders as this has proved to be a key success factor in recent solar auctions held in Cambodia and India. In this regard, consider more actively submitting project proposals to LMAN (Lembaga Manajemen Aset Negara or State Asset Management Agency) to benefit from land acquisition funding under the Land Funding Scheme.
- Continue to improve understanding and capacity of government contracting agencies, including local governments and PLN, to originate, develop and monitor implementation of PPP agreements for clean energy projects. In particular, Indonesia should review public procurement regulations to address barriers to government institutions entering into contracts with developers.

Creating a level playing field between public and private investors in clean energy infrastructure

PLN dominates all segments of Indonesia's power market, acting as a quasi-monopoly (see Chapter 2). IPPs are allowed to own and operate power generation assets but have so far played a limited role as most of the country's fossil-fuel dominated capacity is owned by PLN. However, IPPs own and operate the majority of non-large hydro renewable energy generation assets (see Figure 4.1). While IPPs are legally allowed to directly sell power to consumers (including corporates and households) within a specific business area (also known as a Private Power Utility), most of the power they generate is sold to PLN. Equally, PLN is the sole owner and operator of the transmission and distribution infrastructure, which is closed to private investments (despite rare exceptions) (see Chapter 2).

Figure 4.1. Ownership of Indonesia's power generation assets, 2019

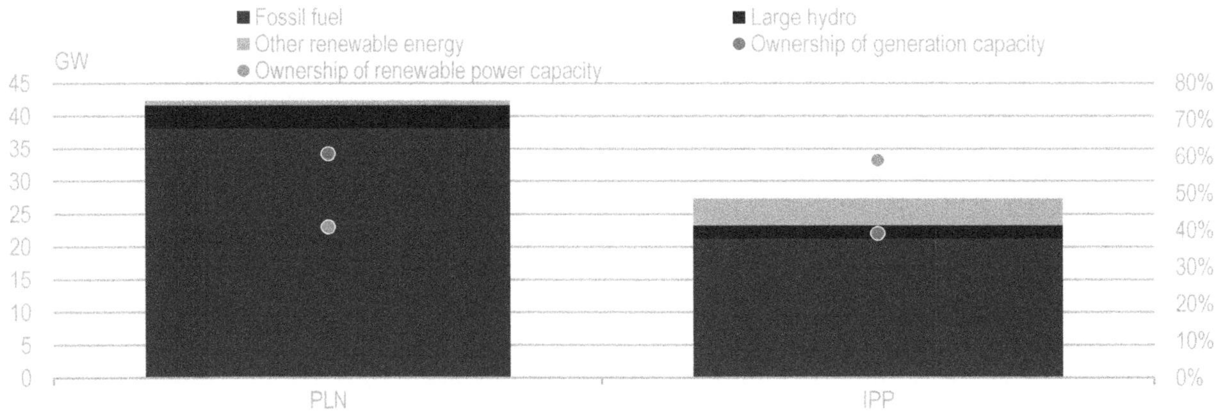

Note: Large hydropower refers to hydro projects with a capacity >10 Mega Watts. GW=Giga Watt.
Source: MEMR and PLN statistics.

StatLink https://stat.link/0g7umf

More efforts are needed to level the playing field between IPPs and PLN

Numerous IPPs have reported difficulties in dealing with PLN. In a stakeholder consultation held in 2019, some IPPs voiced concerns around the patchy and arbitrary application of regulations at the regional level, making it difficult to develop projects; this also reflects potential vertical coordination issues between PLN's central and regional offices. Risk of curtailments of renewables has also been a major concern for investors (Dutt, Chawla and Kuldeep, 2019[1]). Lack of transparency and clarity in PLN's power procurement rules and criteria (from getting projects listed in the RUPTL to tender participation) has also been pointed out as a barrier for renewable energy developers (see next section).

The absence of a powerful, well-resourced and independent electricity market competition authority has made it difficult to address these issues in a fair and transparent way. Indeed, while MEMR (through the Directorate General of Electricity) acts as the *de facto* power regulator, it effectively holds little authority over PLN's operations and management (its performance being supervised by the Ministry of State-Owned Enterprises) as well as on competition-related matters; it also lacks political independence adding to investors' concerns. Instead, competition matters (including for public tenders) fall under the responsibility of the Indonesian Competition Authority, which in practice has played a very limited role in the power sector. To tackle these concerns, Indonesia established a Grid Management Committee for the Java-Bali-Madura grid in 2007, chaired by a number of relevant stakeholders (including PLN and IPPs) which reviews grid rules and their implementation, publishes interpretations and guidelines on grid rules and makes recommendations for changes to grid rules. Then again, the committee has lacked the authority to effectively address competition issues between PLN and private developers.

There is a need to create a more transparent, clear and predictable procurement process

PLN's procurement process, conducted by direct appointment and direct selection (**see Chapter 3**), follows the generation capacity plans in the RUPTL (**see Chapter 2**). Notably, MEMR Regulation No. 50/2017 on the Utilisation of New and Renewable Energy (amended by MEMR Regulation No. 4/2020) allows PLN to award the development of geothermal and waste-to-energy power projects (as well as most fossil fuel technologies) to IPPs. While this direct appointment can be organised in the form of a public tender, as has been the case for a number of geothermal projects over the last decade, there is virtually no obligation for PLN to do so. In the case where developers submit project proposals on an unsolicited basis (to then be appointed via direct appointment), PLN is responsible for reviewing, approving and ultimately listing approved proposals in the RUPTL. However, IPPs submitting unsolicited project proposals under direct appointment have sometimes faced challenges in getting their projects listed in the RUPTL.

For all other renewable energy technologies, direct selection allows PLN to tender projects out to a limited number of eligible project developers based on technology capacity quotas (defined in the RUPTL). To be eligible, developers must participate in a prequalification process in order to be shortlisted (or pre-qualify) against a set of pre-defined criteria (**see Chapter 3**). Yet, while this process aims at filtering out developers with poor financial credentials and limited experience, pre-qualification processes have been held on an irregular basis over the years and their criteria varied year on year (PwC, 2018[2]). Direct selection also allows PLN to arbitrarily invite eligible developers to bid for projects, whereas unsolicited project proposals are not allowed under direct selection.

PLN's power procurement mechanisms under MEMR Regulation No. 50/2017 are complex, long and opaque. Very few pre-qualifications have been held over the last two years under direct selection and, when this is the case, results were announced with a long delay in the process (e.g. one year for the 2017 pre-qualification) (Burke et al., 2019[3]). Pre-qualification criteria have also been unclear and inconsistent across prequalification processes, with questionable impact: in 2017, around 27 clean energy power purchase agreements (PPAs) did not reach financial close, partly because winning IPPs lacked creditworthiness as well as the ability to develop credible feasibility studies (IESR, 2019[4]; PwC, 2019[5]). The result is that some developers have opted for partnering with PLN's subsidiaries (as this does not require listing in the RUPTL). Yet, with no legal basis in place for such partnerships, few financial institutions or development finance institutions are willing to provide financing for these projects.

On a positive note, Indonesia has taken steps to simplify PLN's procurement process through MEMR Regulation No. 04/2020. The regulation notably reinstates the possibility to procure all renewables through direct appointment under specific conditions, e.g. if there is only one bidding IPP. This is welcome, although further steps will need to be taken to simplify procurement, in particular, systematically adopting open competitive tenders to procure renewables. Aside from geothermal, Indonesia had already designed a competitive tender programme for solar projects in 2013 (MEMR Regulation No. 17/2013) but the regulation was later rescinded due to pressure from PLN and local manufacturing associations (Kennedy, 2018[6]). Building from that experience, Indonesia should gradually move towards a competitive auction system for the procurement of all renewables, particularly as recent auctions held in India (under the National Solar Mission) or Denmark (for wind power) proved successful in pushing down the cost of renewables (**see Chapter 5**).

Promoting equal treatment of foreign and domestic investors in clean energy

Indonesia's dynamic economy and large domestic market makes it a key destination for FDI, which has been on an upward trend over much of the last decade and a half, despite a recent slowdown. While manufacturing and services have been the largest FDI recipients, the energy sector – including clean energy – has also been a coveted sector due to the country's tremendous potential. Yet, FDI inflows have slowed as of late and remain below the level of neighbouring countries such as Viet Nam and Cambodia, which have been accounting for growing shares of FDI inflows in ASEAN countries, in the backdrop of US-China trade tensions, and has been integrating at a much faster pace in global value chains than Indonesia. This also holds true in the clean energy sector, where the share of greenfield FDI flows in renewables of countries such as Cambodia, Laos or Viet Nam, have far exceeded that of Indonesia over the last decade and a half (The Jakarta Post, 2019[7]; OECD, 2020[8]).

In the face of these issues, the Indonesian President, Joko Widodo, reiterated commitment to accelerate inwards FDI in Indonesia and improve the ease of doing business in the country. Acting on such commitment and in the context of the COVID-19 crisis, Indonesia passed the Omnibus Law on Job Creation in October 2020 in a bid to repeal a number of overlapping regulations, ease restrictions on FDI (including in the negative investment list) as well as centralise and streamline business licensing and land acquisition procedures. While this is a welcome step (albeit one faced with strong labour and civil society opposition), the impact of the law on the business environment for clean energy will eventually depend on ensuing implementing regulations. Importantly, these reforms should not undermine environmental safeguards for projects (including public consultation) and should support Indonesia's efforts to green its economy and widen corporate access to clean energy. These efforts are paramount to ensure Indonesia is not left behind as global investors are increasingly aware and committed to sustainability. For example, following the passing of the Omnibus Law and upcoming implementing regulations, a group of 36 investors with around USD 4.1 trillion in assets under management urged the government to "support the conservation of forests and peatlands; uphold human rights and customary land rights of indigenous peoples; hold proper consultations with environmental and civil society groups and investors on the Law and its implementation; and take a long-term approach to recovery from the pandemic" (OECD, 2020[8]).

Indonesia is making considerable efforts to liberalise its FDI regime for clean energy

Prior to 2021, Indonesia had a large number of FDI restrictions in place, most of which were set out in the negative investment list. As mandated by the 2007 Investment Law, the negative investment list (lastly revised in 2016) listed a number of power business fields closed to private (both foreign and domestic) investment as well as open under certain restrictions (including foreign ownership restrictions)(see Table 4.1). The list sometimes granted more favourable treatment to ASEAN investors (in the form of higher equity ownership limit), although this did not apply in the aforementioned sectors.

With the passing of the Omnibus Law in 2020, the negative investment list was re-conceptualised into a "positive investment list" as set out in Presidential Regulation No. 10/2021 on Investment Business Lines, thereby liberalising numerous business fields to foreign investment. The general principle of the positive investment list is that a business field is open to 100% foreign ownership unless otherwise specified. The new list categorises business sectors into three broad categories: 1) priority sectors (defined based on a set of criteria), benefitting from a number of fiscal and non-fiscal incentives (245 business fields); 2) business fields allocated to or reserved for partnership with, local cooperatives and micro, small and medium-sized enterprises (MSMEs); and 3) business fields open to foreign investment but subject to certain limitations or requirements. Under this list, most power business fields are now classified as "priority sectors" (see Table 4.1). Most notably, this means that foreign IPPs are now eligible for certain fiscal incentives (including tax allowance and tax holiday) as well as non-fiscal incentives (e.g. ease of obtaining business permits, provision of supporting infrastructure, guarantees on availability of raw materials, immigration and others) (**see Chapter 5**).

Nevertheless, power projects below 1 MW remain closed to foreign investment and so do certain electric power installations and construction services. While Indonesia's rationale to impose such restrictions to promote the development of domestic small-scale IPPs is understandable, it should nonetheless account for local capacity and resource constraints in the clean energy sector. This is particularly key given that in recent years, numerous domestic, small-scale IPPs have faced considerable capacity and creditworthiness issues (especially in developing mini and micro hydro projects) (IESR, 2019[4])

Table 4.1. Foreign equity restrictions apply to a range of renewable energy-related areas

Business sectors	Foreign equity limitations	
	2016 negative investment list	2021 positive investment list
Geothermal drilling services	95%	Up to 100%
Geothermal operating and maintenance services	90%	Up to 100%
Power generation below 1 MW	Closed to foreign ownership	Closed to foreign ownership reserved for cooperatives and MSMEs
Power plant between 1-10 MW	49%	Up to 100%
Geothermal power plant up to 10 MW	67%	Up to 100% Closed if below 1 MW
Power plant beyond 10 MW	95% (100% if as part of PPP during concession period)	Up to 100%
Geothermal surveying services	95%	Up to 100%
Construction and installation of electric power: Installation of electric power supply	95%	Up to 100% (if high voltage) Closed if low/medium voltage

Source: Presidential Regulation No. 44/2016 "Negative Investment List". Presidential Regulation no. 10/2021. PPP=Public Private Partnerships.

While the loosening of foreign equity limits is a commendable effort, there remains other significant restrictions to FDI in place (also applying to the clean energy sector). Among other restrictions are limits on the employment of foreign personnel in key management positions as well as minimum capital requirements for foreign-invested companies (set at IDR 10 billion or around USD 700 000 excluding land and buildings, 25% of which should be paid-up in full before starting a business). Such capital requirements are 200 times what is required from local companies, which is rather exceptional given few countries impose requirements at such a high-level worldwide (and these are rarely discriminatory) (OECD, 2020[8]). There can be certain exemptions in Special Economic Zones, however. Minimum capital requirements could represent a significant barrier for foreign small-scale IPPs and clean energy small and medium enterprises, despite the high innovative potential that many of these small-scale investors can bring (OECD, 2015[9]).

LCRs drive up projects' investment costs

Indonesia continues to impose stringent local content rules for a number of clean energy projects. In a bid to support national industrial development and job creation, the Ministry of Industry has set out minimum LCRs for solar, geothermal and hydro power projects (as well as most fossil fuels and network infrastructure), which are considered as part of renewable power procurement. Most notably, MEMR Regulation No. 05/2017 (amending MEMR Regulation No. 53/2012 on LCR for Power Infrastructure and based on Ministry of Industry Regulation No. 54/M-IND/Per/3/2012) imposed a 40% minimum LCR target for solar PV projects in 2017 that was later increased to 60% in 2019. Given the limited capacity of the local manufacturing base for solar components, project developers struggle to comply with the target, with current local content of solar projects hovering around 43% in 2020.

Table 4.2. Indonesia imposes a number of LCRs for geothermal, hydro and solar technologies.

	MW	LCR (Goods and Services combined)
Solar PV	-	60% (set at 43.85% over 2012-19)
Geothermal	<5	42%
	5-10	40.45%
	10-60	33.24%
	60-110	29.21%
	>110	28.95%
Hydro (excl. pump storage)	<15	70.76%
	15-50	51.60%
	50-150	49%
	>150	47.6%

Source: MEMR regulation no. 05/2017 and MEMR regulation no. 53/2012 based Minister of Industry regulation 54/M-IND/Per/3/2012.

There is wide evidence that LCRs significantly increase project costs, especially when local manufacturers produce at higher costs than international competitors, thereby making the cost of intermediate input more expensive. This is the case of Indonesia's solar PV industry where locally-produced module prices average USD 0.47/Wp (Watt peak) compared to imported module prices ranging from USD 0.25 - 0.37/Wp. This, in turn, has contributed to slowing solar PV market expansion, making downstream investment more expensive (IESR, 2019[4]). In this regard, IESR estimates that accessing module price at the international market price would lower the solar Levelised Cost of Electricity (LCOE) by up to 50% (IESR, 2019[10]).

While Indonesia's job creation and industrial development goals are commendable, global evidence shows that LCRs are not the most effective tool to realise these. Experience from India's National Solar Mission Programme since 2010, for instance, shows that projects tied to LCRs registered a significant cost increase (e.g. a USD 68-88 million top-up per installed GW over 2014-17) while having overall mixed (short-term) effects on manufacturing of solar PV (particularly crystalline-silicon) over 2010-17 (Probst et al., 2020[11]). This can be explained by the fact that the manufacturing segment of solar PV and wind production, generates relatively less value and employment than downstream activities (i.e. project development, construction, installation, operation and maintenance). Indeed, evidence from the solar PV production value chain in the US shows that more than half of the value generated from solar production lies downstream of module production, with that segment also accounting for the bulk of employment (70% for silicon-crystalline solar PV). Therefore LCRs could also have a negative impact on downstream job creation through affecting demand. They could also further slow Indonesia's integration in global value chains (OECD, 2015[12]).

Facilitating land access for renewable energy projects

Project developers are responsible for securing land for a project's site as well as associated network infrastructure to connect the project to the nearest substation (which can be 20 to 40 kilometres long). Before accessing land, developers must obtain a location permit, granted upon compliance with power infrastructure and other regional spatial plans (referring to national plans) as well as approval from the Ministry of Environment and Forestry (MoEF) in case the project is established in the state forest (which accounts for two thirds of Indonesia's land area; see (OECD, 2019[13]) for more detailed information on state forest). The Land Agency Office is the sole body responsible for granting location permits as well as issuing land rights for power projects. In practice, however, developers are left to directly negotiate with land owners to agree on a purchase price or rent for the land (of not more than five hectares). Additionally, foreigners are not allowed to own land and thus usually rely on a local partner.

Unclear land registry and spatial planning have created uncertainty over land tenure and caused numerous land disputes locally. With a land registry only covering 35% of the country's land – mostly in urban areas – numerous Indonesians continue to hold informal land rights (or exert *de facto* control over it) making it a challenge for developers to access land (OECD, 2020[8]). For instance, the country's second large-scale on-shore wind project had to deal with no less than 500 landowners and 100 sharecroppers (spread across 8 villages and 4 districts) in order to access land (Kennedy, 2020[14]). Compounding this issue, inconsistent and often overlapping sectoral spatial plans, alongside fragmented land administration, have caused numerous infrastructure projects to be granted land rights over the same tracts of land, leading to land disputes (OECD, 2019[13]; Dutt, Chawla and Kuldeep, 2019[1]). This, in turn, has made land acquisition one of the longest lead items in renewable energy project development.

In the face of these issues, Indonesia has been taking important steps to improve land tenure and facilitate land access. Important land reforms were started in 2019 through the One Map Policy, which aims to improve consistency across spatial plans using a centralised geospatial data repository (e.g. land tenure and use, and topography) which should help avoid overlapping land right issues (**see Chapter 2**; (OECD, 2019[13])). Efforts to register land are also being accelerated under the Minister of Agrarian and Spatial Planning Regulation No. 12/2017 on Complete Systematic Land Registration Acceleration. These measures are welcome but will take time to implement given current land registration capacity (OECD, 2020[8]). In the same spirit, the MoEF, in 2015, allowed the establishment of geothermal concessions in protected areas as more than half of the country's geothermal resources lie in such areas (MEMR, 2017[15]). While the environmental impact of geothermal power plants is usually minor, these could still cause some disturbances to local ecosystems, particularly if not complemented by robust environmental management systems (Dhar et al., 2020[16]).

In addition, the government has been implementing a number of regulations to facilitate land acquisition. These notably include Law No. 2/2012 on Land Acquisition[1], which formalises legal procedures for land acquisition and limits its duration to 583 days; Presidential Regulation No. 04/2016 on the Acceleration of Power Infrastructure Development, which further clarifies and formalises land acquisition for power infrastructure projects; as well as Presidential Regulation No.38/2015 on Public Private Partnerships (PPPs), that notably obligates government contracting agencies to secure land prior to the tendering of PPP projects.

As more land is required to attain clean energy targets – e.g. around 8000 km^2 is needed to develop 1.5 GW of solar PV – Indonesia needs to step up efforts to facilitate land access under the implementation of the Omnibus Law (Kennedy, 2020[14]). Securing tracts of land prior to project tenders will be critical to reduce project lead time and accelerate investment. Experience in facilitating land access for toll road projects through the LMAN (Lembaga Manajemen Aset Negara or State Asset Management Agency) and under India's Solar Park Schemes could provide useful lessons for Indonesia's renewable sector, in this regards (see Box 4.2).

Box 4.2. Experiences in facilitating land acquisition for renewable energy projects

Indonesia's Land Funding Scheme for national strategic projects

In the face of land acquisition issues for toll road projects and other large-scale infrastructure projects, Indonesia's Minister of Finance launched the Land Funding Scheme in 2016 to help fund land acquisition for infrastructure projects. The scheme is managed and operated by the State Assets Management Agency (LMAN), which was established in 2015 to manage state assets to generate and improve financial and nonfinancial benefits as well as, since 2016, act as a *de facto* national land bank (The Jakarta Post, 2017[17]).

Land funding under the scheme can be provided in two ways: direct disbursement, whereby LMAN directly indemnifies land owners for the land to be acquired; and an indirect disbursement, whereby project developers get a refund for their land acquisition expenses. To be eligible for the Land Funding Scheme, projects must be categorised as "national strategic projects" as specified in Presidential Regulation No. 66/2020 on Funding of Land Acquisition in Public Interest for Purposes of Executing national strategic projects (amending Presidential Regulation No. 102/2016). To be categorised as national strategic projects, projects must fulfil a certain set of criteria including, but not limited to, having a strategic role (including for the economy, social welfare, the environment and employment) and having an investment value above IDR 100 billion (around USD 7 million). In the case of power projects, those listed in the RUPTL are all classified as national strategic projects as set out in Presidential Regulation No. 04/2016 on the Acceleration of Power Infrastructure Development. To obtain LMAN support, project proposals can only be submitted by a state entity to the Committee for Acceleration of Priority Infrastructure Delivery (Komite Percepatan Penyediaan Infrastruktur Prioritas or KPPIP), which is responsible for supporting and approving eligibility of national strategic projects for LMAN.

Since the inception of the Land Funding Scheme, LMAN supported 27 toll road projects as well as 26 dams across the country. As of 2021, however, no clean energy projects benefited from LMAN support as neither MEMR nor PLN have yet submitted RUPTL-listed projects to the KPPIP. Given the invaluable financial support LMAN could provide to land-based clean energy projects (and hence help lower their investment costs), MEMR and PLN should seek to play a more active role in championing strategic clean energy projects and obtain LMAN's support.

India's Solar Park Scheme

Power evacuation and land acquisition represent significant risks for power project development in India. To lower these risks, the Indian government implemented the Solar Park Scheme in 2015, consisting in securing land and power evacuation infrastructure prior to competitive tenders for large-scale solar parks. While the scheme exclusively addressed solar PV over 2015-19, the government expanded the scope of the scheme to other renewables in 2019 (Economic Times, 2019[18]).

Following a 'plug-and-play' model, the Solar Park Scheme transfers the land acquisition and power evacuation risks on to India's Ministry of New and Renewable Energy (and since 2019, to the Ministry's SOE, the Solar Energy Corporation of India) thereby making the SOE responsible for acquiring land and developing evacuation infrastructure prior to tendering out solar parks through competitive auctions. This is done in exchange for a usage fee, which in practice has represented a significant price premium for solar-park vs. non-solar park projects, sparking concerns among certain developers. Nevertheless, the Solar Park Scheme helped achieve considerable economies of scale given the large size of projects established in solar parks and contributed to a significant decline in power tariffs, with the lowest prices for the entire solar PV sector registered in solar park capacity auctions.

All in all, India's solar park scheme has been instrumental in accelerating solar market development in the country, with the share of solar park projects rising from over 38% in 2015 to around 55% of total capacity awarded in 2017 (almost a 3 GW increase). The scheme has helped attract international IPPs (which made up 45% of solar parks against 17% in other renewable projects in 2017) as well as large local IPPs, with the wherewithal to bear the premium and develop large-scale projects. Nevertheless, over 2017-19, India struggled to maintain the high pace of solar park development under the scheme as acquiring the tremendous amount of land needed to develop large-scale projects proved challenging. This caused the share of solar park projects to drop to 7% in 2019.

Despite this challenge, India's Solar Park Scheme still provides useful lessons to help facilitate land access. First, India's experience shows that transferring land acquisition and power evacuation risk to the state (beyond funding aspects) can go a long way to accelerate clean power investment. Second, it also shows that land acquisition facilitation alone does not suffice and should be pursued in tandem with efforts to improve land management in order to be effective.

Source: (Chawla et al., 2018[19]) (MoF, 2020[20])

Harnessing public-private partnerships (PPPs) for clean energy

Indonesia has so far made very limited use of PPPs in the clean energy sector

Indonesia has been making efforts to revamp its legal and institutional framework for PPPs in a bid to scale up private investments in infrastructure development under PPP arrangements, so far dominated by SOEs. To that end, Indonesia created a number of institutions (e.g. IIGF, PT SMI, LMAN) as well as developed a comprehensive and unified regulatory framework for PPPs in 2015 through Presidential Regulation No. 38/2015 on cooperation between the government and businesses, appointing Bappenas as the lead coordinating ministry for PPPs. The presidential regulation notably formalises the PPP implementation stages (from the preliminary study stage through to financial closure) and sets out a number of eligible sectors for PPPs, including energy conservation and power generation. The regulation allows private project proponents to submit proposals on a solicited or unsolicited basis. In all instances, however, the selection process must be conducted through an open, competitive tender, preceded by a *value for money* evaluation (using a Public Sector Comparator[2] method) (APEC, 2019[21]). In 2016, the PPP Joint Office was established to coordinate and assist line ministries, government contracting agencies and investors, and to serve as a de-facto one-stop shop for PPP-related issues.

The regulation also introduced a number of instruments to support PPP projects. Most notably, projects can benefit from government guarantees (through the IIGF; **see Chapter 6**); a Viability Gap Fund, to improve the financial viability of projects (important as only 10% of PPP projects are fully financially feasible) through contributing up to 49% of the construction, equipment and installation costs; a Project Development Facility to assist projects in the preparation phase; as well as partial construction support. Additionally, the regulation makes land acquisition an obligation of the government contracting agency and allows projects categorised as a national strategic project to benefit from the Land Funding Scheme (see Box 4.2; (APEC, 2019[21])).

While there is an increasing number of infrastructure projects developed under PPP arrangements, there have been very few in the clean energy sector. There have so far been a few waste-to-energy projects developed in five cities, which could have a great demonstration effect and help realise the President's target to develop and operate 12 waste-to-energy power plants in 12 municipalities by 2022 (which, combined, should create up to 234 megawatts of electricity using 16,000 tonnes of waste a day). In the energy conservation sector, there are three on-going street lighting projects in Madiun, West Lombok and

Surakarta city (see Box 4.3). While limited in number, these projects are promising examples of PPP energy saving models that could be replicated in other cities and help familiarise government institutions with such projects.

Overall, a number of elements explain why few clean energy projects have taken off under PPP arrangements. First, PPP contracts are often very complex and require extensive co-ordination across a range of stakeholders, making their implementation particularly challenging. Second, government contracting agencies continue to lack both familiarity with clean energy projects as well as the skills and experience to undertake PPPs. Equally, the fact that current PPP documents and procedures are still geared towards traditional, large-scale infrastructure projects and lack standardisation has made it difficult to develop energy efficiency projects through PPP models (**see Chapters 3 and 5**).

Box 4.3. The Surakarta Street Lighting project

The Surakarta's street lighting project was initiated by the municipality of Surakarta in 2018 in a bid to revamp and extend previous public street lighting infrastructure covering around 976 km (of which, 335 km are strategic roads). The project was undertaken following a 2016 survey showing both qualitative and quantitative shortcomings of previous public lighting infrastructure. On the one hand, the survey showed that numerous lamps and poles were non-compliant with national standards and that significant savings could be achieved through replacing existing lamps with more energy-efficient LED lamps. On the other hand, the survey highlighted that previous lighting infrastructure did not satisfy actual needs estimated at around 31,890 lamp points (against 21,222 in 2016).

The project is being prepared under PPP arrangements (following Presidential Regulation No. 38/2015) with the municipality of Surakarta as the government contracting agency. The municipality completed and submitted a final business case to prospective developers in mid-2020. Following a pre-qualification process held at the end of 2020, three consortia of local and international companies are expected to bid for the 17-year concession. The winning bidder will be responsible for building, financing, operating and maintaining Surakarta's public street lighting. The project's forecasted internal rate of return was estimated at 13.24% over 17 years, which is lower than rates observed for energy efficiency in Singapore and the Philippines, often in the upper teens. The project's indicative financial information is summarised in the table below:

Table 4.3. Surakarta public lighting project financial information

Estimated project cost	USD 25.7 million (17 years)
Debt level	70%
Equity level	30%
Project IRR	13.24%
Equity IRR	15%

Note: IRR= Internal Rate of Return*. The internal rate of return is a financial metric used to estimate the profitability of potential investments. It represents the discount rate that makes the net present value of a project's cash flows equal to zero in a discounted cash flow analysis.

The project will benefit from the Ministry of Finance's assistance under its Project Development Facility and is expected to reach financial close in 2022. The project will also benefit from a government payment guarantee administered by the IIGF to guarantee availability payment by the Municipality.

Figure 4.2. Financing structure of the Surakarta public street lighting project

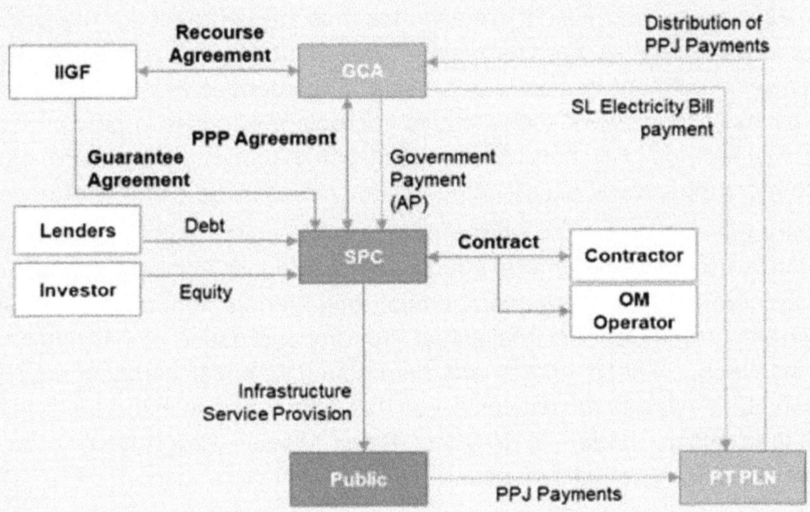

*AP=Availability Payments. GCA=Government Contracting Agency. OM= Operation and Maintenance. PPJ= Pajak Penerangan Jalan or Street Lighting Tax.SL= Street Lighting. SPC=Special Purpose Company.

Source: Bappenas and PT SMI.

Other investment-related issues

Other issues relating to intellectual property, contract enforcement and investment treaties play an important role in creating a healthier regulatory climate for investment. The OECD *Investment Policy Review of Indonesia 2020* discusses Indonesia's progress on these issues in more detail and identifies potential areas for improvement. While the report's messages are not specific to clean energy, they have important implications. The following list highlights selected messages from the Investment Policy Review on aforementioned issues with implications for clean energy:

- The 2007 Investment Law guarantees "to provide the same treatment to any domestic and foreign investors, by continuously considering the national interest" and to provide "equitable treatment to all investors of any countries that carry out investment activities in Indonesia in accordance with provisions of laws and regulations." (Article 6). As explained in this chapter, however, these non-discrimination guarantees are not always enforced in practice in the clean energy sector, although on-going reforms are a step in the right direction.
- Indonesia's dispute resolution mechanisms have a good track record overall, although there have been concerns over the court system's transparency and fair treatment as well as the effectiveness of contract enforcement. Concerning contract enforcement, the process often appears lengthier and costlier than in some neighbouring countries. The World Bank, for example, ranks Indonesia 139th out of 196 countries in terms of "contract enforcement"[3] as part of its Ease of Doing Business index. While efforts are underway, continuing to improve the access and efficiency of local courts is critical in order to ensure predictability in commercial relationships as well as ensure an effective and clear contract enforcement process. This is particularly important for clean energy investment, given the high number and often complex contractual arrangements involved in project development.

Indonesia has 36 investment treaties in force today, covering around 41% of its inward FDI (almost half of that share being covered by the ASEAN Comprehensive Investment Agreement treaty). Yet, a significant number of these treaties contain vague investment protections that may create unintended consequences. As in many countries, Indonesia has thus started to modernise and renegotiate some of these treaties (e.g. 23 treaties were terminated over 2014-16) and is about to enter into new ones. Nevertheless, while investment treaties can provide much-needed investor protection and contribute to a friendlier business environment, these should not replace efforts to improve the current investment framework (e.g. FDI regime, LCR, court system, intellectual property etc.) which, as nascent evidence shows, could be more effective at accelerating FDI (including in the clean energy sector).

- Indonesia's intellectual property legal framework is overall solid, regularly amended and in line with international standards. However, more efforts are needed to improve intellectual property rights protection and enforcement, as the implementation and enforcement of existing laws remain overall weak. Cutting down currently lengthy Intellectual Property application processing times is also needed to incentivise innovation. These efforts are paramount to boost clean energy innovation, which ultimately will contribute to slash project costs – as has been the case in India where solar PV patenting has increased dramatically under its National Solar Mission Programme – as well as improve Indonesian manufacturers' competitiveness.

References

APEC (2019), *Peer Review and Capacity Building on APEC Infrastructure Development and Investment: Indonesia*, Asia Pacific Economic Cooperation, https://www.apec.org/Publications/2019/11/Peer-Review-and-Capacity-Building-on-APEC-Infrastructure-Development-and-Investment-Indonesia (accessed on 23 December 2020). [21]

Burke, P. et al. (2019), *Overcoming barriers to solar and wind energy adoption in two Asian giants: India and Indonesia.* [3]

Chawla, K. et al. (2018), *Clean Energy Investment Trends: Evolving Landscape for Grid-Connected Renewable Energy Projects in India*, CEEW and OECD/IEA, New Delhi. [19]

Dhar, A. et al. (2020), "Geothermal energy resources: potential environmental impact and land reclamation", *Environmental Reviews*, pp. 1-13, http://dx.doi.org/10.1139/er-2019-0069. [16]

Dutt, A., K. Chawla and N. Kuldeep (2019), *Accelerating Investments in Renewables in Indonesia Drivers, Risks, and Opportunities*, Council on Energy, Environment and Water. [1]

Economic Times (2019), *Govt modifies solar park scheme to ease land, evacuation constraints*, https://energy.economictimes.indiatimes.com/news/renewable/govt-modifies-solar-park-scheme-to-ease-land-evacuation-constraints/68374675 (accessed on 17 December 2020). [18]

IESR (2019), *Indonesia Clean Energy Outlook - Tracking Progress and Review of Clean Energy Development in Indonesia*, Institute for Essential Services Reform , Jakarta, http://www.iesr.or.id (accessed on 16 November 2020). [4]

IESR (2019), *Levelized Cost of Electricity in Indonesia - Understanding The Levelized Cost of Electricity Generation*, http://www.iesr.or.id (accessed on 6 April 2020). [10]

Kennedy, S. (2020), *Research: land use challenges for Indonesia's transition to renewable energy*, The Conversation, https://theconversation.com/research-land-use-challenges-for-indonesias-transition-to-renewable-energy-131767 (accessed on 6 November 2020). [14]

Kennedy, S. (2018), "Indonesia's energy transition and its contradictions: Emerging geographies of energy and finance", *Energy Research and Social Science*, Vol. 41, pp. 230-237, http://dx.doi.org/10.1016/j.erss.2018.04.023. [6]

MEMR (2017), *Lampu Hijau Untuk Geothermal Di Kawasan Konservasi (Green Light for Geothermal in Conservation Areas)*, https://ebtke.esdm.go.id/post/2017/03/16/1592/lampu.hijau.untuk.geothermal.di.kawasan.konservasi (accessed on 4 March 2021). [15]

MoF (2020), *National Strategic Project as Regional Public Goods in Indonesia*, https://www.djkn.kemenkeu.go.id/kanwil-sulseltrabar/baca-artikel/13173/National-Strategic-Project-as-Regional-Public-Goods-in-Indonesia.html (accessed on 21 December 2020). [20]

OECD (2020), *OECD Investment Policy Reviews: Indonesia 2020*, OECD Investment Policy Reviews, OECD Publishing, Paris, https://dx.doi.org/10.1787/b56512da-en. [8]

OECD (2019), *OECD Green Growth Policy Review of Indonesia 2019*, OECD Environmental Performance Reviews, OECD Publishing, Paris, https://dx.doi.org/10.1787/1eee39bc-en. [13]

OECD (2015), *Overcoming Barriers to International Investment in Clean Energy*, Green Finance and Investment, OECD Publishing, Paris, https://dx.doi.org/10.1787/9789264227064-en. [12]

OECD (2015), *Policy Guidance for Investment in Clean Energy Infrastructure: Expanding Access to Clean Energy for Green Growth and Development*, OECD Publishing, Paris, https://dx.doi.org/10.1787/9789264212664-en. [9]

Probst, B. et al. (2020), "The short-term costs of local content requirements in the Indian solar auctions", *Nature Energy*, Vol. 5/11, http://dx.doi.org/10.1038/s41560-020-0677-7. [11]

PwC (2019), *As many as 21 PPAs for new and renewable energy power plants planned to be signed this year*, https://www.pwc.com/id/en/media-centre/infrastructure-news/april-2019/planned-to-be-signed-this-year.html (accessed on 9 November 2020). [5]

PwC (2018), *Power In Indonesia - Investment and Taxation Guide*, http://www.pwc.com/id (accessed on 19 July 2019). [2]

The Jakarta Post (2019), *Foreign investments flow to neighbors instead of Indonesia: World Bank*, https://www.thejakartapost.com/news/2019/09/10/foreign-investments-flow-to-neighbors-instead-of-indonesia-world-bank.html (accessed on 20 November 2020). [7]

The Jakarta Post (2017), *LMAN gets down to business on promised land*, https://www.thejakartapost.com/news/2017/04/06/lman-gets-down-business-promised-land.html (accessed on 21 December 2020). [17]

Notes

[1] Later amended by Presidential Regulation no. 148/2015.

[2] As part of a value-for-money assessment of a potential PPP project (against traditional procurement or fully-private development) , a 'public sector comparator' (PSC) is a common method used to estimate the hypothetical risk-adjusted cost of that project was it to be financed, owned and implemented by the Government.

[3] The cost dimension of the indicator on contract enforcement refers to average cost of court fees, attorney fees (where the use of attorneys is mandatory or common) and enforcement fees expressed as a percentage of the claim value. The time it takes to resolve a dispute is counted from the moment the plaintiff decides to file the lawsuit in court until payment, and covers both the days when actions take place and the waiting periods in between.

5 Investment promotion and facilitation

This chapter examines investment promotion and facilitation policies in place in Indonesia. It analyses the use of targeted incentives and financing for energy efficiency and renewable energy development, and provides insights into good practices in other countries. It highlights key measures implemented by the government to improve the business environment for clean energy projects, as well as areas of untapped opportunity to attract further investment. It also examines the role that public procurement of energy efficiency services and corporate sourcing of renewables can play to jump-start market-based instruments and foreign investment in clean energy projects. The chapter identifies remaining challenges and proposes recommendations to address them.

The Government of Indonesia has introduced multiple regulatory changes and policy measures in recent years to encourage clean energy development (**see Chapter 3**). It has also taken a number of reforms targeting investment facilitation, such as the creation and on-going development of its Online Single Submission (OSS) business licensing system, which is working to improve transparency, streamline licencing and ease the business development process. These measures, alongside targeted incentives such as the import duty exemptions for renewable energy machinery passed by the Ministry of Finance (MoF) in 2010 and the use of tax holidays or tax allowances for certain projects, are helping to stimulate growth in renewable energy and energy efficiency investments in Indonesia.

At the heart of overall investment promotion and facilitation is the Indonesian Investment Co-ordinating Board (Badan Koordinasi Penanaman Modal, or BKPM). Notably, its role includes co-ordinating across the various ministries and related entities that influence investment policies and their implementation (OECD, 2020[1]). In more recent years, its focus has been to simplify licensing, facilitate investment projects and improve conditions to attract investments, though this can be a challenging task, given the number of actors involved (**see Chapter 2**).

While progress in co-ordinating, facilitating and promoting investment is encouraging, the current level of investment in clean energy is still not sufficient to meet Indonesia's ambitious targets by 2025 and beyond. In practice, procedures and requirements can still be rather complex, for instance requiring obtaining licences and permits from line ministries and regional administrations beyond what is processed in the OSS. New regulations stemming from the recent Omnibus Law are working to harmonise and ease the business process further, and subsequent implementing regulations should help to operationalise those ambitions. For example, a new version of the OSS that integrates via a single portal business and risk-based assessment licensing (taking into account health, safety, environmental security and resource risks, as per Government Regulation No. 5 of 2021) is expected to be launched in June of 2021.

Ensuring these policy measures create an enabling environment that promotes and facilitates investment (while equally ensuring compliance with environmental impact assessment requirements) will therefore be critical to scale-up clean energy deployment in Indonesia. Encouraging and rewarding early adopters, diminishing obstacles for investors and incentivising innovative solutions and market-based services will also be critical to promote and facilitate the required scale-up in clean energy investment.

Assessment and recommendations

Indonesia should continue to see through its fossil fuel subsidy reform

Progress made since 2014 is commendable, though ensuring cost-reflective market pricing for all energy products is critical to meeting Indonesia's clean energy targets. Phasing-out remaining fossil fuel subsidies will not only create a more level playing field for clean energy projects but also will signal to investors the government's steadfast commitment to clean energy development. The reform can also be targeted in a way that achieves longer lasting impact for poor households, for instance by sensibly redirecting financial support to energy efficiency and renewable energy solutions, rather than to annual price subsidies.

Time to 2025 ambitions is short, but near-term measures can get projects off the ground

Indonesia can promote and facilitate clean energy development by focusing or expanding its use of cost-based tax incentives and accelerated depreciation rules. It can also develop more targeted support for clean energy projects, for instance using the Perseroan Terbatas Sarana Multi Infrastruktur (PT SMI) fund to provide a de-risking or credit enhancement mechanism to lower collateral requirements for renewable energy project developers or by designing specific procedures within the Indonesia Infrastructure Guarantee Fund (IIGF) risk guarantee for energy efficiency projects. These incentives and support mechanisms can help address market barriers and encourage uptake of clean energy solutions and services. Complementing those measures with longer-term policy signals, such as progressive ratcheting up of energy performance requirements, will help create a pipeline of clean energy projects to 2025 and beyond.

Lack of incentives give limited reason to adopt current voluntary standards

Complementing regulatory measures with grants or financial incentives can create a "carrot and stick" approach – encouraging adoption of efficient products to then drive out least-efficient ones – that has been successful in other countries such as Denmark, Japan and Australia. Current lack of tax credits or other financial incentives in Indonesia limits uptake of energy efficiency, especially given most current standards are voluntary. Incentives will encourage adoption of voluntary regulations such as national non-residential building codes, creating momentum and confidence in the market that can then be used to transition to mandatory requirements and to expand regulations to other sectors, such as residential buildings. Market-based instruments, such as the tradable energy savings (white) certificates used in Europe, can also encourage adoption of energy efficiency solutions and best practices.

Channelling finance and investment to energy efficiency requires more targeted support

Government support and incentives to date have not sufficiently targeted energy efficiency development, which continues to lag behind. In particular, low capacity in the market to propose "bankable" projects creates a critical barrier to finance and investment. To improve this situation, Indonesia can provide more targeted support to stakeholders involved in preparing energy efficiency projects, such as the informational guide by the Sustainable Energy Authority of Ireland[1] for public and private actors preparing energy performance contracting. Additional support can include measures to enable energy service companies (ESCOs), such as continued training on investment grade energy audits and development of certification of third-party monitoring and evaluation. These measures will help to ensure a standardised investment environment without need for investors to treat financing on a case-by-case basis.

Demonstrating support of clean energy projects is critical to create market confidence

Support through financing products like the Kredit Usaha Rakyat (People's Business Credit), which provides a guarantee scheme and subsidised interest rates for small businesses, can help overcome barriers such as high collateral requirements, making it easier for businesses to establish or expand their offerings. Government efforts should focus on expanding financial support for clean energy development, with immediate focus on enabling successful projects that address perceived risks and that encourage market replication. The government can help jump-start the market through initiatives such as pilot ESCO projects with state-owned enterprises (e.g. by extending the current IIGF scope beyond public-private partnership [PPP] models). It can also focus on deploying clean energy solutions in specific clusters, for example, by partnering with energy-intensive industries to facilitate renewable energy procurement. Efforts to demonstrate successful applications will increase market confidence and create more attractive conditions for clean energy finance and investment.

Support should aim to diminish obstacles to renewable energy finance and investment

Effort is needed to address obstacles preventing growth in the renewable electricity market in Indonesia. One such example is the present framework for wheeling of power, which makes corporate sourcing of off-site renewable electricity generation both complex and challenging. The current system to determine feed-in tariffs for net metering likewise does not provide transparency in the calculation of cost and can put renewables at a disadvantage, compared to other generation assets. Perceived risks, such as lack of transparency in power purchase agreement (PPA) prices as well as uncertainties around government force majeure (GFM) and natural force majeure (NFM), also create uncertainty for investors and can lead to high costs of capital for clean energy projects. Addressing these types of barriers requires establishing transparent rules and processes (e.g. for power wheeling) that will complement on-going support for renewable energy business development, ensuring there is on the one hand ample demand for renewable energy projects and on the other hand a fair and competitive market offering those solutions.

Indonesia has shown it can be innovative in enabling renewable energy investment

One such example is the recently announced project between the state electricity company, Perusahaan Listrik Negara (PLN), and the Abu Dhabi-based renewables firm, Masdar, to develop a 145 megawatt (MW) floating solar photovoltaic (PV) plant in the Java-Bali system (Harsono, 2020[2]). The project will be a hybrid system, located on a reservoir behind a hydroelectric power plant, designed using smart controllers to ensure the hydroelectric power can balance the variable production of the solar PV, thus making the installation more flexible, reliable and cost-effective with capacity to add additional renewable assets in the future. The project also highlights a potential synergistic opportunity to address the challenging issue of land access for renewable energy development. Efforts to enable similar bankable solutions, including recent developments by PLN to apply renewable energy certificates (RECs), will make Indonesia a more attractive destination for clean energy finance and investments.

Long-term effort should focus on creating conditions for a flexible and dynamic market

This will require co-ordinated oversight and planning, building upon success and addressing enduring challenges to ensure the overall facilitation and compatibility of clean energy investments (e.g. grid and generating assets). Medium- to long-term efforts should focus on enabling innovative finance and market-based mechanisms such as energy savings performance contracting, open and tradeable energy attribution certificates, and energy-as-a-service models. These can all enable large-scale engagement of private capital for clean energy projects, so long as Indonesia addresses gaps and weaknesses impeding market development (e.g. ensuring a transparent, straightforward process for licensing and permitting of renewable energy projects). Enabling uptake of market-based mechanisms may also require government support to enable their operability, for example by providing risk guarantees or insurance products until the market is sufficiently familiar and comfortable with those financial instruments.

Box 5.1. Main policy recommendations on investment promotion and facilitation

- Review with PLN current operational regulations for power wheeling in comparison to international best practises for grid access in order to develop a more transparent process that fits the specific Indonesian context and that encourages greater corporate sourcing of renewable electricity, especially from businesses looking to procure off-site renewable generation.
- Mandate public institutions and local authorities to identify energy savings opportunities to help jump-start the current energy efficiency market, while equally enabling public actors to engage in procurement of those solutions and services. This could include relaxing rules on multi-year contracts or identifying suitable accounting practices that allow public authorities to engage in those energy efficiency investments.
- Identify levers such as risk guarantee mechanisms that help clean energy projects and investors to overcome risks to finance, and address shortcomings in existing funds such as the IIGF to provide more targeted support to clean energy projects. This can include working with partners to create a dedicated clean energy fund or a risk-sharing facility such as the one support by the Small Industry Development Bank of India to help lower the cost of capital and mobilise investments for energy efficiency and renewable energy.
- Improve the clean energy investment environment by speeding up decision making and facilitating market-based solutions. Building on recent OSS efforts, work to provide simple and straightforward access to rules and guidelines to facilitate project developer and investor engagement, while also prioritising co-ordination across governance institutions involved in clean energy projects.
- Clarify intentions on the short, medium and long-term expectations for energy regulations, subsidies, tax regimes and other targeted incentives, for instance by enshrining these objectives in the anticipated presidential regulation on renewable energy. Also ensure policies are transparent to enable project developers, financial institutions and investors considering or engaged in clean energy development to make informed decisions and risk assessments, as these currently hinder wide-spread renewable energy and energy efficiency deployment.
- Consider aligning feed-in tariff calculations with international net-metering practices, ensuring that grid tariff structure is not an unfair barrier to deploy renewable energy. Also consider expanding current incentives for renewable electricity development, such as the tax holiday for large-scale clean energy investments, to facilitate and encourage investment at a smaller scale.

Energy subsidy reform and carbon pricing

Energy subsidies, including both fossil fuel and electricity price subsidies, have constituted a large share of government expenditure in Indonesia, representing as much as 4% of gross domestic product (GDP) since 2005 (Figure 5.1). This share is not certain, though, as Indonesia did not have a comprehensive inventory taking stock of the subsidies and their associated costs.

Nevertheless, the question of reform was inevitable, given the sizeable fiscal burden of the subsidies (OECD, 2019[3]), and the government consequently kicked off major reforms in 2014, for instance linking domestic transport fuel prices to international prices and applying more targeted electricity subsidies. The result was a rapid cut in expenditures, saving an estimated USD 9 billion, or 8% of state revenues, in 2015 alone (IEA, 2017[4]).

Figure 5.1. Government expenditure on energy consumption subsidies, 2007-19

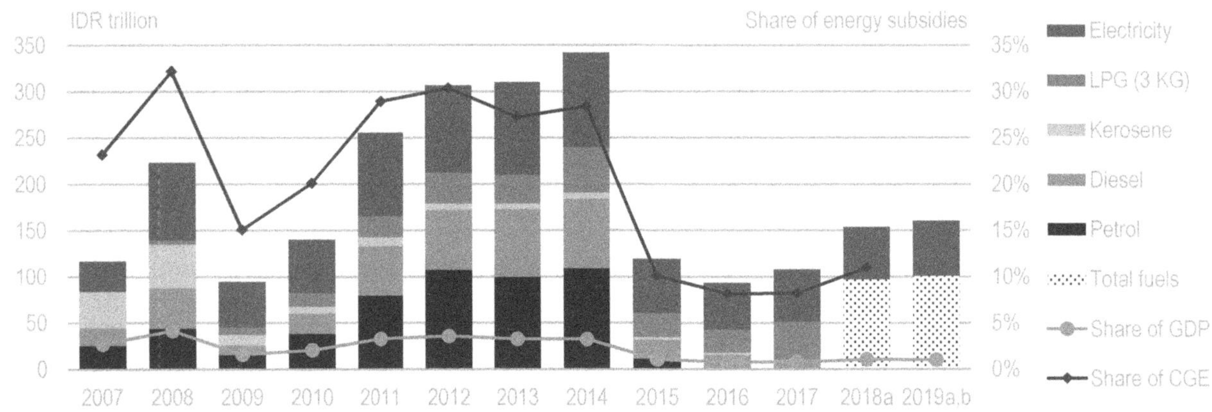

Note: LPG = liquefied petroleum gas; CGE = central government expenditure; a) detailed breakdown for fuel subsides not available; b) data refer to planned budget.

Source: (OECD, 2019[3]) *Green Growth Policy Review of Indonesia 2019*; MoF (2019), *Indonesia's Effort to Phase out and Rationalise its Fossil-fuel Subsidies: A Report on the G20 Peer-review of Inefficient Fossil-fuel Subsidies that Encourage Wasteful Consumption in Indonesia.*

StatLink https://stat.link/30tgra

By 2016, 12 consumer classes of electricity subsidies had been phased out, targeting removal from higher-income households and supporting instead the two lowest consumption classes of 450 volt-ampere (VA) and 900 VA customers. The initial effect of the electricity subsidy reform, in addition to cutting annual government subsidy spending by around USD 5.6 billion (IEA, 2017[4]), was around 7% lower overall household electricity consumption (Burke and Kurniawati, 2018[5]). Further reforms were planned to phase out subsidies for 900 VA customers, but the government announced intentions to keep those electricity prices constant until at least 2019 due to fears of social unrest (OECD, 2019[3]). There were also plans to adjust the tariff for 450 VA customers that are not listed in the poor and vulnerable household database, but those reforms have not yet occurred (Afut Syafril and Sri Haryati, 2020[6]; Massita Ayu, 2020[7]).

The government has also been working to improve the subsidy mechanisms for LPG, which is estimated to have cost the government around USD 664 million in fiscal support to the coal industry in 2015 (Bridle et al., 2018[8]). Just like electricity subsidy reforms, LPG reforms will target support only to poor and vulnerable households, although to date the price subsidy has remained in place.

Broadly speaking, fossil fuels still benefit from a number of fiscal incentives such as tax incentives to the mining and processing industries. Fossil-fuel production is also supported through the domestic market obligations (DMOs), which require oil, natural gas and coal producers to sell part of their output (generally between 15% and 25%) to the domestic market at heavily discounted prices (OECD, 2019[3]). Coal-fired electricity generators can also benefit from support such as preferential loans, loan guarantees and subsidised credit, and in 2020, the government announced its plans to move forward with coal downstream industry development, which could increase spending on coal support (Arinaldo et al., 2021[9]).

In terms of monitoring, fossil fuel subsidies are now scrutinised on a monthly basis, accounting for fuels consumed and the respective subsidy amounts. This helps to ensure subsidies remain within the agreed quota, and the tally is used to design subsidy policy and possible reforms for the next budget year. It is important to note that the quota, budget and subsidy policy are all subject to parliament agreement.

While Indonesia has made great progress in reducing its fossil-fuel and electricity price subsidies since the mid-2000s, not all price reforms have been implemented as announced, and the continued use of these subsidies (including indirect support such as industry tax incentives and DMOs) are holding back Indonesia's transition to a sustainable energy system (OECD, 2019[3]). A clear, transparent strategy on the government's intentions and commitment to follow through with energy subsidy reform will thus send important signals to market, helping to encourage energy efficiency and renewable energy investment.

The government is also considering the implementation of a carbon price on fossil fuels, after several years of discussions for it. A green paper published by MoF in 2009 identified policy options that would help reach the country's climate change commitments, including the introduction of carbon pricing alongside gradual removal of energy subsidies (Keuangan, 2009[10]). The paper proposed applying an initial carbon tax on fossil-fuel combustion for electricity generation and large industrial installations as of 2014, although no legislation was introduced to impose the tax. Nonetheless, Presidential Regulation No. 77 of 2018 did provide a legal framework for carbon trading, and the government studied potential carbon pricing mechanisms, including a cap-and-trade system for the power sector, the pulp and paper industry and the cement sector (OECD, 2019[3]).

Several discussions and studies, with support from international co-operation such as the Partnership for Market Readiness (PMR) programme[2], have also looked to enhance market readiness for a carbon market in Indonesia and to initiate domestic links to other carbon markets. There also were inter-ministerial discussions throughout 2020 on the topic of carbon pricing, and a presidential regulation may be announced in 2021.

In March of 2021, the Ministry of Energy and Mineral Resources (MEMR) announced that it would begin an initial trial of a carbon trading scheme for the electricity sector (Meilanova, 2021[11]). Around 80 coal-fired power plants will participate in the first year of the trial, including 19 plants with more than 400 MW of electricity generation capacity and another 51 plants with between 100 MW and 400 MW capacity. To monitor participants, MEMR Directorate General of Electricity created a monitoring tool called APPLE (Aplikasi Pelaporan dan Perhitungan Emisi, or the Emission Reporting and Calculation App). Participants exceeding the emissions cap will be able to: substitute fuel (e.g. using biodiesel co-firing); convert generation capacity to renewable electricity; or replace old technology to make the power plant more efficient. Further details for the trial are in preparation.

MEMR Minister Arifin Tasrif also launched a new category for Greenhouse Gas Emissions Reduction and Trading at the 2021 Subroto Award for Energy Efficiency (Riana, 2021[12]). The new award aims to reward power plants participating in the carbon trading trial and those that have succeeded in reducing their emission levels. The trial and awards are intended to serve as a learning tool for the development of a broader emissions trading scheme expected under the presidential regulation on carbon pricing.

Targeted incentives and funds for energy efficiency investment

Tax incentives are one of the commonly used tools to attract investment for development. In Indonesia, these incentives to support investment in the country are among the most generous in the region (OECD, 2020[1]). Unfortunately, they are not specific to energy efficiency development.

In principle, tax holidays given for investment in certain sub-sectors of industry could be used for energy efficiency investments, but these are not noted explicitly as eligible expenses. In the same way, a luxury goods value-added tax (VAT) policy can consider, in theory, energy efficiency as one of the bases for determining tax rates (e.g. VAT of luxury vehicles may vary depending on emissions and the efficient use of fuel), but again this is not specific to energy efficiency.

Other incentives, such as some local tax benefits for green building construction, are available in a few cities but are rather limited in size and scope (APEC, 2017[13]). For instance, Bandung's energy performance requirements for small buildings include incentives via reduced land and property taxes for buildings meeting two and three star ratings (Pahnael, Soekiman and Wimala, 2020[14]). Otherwise, there are no specific financial incentives (e.g. dedicated lines of credit, concessional financing or project finance) used to encourage energy efficiency in Indonesia, thus further contributing to a limited project pipeline.

Lack of incentives compounds other challenges affecting energy efficiency investment

Progress in developing and implementing new energy efficiency regulations, such as the planned minimum energy performance standards for 10 new appliance and equipment categories, is encouraging, as is improved compliance with regulations in recent years (**see Chapter 3**). Improved monitoring, verification and enforcement of energy efficiency policy will help to increase uptake and compliance, but lack of incentives (e.g. rebate schemes, tax reductions and VAT exemptions) fails to encourage early adopters and market awareness for energy efficiency solutions.

Incentives can play a critical role in creating a "carrot and stick" approach for energy efficiency that has been successful in many countries. For example, the Italian government created an incentive programme in 2010 offering 50 percent tax deduction for replacement of household appliances such as refrigerators, washers, dryers, ovens and freezers with more efficient new units. Mexico similarly provided government-funded subsidies to consumers to cover a portion of the purchase of new, energy-efficient refrigerators and air conditioners. Other examples, such as the "Carbon Cashbag" programme in Korea, which created credits for energy-efficient and low-carbon products that could then be used for things like discounts on public transportation, have been used to incentivise energy efficiency uptake (de la Rue du Can et al., 2014[15]), while more innovative approaches include examples such as the on-wage financing scheme launched by Ghana to improve the accessibility and affordability of energy-efficient appliances in line with the countries new energy efficiency standards and labelling regulations (U4E, 2020[16]).

Lack of incentives (e.g. reduced property taxes or enhanced capital allowances) similarly fail to encourage businesses, facility owners and asset managers to seek out energy efficiency, though they often are aware of its value. Programmes such as Germany's tax relief for energy-efficient refurbishment of buildings can help encourage asset owners and property managers to engage in energy saving activities (IEA-UNEP, 2019[17]). At the same time, awareness and incentives may not suffice to overcome additional barriers such as inadequate human resource capacity (e.g. to carry out investment grade energy audits), and so capacity building efforts may also be needed to enable "bankable" energy efficiency opportunities (**see Chapter 7**).

Mainstream financial institutions also commonly lack familiarity of the notions and (financial) benefits of energy efficiency measures, which can also include not knowing how to structure financial products for those investments, and they do not necessarily have real incentive to seek out energy efficiency projects. In fact, even when institutions are familiar, credit regulations (established to protect against risky lending practices) do not incentivise them to finance those projects. Thus, while banks may currently be the main funders of energy efficiency projects in Indonesia, this generally is through corporate finance to existing customers and usually requires collateral that covers 80-120% of the project cost (APEC, 2017[13]).

In response, the government of Indonesia has supported a number of activities to try and improve this situation, for example by creating its Partnership Program on Energy Conservation, which supports energy efficiency uptake by providing government-funded energy audits for buildings and industry. Through this programme, 28 investment grade energy audits have been carried out since 2014 to profile energy efficiency opportunities and investment needs. In the finance sector, Otoritas Jasa Keuangan, Indonesia's financial services regulator, has also made significant efforts supported by MEMR to raise awareness raising and do capacity building, for instance designing guidelines for energy efficiency projects and running training modules to improve knowledge on energy efficiency technologies for local banks.

The government has also announced intentions to introduce a number of measures supporting energy efficiency investment as part of its update of the 2009 Regulation on Energy Conservation, which is expected in 2021. Those measures include: further details on the ESCO business model; support to improve investment grade energy audits as well as measurement and verification protocols; fiscal and non-fiscal incentives for energy efficiency development; mandatory energy management requirements for certain large energy users and providers; improved capacity building programmes; and other efforts to de-risk energy efficiency projects.

In addition to these measures, the government can further incentivise energy efficiency investment through existing initiatives, notably by explicitly targeting energy efficiency development to address barriers to the development of energy efficiency projects under those schemes. For instance, existing guarantees under the IIGF and the project development facility from PT SMI already acknowledge energy efficiency as an eligible project type, but have seldom been used for energy efficiency (as it has traditionally been achieved through conventional procurement). This is due, in part, to a PPP framework whose due diligence requirements can make public procurement of energy efficiency services and solutions complex and costly (**see Chapter 3**), thus making it challenging to access those guarantees, which were designed to have an element of public ownership. Addressing these barriers, for instance through standardised PPP documentation to help facilitate the public procurement process, can help to unlock those risk guarantees and other financial support mechanisms for energy efficiency development.

The government could also consider establishing a dedicated energy efficiency fund that could support long-term concessional finance and/or a risk-sharing facility to address barriers like lack of collateral for ESCOs and facility owners looking to finance energy efficiency investments. For example, this could be through the SDG Indonesia One Blended Finance Platform managed by PT SMI, working with potential financiers like the Green Climate Fund or the Asian Development Bank. The fund could be used as a line of credit with financial partners using a list of eligible projects and/or technologies, which would concurrently help build awareness and confidence in those solutions in the market, as it has in other countries like India (Box 5.2). The fund equally could be built around a "lending plus" approach, providing non-financial support (e.g. technical assistance or support in preparing contractual structures) where needed. This may be especially helpful in kick-starting the nascent energy efficiency market in Indonesia.

Box 5.2. India's partial risk sharing support is enabling growth in energy efficiency services

Like Indonesia, India has substantial untapped potential for energy efficiency developments that have been hindered by market barriers impeding access to finance, such as perceived risk by commercial banks. To help mobilise capital for investment in energy efficiency initiatives, the Government of India and the World Bank via the Global Environment Facility launched a USD 43 million grant and guarantee agreement in 2015 to support the Partial Risk Sharing Facility (PRSF) managed by the Small Industries Development Bank of India (SIDBI). This builds upon SIDBI's experience in supporting energy efficiency finance and investments through various forms of financial support (e.g. lines of credit, micro-loans, guarantees and a "credit plus" approach providing both finance and technical advisory services).

The PRSF programme has the objective to transform India's energy efficiency market by promoting and enabling increased investment in energy efficiency projects, notably through ESCOs and energy service performance contracting. In particular, the programme aims to overcome gaps from complex contractual structures, lack of collateral or tangible assets, and limited market experience with ESCOs.

To address these barriers, the programme has supported loans guaranteed by various participating financial institutions using partial credit guarantees to cover a share of the default risk (up to 75%) faced when extending loans to eligible energy efficiency projects. A technical assistance component also provides capacity building activities and other operational support to prepare projects for finance.

As of 2020, the programme had applied around USD 14 million in guarantees for total project investment of nearly USD 50 million (Bharti, 2020[18]). These projects are helping to demonstrate the viability of ESCOs and energy savings performance contracts in India, for example to deliver energy efficiency measures for street lighting, school, hospitals, utility facilities and industry. Indonesia could look to create a similar facility or support mechanism, which would help create confidence in the energy savings model and support increased flows of finance to the currently limited and nascent ESCO market.

Public procurement for energy efficiency investments can propel market demand

Presently, use of public procurement for energy efficiency investments in Indonesia is limited. Financial support by the government, essentially for PPPs, has mostly been for large-scale infrastructure projects, although the government is currently preparing some strategies to encourage the implementation of smaller scale projects under the PPP scheme. In addition, local authorities and public entities cannot easily engage in contractual arrangements that are longer than one year, due to budgetary regulations, thus limiting local energy efficiency procurement, for instance through energy savings performance contracts (**see Chapter 3**).

Nevertheless, a few examples of public procurement of energy efficiency exist. This includes a public procurement project for public street lighting that is currently being implemented across Indonesia. The programme will fund the replacement of 12 437 halogen street lights by light-emitting diode (LED) lamps in 93 cities and regencies, including use of 5 005 solar-powered LED street lights (MEMR, 2020[19]). It is financed by annual state budgets and implemented through procurement that is managed by the government's procurement agency, Lembaga Kebijakan Pengadaan Barang/Jasa Pemerintah.

A similar project for public street lighting using a PPP model exists in Surakarta (**see Chapter 4**). The programme is not fully implemented, but it illustrates the potential for public engagement to accelerate energy efficiency deployment in Indonesia, similar to successful PPPs and other public procurement programmes in other countries. For example, in India, the publicly-owned Energy Efficiency Services Limited super ESCO used bulk procurement to deliver energy-efficient LEDs to market at less than USD 1, which is 80% lower than the previous market price, thanks to bulk purchase of around 330 million LEDs (IEA, 2018[20]). In the United States, the federal government, which represents a considerable purchasing power, has procurement rules that require the purchase of high efficiency ENERGY STAR equipment (IEA, 2019[21]).

Indonesia's government can similarly create business opportunities for energy efficiency services and technology providers by creating momentum in the market. For instance, the government could mandate state-owned facilities such as schools and hospitals to engage in a transparent and standardised process for procurement of energy-efficient products (e.g. retrofitting with LEDs and high-efficiency air conditioning equipment) or energy efficiency services (e.g. through ESCO models). These projects would not only help achieve energy conservation (and related financial savings) for public entities, but also would help the market to recognise how monetised energy savings can be used to finance energy efficiency projects, which is particularly important for project finance development in Indonesia.

Market-based instruments can help to promote energy efficiency investment

Market-based instruments such as energy saving obligations for industry or utilities, white certificate (or energy saving certificate) programmes, and energy efficiency auction mechanisms are not currently in use in Indonesia. These instruments can be an effective tool to drive investment in energy efficiency measures, helping to creating a market-based (e.g. tradable) approach to achieve energy savings through a market-based, cost-effective approach that has been used in other countries (IEA, 2017[22]).

For example, in China, the State Grid Corporation created ESCOs in all 26 provinces within its service territory in response to the country's 2010 energy obligation programme, while the Southern Grid Company likewise established a single ESCO at the corporate level, covering all four provinces within its service territory. These ESCOs implemented energy efficiency projects, delivered specialised energy and consultancy services, and helped organise workshops and seminars to engage costumers in energy efficiency programmes. Between 2012 and 2016, the two grid companies exceeded their cumulative electricity savings target (around 55 gigawatt-hours of electricity reductions) by over 13 gigawatt-hours in additional savings (IEA, 2018[23]).

While no market-based instruments exist currently in Indonesia, the government has been working alongside the World Bank and United Nations Development Programme since 2013 through the PMR programme. There were delays in the original implementation schedule, but the programme has been working with stakeholders from the power and industry sectors since late 2017 to consider carbon pricing issues and prepare Indonesia's capacity and readiness to implement market-based instruments such as energy efficiency certificates and cap and trade programmes.

As the government prepares its update of the 2009 Regulation on Energy Conservation, including announced mandatory energy management requirements for certain large energy users and providers, it could consider developing incentives and market-based instruments (e.g. tradable energy savings certificates) to support development of energy efficiency projects in Indonesia. This would help address barriers to energy efficiency development such as facility owners' unwillingness to finance energy efficiency projects. The combination of energy performance obligations with use of market-based instruments would also encourage large energy users to take up "low-hanging fruits" in the immediate term, while a programmed ratcheting-up of energy savings requirements over time would push them to identify cost-effective energy efficiency solutions for the future.

Promotion of an energy services market can unlock energy efficiency development

The energy services market in Indonesia is fairly limited. There is a small number of ESCOs operating in the country (MEMR, 2019[24]), and they tend to be small engineering firms providing services to industry or businesses, for instance to identify energy savings opportunities (APEC, 2017[13]). Most of these ESCOs have very limited capital and access to corporate finance due to lack of collateral, which consequently limits their potential to grow.

Growth of the energy services market is limited further by low market familiarity with the ESCO model and poorly perceived credibility, for instance because of inadequate human resource capacity to prepare proper investment grade energy audits and third-party verification. These limitations are due, in part, to the lack of regulatory conditions (e.g. standardised energy savings performance contracts) targeted at the development of an energy services market in Indonesia, as MEMR revoked its regulation aimed at regulating and promoting an ESCO market (**see Chapter 3**).

Good practice in other countries shows that regulatory frameworks are central in addressing legally robust energy services contracting. For example, Dubai's Regulatory and Supervisory Bureau for Electricity and Water launched a regulatory framework for ESCOs in 2014 that provided an official system to approve ESCOs, while also establishing standardised methods of measuring and documenting energy savings and equally providing standards for energy performance contracts as well as a clear and transparent mechanism for settling disputes (Construction Week, 2014[25]) In other countries, accounting rules (e.g. for ring-fencing of savings) and other policies such as restrictions for public debt and deficit have needed to be amended in order to eliminate regulatory barriers to engagement in energy performance contracting.

As noted previously, regulations on public financing in Indonesia do not allow local government institutions to enter into multi-year contracting. Officially, Presidential Regulation No. 38 of 2015 on PPPs does allow certain forms of multi-year contracts, but it does not specifically mention ESCOs. ESCOs can participate in PPP projects through an available payment fee structure[3], but specific details are left to line ministries to regulate in sectoral regulations (e.g. leaving MEMR to regulate technical provisions for PPPs in the energy sector). The sector regulations in turn need to be in line with the general regulation on PPP development under Bappenas Regulation No. 02/2020. Overall, this policy environment limits development of the nascent market for ESCO services in Indonesia, where globally most robust ESCO markets generally exist only where there is considerable public sector use of the energy services business model (e.g. for public buildings or street lighting using paid-from-savings contracting).

Indonesia's government can help create demand for an ESCO market through a number of measures, including addressing current limitations for public sector engagement in energy savings performance contracting, which has helped to drive ESCO market development in other countries. It can also work to provide legal and regulatory guidance and energy performance contracting (e.g. on baseline calculations, measuring of energy savings, and resolution of disputes) to support businesses in engaging with ESCOs, for instance as the government lowers the energy intensity threshold for industry and requires stricter energy management by those companies.

The government can also build upon its awareness and capacity building efforts, such as the trainings carried out with the Asian Development Bank on investment grade energy audits and energy saving verifier certification. It likewise could provide standard contracting documents and guidelines for public sector engagement with ESCOs, such as those used in Australia. Inspiration can also be taken from innovative programmes in other countries, such as the ColdHubs cooling as a service model in Nigeria (Box 5.3), where support by Indonesia's government for development of similar energy service models can enable replication in the market.

The government could also provide targeted financial support to address the creditworthiness of ESCOs in the country. For instance, IIGF can provide credit guarantees for a contracting agency (e.g. a state-owned enterprise). To date, ESCOs have received very limited support from IIGF and PT SMI. Yet, given ESCO difficulties to access debt financing in Indonesia, support from those funds (e.g. through risk guarantees) would help address known financing barriers like high required levels of collateral (e.g. 120% of the loan value) and high interest rates.

Box 5.3. The ColdHubs model is helping to scale up energy-efficient cooling solutions in Nigeria

Innovative financing using cooling as a service (CaaS) models[4] have gained traction in recent years, helping implement energy efficiency measures without businesses having to use directly upfront capital. One such example is ColdHubs[5], a social enterprise in Nigeria that designs, installs, commissions and operates energy-efficient walk-in cold rooms using 100% solar power for farm clusters.

Notably, ColdHubs provides a pay-as-you-go model for small-scale farmers, providing them with a shared cold storage facility to keep their produce and other perishable items fresh. Farmers pay roughly USD 50 cents per day to store food in a 20 kilogram crate, where the "hub" is operated by a local female operator, who collects the fees and builds relationships with local farming clusters. There is no contract, making the model simple and accessible, while also providing much needed cold storage to reduce risk of food spoilage and support the livelihood of local farmers.

By 2019, ColdHubs were operating 24 facilities serving over 3 500 farmers and helping to save around 24 000 tonnes of food from spoilage (Cool Coalition, 2020[26]). Similar CaaS projects have been launched recently in other countries, such as the cooling systems for octopus fishing activities in Kilwa, Tanzania[6]. Indonesia could support development of comparable CaaS financing models that can help facilitate deployment of energy-efficient and low-carbon cooling technologies, particularly across Indonesia's many islands that have similar cold storage needs (e.g. for fisheries and farming).

Targeted incentives and enabling environment for renewable electricity

Indonesia has applied a combination of incentives and pricing schemes to encourage development of renewable electricity over the last decade. For example, MoF implemented a tax holiday on clean energy investments under which new power plants that generate clean energy with a minimum investment value of IDR 100 billion (around USD 7 million) are eligible for a tax holiday. This can range from 5-20 years in corporate income tax exemption, where the length is determined by the investment value. Additional incentives have been added under the Omnibus Law and subsequent Presidential Regulation No. 10/2020 on Investment Business Activities, which came into force in March of 2021 (Table 1.2). Import duty and VAT exemptions are also available for certain components for renewable energy power generation.

Table 5.1. Power sector tax incentives under Presidential Regulation No. 10 of 2021

	Tax holiday	Mini tax holiday	Tax allowance
Reference regulations	MoF Regulation 130/PMK.010.2020 and BKPM Regulation No. 07/2020		Government Regulation No. 78/2019; MoF Regulation No. 96/PMK.010/2020
Eligible business activity	New and renewable energy power plants		Micro power plants; mini power plants with investment value below IDR 100 billion (around USD 7 million)
Tax Benefit	Corporate income tax exemption Minimum CAPEX: IDR 500 billion (around USD 35 million) between 5 and 20 years (depending on CAPEX size)	50% corporate income tax discount CAPEX: IDR 100 billion to less than IDR 500 billion (USD 7 to 35 million) for 5 years	Net income / earning before tax reduction by 30% of CAPEX, in instalment over 6 years at 5% per annum
Additional benefits	50% corporate income tax discount for following 2 years	25% corporate income tax discount for following 2 years	Accelerated depreciation / amortisation Withholding tax for dividend, lowered to 10% (or based on tax treaty) Losses carried forward for 5-10 years

Note: CAPEX = capital expenditure.
Source: OECD communication (April 2021) with BKPM on Implementing Regulations of Law 11/2020 on the Clean Energy Sector

Renewable electricity procurement practices need to sufficiently encourage investment

The government has also applied several different methods of remunerating renewable energy over the past decade, including the previous feed-in-tariff (FiT) scheme and the latest system of remuneration governed by MEMR Regulation No. 50/2017 and the more recent MEMR Regulation No. 04/2020 (**see Chapter 3**). The measures have aimed to encourage renewable electricity deployment, though these have not always provided real incentives to project developers. In particular, the 2017 changes introduced the controversial tariff scheme using the average cost of electricity production (Biaya Pokok Penyediaan, or BPP) which has proven to deter certain renewable energy investments. While the BPP calculation was designed in principle to enable renewable energy to enter into the electricity system and contribute to lower average prices of electricity generation, in most parts of the country the regulation effectively establishes price ceilings that can be too low for renewable electricity projects to compete with fossil fuels (Figure 5.2).

The lack of transparency in the value of exported renewable electricity in Indonesia is also seen by renewable electricity proponents as a barrier to investment, effectively creating a shadow price regulatory framework that can deter project developers. Other electricity market regulations, such as the current room for negotiation between independent power producers (IPPs) and PLN, similarly do not give strong incentive to invest in renewable energy projects. Lack of a standard PPA allows an unfair playing field across investors, and current, complex PPA negotiations can act as a barrier for new developers establishing themselves in the country. These barriers may limit Indonesia's ability to mobilise competitive investment in renewable energy, unlike best practice in other countries that has supported investor engagement (Box 5.4).

PPA risk allocation changes introduced in MEMR Regulation No. 10/2018 is another point of contention. Political risk is always a consideration in the early development phase of clean energy projects. However, in low-risk countries, policy changes do not impact existing agreements, meaning there is no retroactive application of new rules or policies. This guarantee around changes in policy is a critical factor in the assessment of the economic viability of projects (e.g. eventual changes to tariffs), where signalling changes well in advance gives projects time to prepare (and does not affect those that are far into the development process).

Figure 5.2. Renewable energy projects may be uncompetitive in the most populated areas

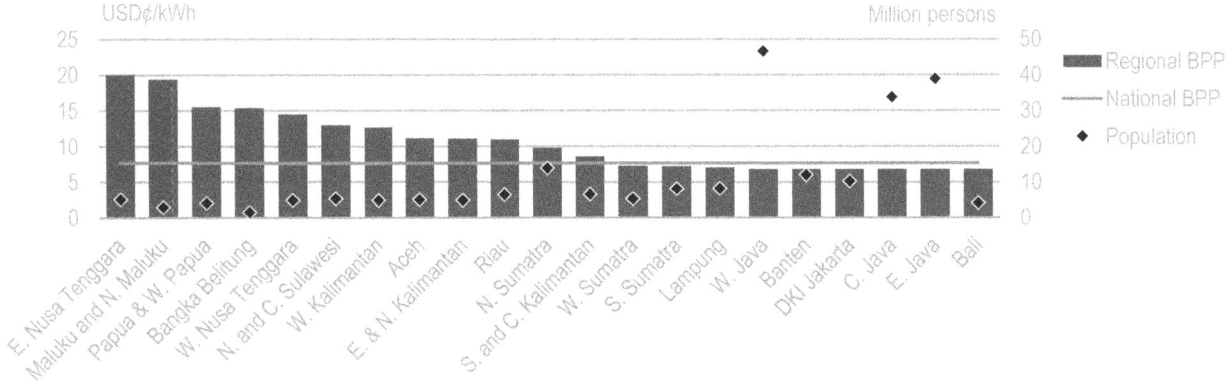

Note: kWh = kilowatt-hour; E = East; N = North, W = West; C = Central; S = South; exchange rate assumption: IDR 13 307 per USD; many provinces have several electricity grids with different average generation costs, where for reasons of simplification this figure presents average costs in the province or region as a whole.

Source: Adapted from (OECD, 2019[3]) *Green Growth Policy Review of Indonesia 2019*; MEMR (2018), Ministerial Decree No. 1772 K/20/MEM/2018; BPS (2018), "Population Projection by Province, 2010-2035", Statistics Indonesia (database).

StatLink https://stat.link/1sjnpe

Box 5.4. Transparent electricity procurement in Mexico led to record-breaking price reductions

Mexico launched an energy reform in 2013, opening up the power sector to participation by the private sector and introducing competitive electricity markets for capacity and clean certificates. In 2015, the Ministry of Energy published rules for long-term energy auctions to support renewable electricity development, where the auctions and resulting PPAs were designed to help generators avoid risks of volatile prices, thus benefitting from stable revenues to finance their investments (Rio, 2019[27]).

Mexico ran three successful auctions for renewable energy in 2015, 2016 and 2017. They were run by the unbundled system operator CENACE, which allowed the incumbent state-owned enterprise to compete on a level playing field with other investors. The auctions resulted in progressive price reductions, which were record-setting at the time (BNEF, 2016[28]), and helped to attract several international investors.

One of the main features of the auctions was that pricing featured a locational component, which would increase or decrease the value of the bid, depending on system friendliness. This had the effect that even if some prices were more expensive, projects would still be selected over other less expensive ones if they had more value for the system (e.g. because the project was located in a place of power scarcity). The effect was that the overall system cost was lowered, where the price resulting from the first auction was USD 47.8 per megawatt-hour (MWh), while the price was reduced to USD 33.5 per MWh in the second auction and then USD 20.6 per MWh in the third.

Another important feature was an evaluation between each round of the auctions' design. This allowed for progressive improvement of the auction system to ensure as many competitive bids as possible. In addition, the three auctions were planned ahead of time, so that developers could see a clear pipeline of projects, which allowed them to assess the business case of developing projects in Mexico.

In total, the three auctions resulted in USD 9 billion of investment, coming from eight different countries. The auctions had more than 50 bidding participants, thus ensuring competition resulting in the record-breaking prices. This approach exemplifies the important role procurement design plays in facilitating competitive and attractive conditions for investment in renewable electricity development.

In general, policy stability and foreseeable certainty, including no retroactive implications, for policy changes are key features of low perceived risk. This stability is also important to bring down the cost of capital for investment in renewable energy. While in theory MEMR Regulation No. 10/2018 accounted for issues created with the previous regulations on GFM, leaving risk-allocation to a case-by-case negotiation can increase both the perceived and real risk of investment for developers. Typically, a PPA is not negotiated without substantial effort, and thus monetary commitment has already been made by the developer in preparing the PPA. The 2018 revision in regulation thus means project developers have to carry force majeure uncertainty while already spending money preparing the project. This may deter developers from considering electricity projects, and likely decreases the perceived bankability of projects.

Extending PPAs in the case of NFM events is also not international best practise. Normally, compensation payment is given to asset owners when prolonged disruptions happen. This gives grid companies an incentive to be as efficient as possible in repairing any outages, both in terms of limiting the timing of the outages but also prioritising repairs based on system efficiency. In so far as disruptions are compensated by PLN, the only risk for investors is the credit worthiness of PLN. However, if the rules are unclear on when compensation is paid, or if risk of prolonged outages are allocated to asset owners, then these provisions will negatively affect PPA bankability and increase the overall cost of capital for renewable investments.

In short, while policy changes in recent years have aimed to simplify the regulatory environment for renewable electricity development, they may in fact create a disincentive for project developers and investors. Transparent rules and processes (e.g. through standardised PPAs) can help to diminish these obstacles, but to be successful, market conditions need to address the bankability of renewable energy projects by addressing risks and remuneration in a consistent and fair manner.

Licensing of renewable electricity projects can be improved to facilitate development

Beyond PPAs and related risk and remuneration concerns, the licensing process for renewable electricity projects in Indonesia is, in theory, relatively straightforward. Before an entity can operate an electricity generation asset, an electricity business licence (Izin Usaha Penyediaan Tenaga Listrik, or IUPTL) must be obtained. The IUTPL allows the entity to supply electricity for public use and is valid for 30 years and extendable. It also can allow the entity to supply electricity for own use with a capacity of more than 200 kilovolts, valid for 10 years and extendable.

Given the expected lifetime of a renewable asset, the process of obtaining a licence for 30 years would not normally create a barrier. However, the 10-year lifetime of a self-supply licence may be a bit low for some businesses. If the expected process for extension is perceived as easy and more or less guaranteed, this should not be a major concern.

Indonesia has taken positive steps in recent years to simplifying the licensing process through its OSS system, which has helped with development of clean energy projects (e.g. with monitoring of the approval process for Analisis Manajemen Dampak Lingkungan, or AMDAL, environmental impact assessments). Applying for an IUPTL in Indonesia has also been facilitated through submission of applications in the OSS system. OSS likewise facilitates newly established businesses to obtain a single business number (Nomor Induk Berusaha, or NIB), as required by Government Regulation No. 24 of 2018.

Feedback from investors is that licensing processes can still be relatively complex, especially for elements that are not presently covered by the OSS system. Additional measures can further improve or streamline project development. For instance, the process of obtaining an Izin Mendirikan Bangunan, or IMB, construction permit can be time consuming and costly (e.g. for wind farms). Land issues also need to be tackled more effectively, and there is general consciousness of the importance of addressing this, for instance through the One Map policy that is expected to play an important role in overcoming handicaps to land acquisition (**see Chapter 4**). Additional measures, such as the forthcoming single portal for risk-based assessment and business licensing under a new online OSS architecture, should help to facilitate some of these challenges. It is equally important that streamlining of licensing procedures do not weaken environmental and social safeguards.

To address these types of administrative barriers to licensing, other countries have made so called "one-stop shops" for permitting and licensing. These one-stop shops often include multiple filing procedures for development projects, such as environmental impact assessments, land permits, business permits and other context specific requirements, through a centralised portal. In this way, investors have a single point of contact in order to obtain needed licences and permits for investing in renewable assets, thus easing the process significantly. This is a key enabling factor in lowering the cost of capital for renewable investments and thus should be considered as a possible solution to build upon positive changes in the OSS system.

Corporate sourcing of renewable electricity remains an untapped opportunity

Around 70 companies in Indonesia have pledged to commit to renewable energy under initiatives like the global RE-100 campaign[7]. While this is encouraging, it is not sufficient to achieve Indonesia's renewable energy targets by 2025, including deployment of 45 gigawatts (GW) of renewable energy capacity by then. Private investments, including international capital flows, are critical to meet the estimated USD 95-100 billion of needed investments by 2025 (and more than USD 525 billion to 2050)[8]. Yet, there are a number of barriers to encourage and enable corporate sourcing of renewables in Indonesia.

Currently, it is possible for industry and businesses to self-generate electricity in Indonesia. Assets that generate electricity for their own use (rather than for sale to PLN) are known as private power utilities (PPUs, sometimes referred to as captive power plants). As regulated in the Electricity Law of 2009, PPUs are allowed to generate for on-site consumption, including use by tenants of an industrial estate. This can include direct sale of power to end customers, but to do so, PPUs bigger than 200 kilovolts must hold an operating licence and get approval from the relevant minister, governor or mayor. They must also be granted an IUTPL as well as an electricity business area (Wilayah Usaha) licence.

MEMR Regulation No. 1/2017 (**see Chapter 3**) also allows PPUs to establish a back-up connection to PLN's grid, but getting that connection can come at a high cost. The requirements include:

- a connection charge: based on existing laws and ministerial regulations
- a capacity charge: calculated as total power generated x 40 hours x electricity tariff
- an energy charge: applied for electricity consumed when PPUs operate in parallel systems, either as a normal charge or as emergency energy charges, which applies in emergency situation that results in PPUs requiring electricity supplied by PLN.

Off-site power generation is also allowed via MEMR Regulation No. 01/2015, which addresses co-operation on the utilisation of power grid (for transmission or distribution). However, off-site generation needs to be transmitted through the PLN grid via a power wheeling agreement, and there currently is no implementing regulation nor technical guidelines on power wheeling to establish the cost of grid connection and the terms for grid use. As a result, power wheeling is uncommon, and where it could be used, the process could be improved (e.g. considering a tripartite agreement with PLN to allow corporate buyers to find a suitable model).

Net-metering is also available (e.g. for rooftop solar photovoltaic), but power exported to the grid is settled at 65% of the BPP. While the number of rooftop customers grew from 351 in 2018 to more than 2000 in June 2020, this pricing structure (accounting for facility services with respect to reliability and power quality) has been seen by some investors as making it uneconomical to invest in self-generation. The grid fee for IPPs can also detract from corporate investment. In fact, the low export tariff has motivated some self-generators to go off-grid and invest in electricity storage solutions instead. Forthcoming changes to MEMR regulation under the recent Omnibus Law are expected to raise the export calculation from 65% to 75%, and to 90% for consumers with battery capacity. However, these tariff rules are still not in line with net-metering schemes globally (**see Chapter 3**).

Recently, PLN looked at how to increase private investment in renewable electricity capacity. One such effort includes a new PLN Service Product that it developed with the Clean Energy Investment Accelerator to provide a tracking system for RECs for customers looking to procure clean electricity. The RECs can be bundled with the purchase of electricity or they can be bought as a separate product (unbundled). RECS are valued as 1 MWh of power and it can be sold within a year of their production. This means that RECs will expire after a year, and they follow international standards using the APX, Inc. Tradable Instrument for Global Renewables registry for tracking the certificates.

PLN's RECs are currently priced at IDR 35 000 (around USD 2.50) and are available to both PLN and non-PLN consumers. If this promising initiative continues towards internationally accepted practice, PLN's RECs market can help attract industries that value green energy to Indonesia, which in turn can incentivise the government to create more ambitious targets for renewable energy.

Further developments for a successful RECs market can include provisions allowing renewable energy producers to get certificates from their production and to sell them in equal competition with the certificates from PLN. In the current PLN structure, it is currently unclear if IPPs can get their energy certified for RECs that can be sold to or through the PLN system. This would be a prerequisite for the new system to attract investment in renewable energy development, as not all investors will want to go through PLN. An open RECs system would also be aligned with international best practise.

While progress on RECs is promising, Indonesia's options and incentives for corporate buyers are still not where they could be compared to other countries. Off-grid captive and on-site captive connected renewables may work well for some companies, but for companies without nearby access to renewable energy, there are limitations. Even for those that are able to do captive production, it is still challenging to meet 100% of their electricity needs, given constraints in total production capacity locally – generally only around 10-15% of electricity needs. RECs are important to companies, but so are robust PPAs and availability of other procurement mechanisms, such as green tariffs. These options are not really available in Indonesia and are limiting broad sources of electricity supply for customers looking to meet renewable energy targets.

A "carrot and stick" approach can also help in engaging corporate sourcing of renewables. This has worked well in other countries, such as Australia, where the renewable energy target scheme with financial incentives (e.g. solar subsidies) and industry obligations helped bring spot prices down for renewable electricity generation certificates and led to 3.5 GW of new renewable generation capacity in 2020, supported by corporate PPAs (Kay, 2020[29]).

Incentives for investments in renewable integration and grid infrastructure can improve

The integration of variable renewable energy in Indonesia's electricity mix is rather low. The share of renewables in electricity generation capacity in 2019 was 9.15% (IEA, 2020[30]). Of the installed renewable capacity, wind and solar made up 150 MW and 140 MW, respectively. With this relatively low amount of variable renewables in the system, there should be little to no system impact due to the variable production of those assets[9] (Figure 5.3). For example, the Java-Bali system has a system peak demand of around

25 000 MW. Even if all the 2019 variable renewable electricity capacity installed in Indonesia was located in Java-Bali, it would still only represent 1.2% of total peak load.

Figure 5.3. Level of renewable energy integration across selected countries in 2019

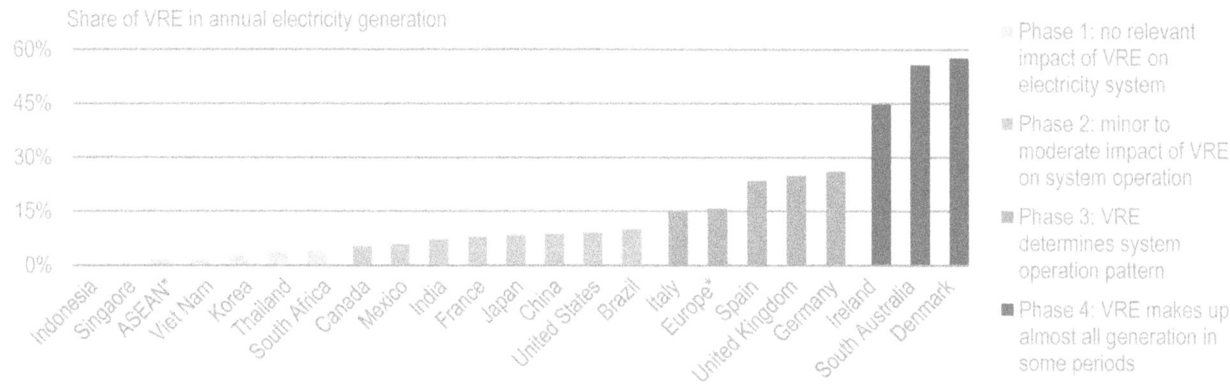

Notes: VRE = variable renewable energy; ASEAN = Association of Southeast Asian Nations; * indicates average across countries.
Source: Adapted from (IEA, 2020[31]), *Power systems in transition: Challenges and opportunities ahead for electricity security*.

StatLink https://stat.link/tyg6i5

The International Energy Agency (IEA) developed a framework to highlight the different challenges of system integration, depending on the phase of transition in a country. Lower phase challenges typically can be addressed by minor changes to operation practises and by using some economic incentives (Figure 5.4). The IEA assesses that Indonesia is still in Phase 1, where there is no measurable impact on the existing power system (though regions within countries can differ from the country average). While Indonesia may be in Phase 1, it is important that the country nonetheless prepare for coming phases, especially given Indonesia's ambitious renewable targets, where suitable policy frameworks and market incentives can ensure phase transitions happen smoothly.

Figure 5.4. Renewable integration transition challenges and enabling options, by phase

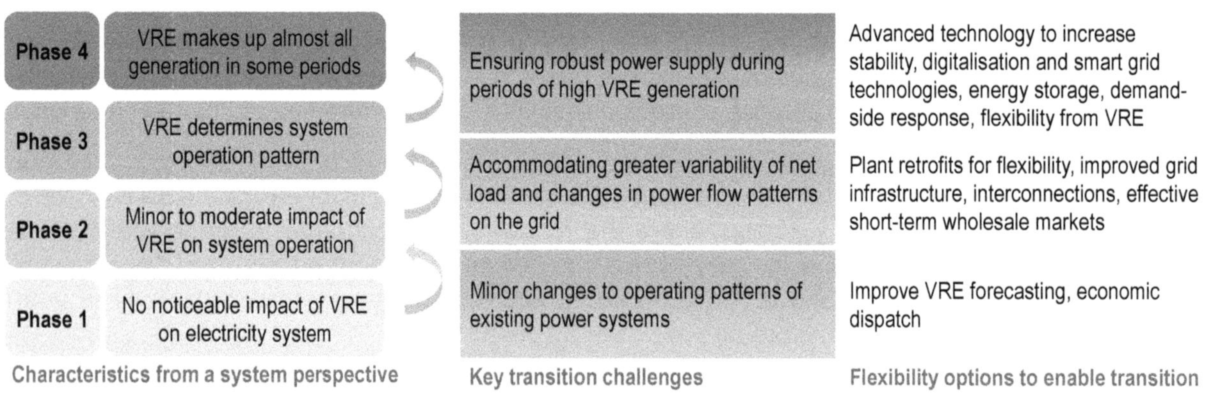

Source: Adapted from (IEA, 2018[32]), *Renewables 2018: Analysis and Forecasts to 2023*.

Currently, there are no incentives to ensure system friendly deployment of renewables in Indonesia, and operational practises are geared overall towards a system composed mainly of dispatchable baseload generation. The planning process in Indonesia has historically catered to this baseload generation, which means that there is no approach developed to ensure grid investments are made in line with development of renewable sources. One such example can be seen in PLN's 2019-28 electricity supply business plan (RUPTL): the target of 23% renewable integration is not complemented by the planned 10% drop in investment for power transmission.

Grids are imperative to the successful integration of variable renewable energy sources, and the planned scale-back in grid investments in the RUPTL is concerning. It is not uncommon to see solar projects halted due to grid constraints, especially outside the main grid of Java-Bali (Hamdi, 2019[33]). Closer links between grid and renewable energy expansion would thus be beneficial to mobilise investments in renewables.

An integrated planning approach is needed to alleviate potential issues with grid constraints. This includes considering electricity demand, generation and grid planning in a holistic approach to ensure responsive feedback is enabled across all elements of Indonesia's electricity ecosystem. In particular, such planning would ensure necessary grid investments are made ahead of renewables deployment, given those developments generally take longer than typical renewable energy asset deployment. For example, green corridors in India and the United States are being developed with grids capable of accommodating high shares of variable renewable energy (Box 5.5).

Future renewable projects under the expected large-scale auctions will be designed by PLN, which means that renewable energy investments can be integrated into the wider electricity system. With the right planning procedures, this can ensure the entire electricity system benefits from those investments. Development also can be planned in a way that helps to avoid costly interruptions for renewable energy generation and the electricity system.

Box 5.5. Green corridors in India are preparing for renewable electricity capacity additions

India has some states that are very rich in renewables potential, where large-scale solar and wind projects can be deployed at low costs. However, that renewable energy will need to be transmitted from resource-rich areas and distributed across the country to electricity load centres. In order to do this effectively, India has introduced the concept of green corridors for transmission projects, which will develop inter- and intra-state transmission lines to utilise resource-rich areas effectually and increase renewable electricity generation for the whole country. In addition, a Renewable Energy Management Centre will be established and advanced forecasting will also be implemented.

The green corridor project illustrates the importance of aligning transmission planning with renewable energy development, helping to avoid potentially "stranded" assets due to grid connection or capacity issues. With well-planned and well-designed grids, the pipeline of renewable energy projects will not be halted due to grid constraints, helping to create an attractive environment for project development and investment. Once built, well-developed grids also make renewable energy integration easier from a system operations perspective.

From an Indonesian perspective, grid development within and between islands is important to utilise and integrate renewable energy efficiently and effectively. System planning, including grid development, will increase investor confidence and ultimately lower the cost of capital for renewable energy investment.

Source: (IEA, 2020[34])

References

Afut Syafril, N. and Sri Haryati (2020), *Government extends electricity-relief scheme until September 2020*, Antara News, https://en.antaranews.com/news/151590/government-extends-electricity-relief-scheme-until-september-2020 (accessed on 18 December 2020). [6]

APEC (2017), *Energy Efficiency Finance in Indonesia Current State Barriers and Potential Next Steps*, https://apec.org/Publications/2017/10/Energy-Efficiency-Finance-in-Indonesia-Current-State-Barriers-and-Potential-Next-Steps (accessed on 8 April 2020). [13]

Arinaldo, D. et al. (2021), *Indonesia Energy Transition Outlook (IETO) 2021*, Institute for Essential Services Reform, Jakarta, https://iesr.or.id/en/pustaka/indonesia-energy-transition-outlook-ieto-2021 (accessed on 4 March 2021). [9]

Bharti, P. (2020), *SIDBI Green Climate & Sustainable Development Initiatives*, Small Industries Development Bank of India, Paris, https://www.slideshare.net/OECD_ENV/pawan-kumar-bharti-sidbi-green-climate-sustainable-development-initiatives-239052077 (accessed on 18 December 2020). [18]

BNEF (2016), "Mexico's second power auction results: Record low prices in Latin America", Bloomberg New Energy Finance, https://data.bloomberglp.com/bnef/sites/14/2017/01/BNEF_MexicosSecondPower_SFCT_FNL_B.pdf (accessed on 17 December 2020). [28]

Bridle, R. et al. (2018), *Missing the 23 Per Cent Target: Roadblocks to the development of renewable energy in Indonesia*, Global Subsidies Initiative, International Institute for Sustainable Development (IISD), https://www.iisd.org/sites/default/files/publications/roadblocks-indonesia-renewable-energy.pdf (accessed on 15 December 2020). [8]

Burke, P. and S. Kurniawati (2018), "Electricity subsidy reform in Indonesia: Demand-side effects on electricity use", *Energy Policy*, Vol. 116, pp. 410-421, http://dx.doi.org/10.1016/j.enpol.2018.02.018. [5]

Construction Week (2014), *Regulatory framework for ESCOs launched in Dubai*, https://www.constructionweekonline.com/article-26310-regulatory-framework-for-escos-launched-in-dubai (accessed on 9 February 2021). [25]

Cool Coalition (2020), *Meet The Global Cooling as a Service Prize Winner: ColdHubs*, United Nations Environment Programme, Kigali Cooling Efficiency Programme, https://coolcoalition.org/meet-the-global-caas-prize-winner-coldhubs/ (accessed on 18 December 2020). [26]

de la Rue du Can, S. et al. (2014), "Design of incentive programs for accelerating penetration of energy-efficient appliances", *Energy Policy*, Vol. 72, http://dx.doi.org/10.1016/j.enpol.2014.04.035. [15]

Hamdi, E. (2019), *Indonesia's Solar Policies: designed to fail?*, Institute for Energy Economics and Financial Analysis (IIEFA), Cleveland, https://ieefa.org/wp-content/uploads/2019/02/Indonesias-Solar-Policies_February-2019.pdf (accessed on 16 December 2020). [33]

Harsono, N. (2020), "UAE's Masdar to support development of Indonesia's largest solar power plant", *The Jakarta Post*, https://www.thejakartapost.com/news/2020/01/08/uaes-masdar-to-support-development-of-indonesias-largest-solar-power-plant.html (accessed on 16 December 2020). [2]

IEA (2020), *India 2020 Energy Policy Review*, OECD Publishing, Paris, https://dx.doi.org/10.1787/9faa9816-en. [34]

IEA (2020), *Power investment trends in indonesia*, International Energy Agency. [30]

IEA (2020), *Power systems in transition: Challenges and opportunities ahead for electricity security*, OECD Publishing, Paris, https://dx.doi.org/10.1787/4ad57c0e-en. [31]

IEA (2019), *Perspectives for the Clean Energy Transition: The Critical Role of Buildings*, International Energy Acency, Paris, https://webstore.iea.org/perspectives-for-the-clean-energy-transition (accessed on 16 December 2020). [21]

IEA (2018), *Energy Efficiency 2018: Analysis and outlooks to 2040*, International Energy Agency, Paris, https://dx.doi.org/10.1787/9789264024304-en. [23]

IEA (2018), *Perspectives for the Energy Transition: The Role of Energy Efficiency*, International Energy Agency, Paris, https://webstore.iea.org/perspectives-for-the-energy-transition-the-role-of-energy-efficiency (accessed on 18 December 2020). [20]

IEA (2018), *Renewables 2018: Analysis and Forecasts to 2023*, International Energy Agency, Paris, https://dx.doi.org/10.1787/re_mar-2018-en. [32]

IEA (2017), *Energy Efficiency 2017*, International Energy Agency, Paris, https://dx.doi.org/10.1787/9789264284234-en. [4]

IEA (2017), *Insights brief: energy utility obligations and auctions*, International Energy Agency, Paris, https://www.iea.org/reports/insights-brief-energy-utility-obligations-and-auctions (accessed on 18 December 2020). [22]

IEA-UNEP (2019), *2019 Global Status Report for Buildings and Construction: Towards a zero-emissions, efficient and resilient buildings and construction sector*, International Energy Agency, United Nations Environment Programme, Paris, https://www.iea.org/reports/global-status-report-for-buildings-and-construction-2019 (accessed on 18 December 2020). [17]

Kay, I. (2020), *Attracting Private Investment for Renewable Energy*, Australian Renewable Energy Agency (ARENA), https://www.slideshare.net/OECD_ENV/ppt-ian-kay-attracting-private-investment-for-renewable-energy (accessed on 16 December 2020). [29]

Keuangan, I. (ed.) (2009), *Economic and fiscal policy strategies for climate change mitigation in Indonesia : Ministry of Finance green paper*, Ministry of Finance, Republic of Indonesia : Australia Indonesia Partnership. [10]

Massita Ayu, C. (2020), *Good News is a Bad News: Indonesia's Electricity Subsidy - The Purnomo Yusgiantoro Center*, The Purnomo Yusgiantoro Center, https://www.purnomoyusgiantorocenter.org/good-news-is-a-bad-news-indonesias-electricity-subsidy/ (accessed on 18 December 2020). [7]

Meilanova, D. (2021), "ESDM Trials Carbon Trading in Steam Power Plants", *Bisnis.com*, p. 1, https://ekonomi.bisnis.com/read/20210318/44/1369262/esdm-uji-coba-perdagangan-karbon-di-pembangkit-listrik-tenaga-uap (accessed on 8 April 2021). [11]

MEMR (2020), *Data & Information of Energy Conservation 2019, 3rd Edition*, Directorate of Energy Conservation, Ministry of Energy and Mineral Resources, http://www.ebtke.esdm.go.id (accessed on 15 December 2020). [19]

MEMR (2019), *Data & Information of Energy Conservation 2018, 2nd Edition*, Directorate of Energy Conservation, Ministry of Energy and Mineral Resources, https://drive.esdm.go.id//wl/?id=cwFohj0AaWgwlWQMNr5Yu68d8ptxTg4o (accessed on 15 December 2020). [24]

OECD (2020), *OECD Investment Policy Reviews: Indonesia 2020*, OECD Investment Policy Reviews, OECD Publishing, Paris, https://dx.doi.org/10.1787/b56512da-en. [1]

OECD (2019), *OECD Green Growth Policy Review of Indonesia 2019*, OECD Environmental Performance Reviews, OECD Publishing, Paris, https://dx.doi.org/10.1787/1eee39bc-en. [3]

Pahnael, J., A. Soekiman and M. Wimala (2020), "Penerapan Kebijakan Insentif Green Building di Kota Bandung (Implementation of Green Building Incentive Policies in Bandung City)", *Jurnal Infrastruktur*, Vol. 6/1, pp. 1-13, http://dx.doi.org/10.35814/infrastruktur.v6i1.1315. [14]

Riana (2021), "Arifin Launched Subroto Award for Energy Efficiency 2021", *Pontas*, p. 2, https://pontas.id/2021/03/18/arifin-launching-penghargaan-subroto-bidang-efisiensi-energi-2021/ (accessed on 8 April 2021). [12]

Rio, P. (2019), *Auctions for the support of renewable energy in Mexico*, AURES II, European Commission, http://aures2project.eu/wp-content/uploads/2019/12/AURES_II_case_study_Mexico.pdf (accessed on 17 December 2020). [27]

U4E (2020), *ECOFRIDGES Green On-wage Financial Mechanism Launched in Ghana by the Energy Commission*, United for Efficiency (U4E), United Nations Environment Programme, https://united4efficiency.org/ecofridges-green-on-wage-financial-mechanism-launched-in-ghana-by-the-energy-commission-unep-and-base-to-make-environmentally-friendly-cooling-products-more-affordable/ (accessed on 16 December 2020). [16]

Notes

[1] For more information, see https://www.seai.ie/business-and-public-sector/business-grants-and-supports/energy-contracting/.

[2] For more information, see https://www.id.undp.org/content/indonesia/en/home/projects/Partnership-for-Market-Readiness.html.

[3] For more information, see http://kpbu.djppr.kemenkeu.go.id/pembayaran-ketersediaan-layanan/ (in Bahasa).

[4] For more information on CaaS, see https://www.caas-initiative.org/.

[5] For more information, see www.coldhubs.com/.

[6] For more information, see https://wwf.panda.org/wwf_offices/tanzania/?349380/New-Project-to-Scale-Up-Efficient-Clean-Cooling-Systems-for-Octopus-Fisheries-Launched-in-Kilwa.

[7] https://www.there100.org/

[8] Renewable energy investment needs as presented by Pak Suryadarma, Chairman of METI-Indonesia Renewable Energy Association, in his presentation to the CEFIM Virtual Review Mission in the Focus Group Discussion on Corporate Sourcing of Renewables (13 October 2020).

[9] It should be noted that low amounts of variable renewable electricity may have an impact in some small systems.

6 Financial market policy

This chapter examines the current status and future requirements of clean energy finance in Indonesia. It reviews the current state of the Indonesian financial markets and highlights the need to deepen capital market development. It highlights financial market regulation, including the role of sustainable finance policies and targeted green finance instruments in mobilising finance for clean energy projects. The chapter also examines the role of development finance in mobilising private capital and opportunities for institutional innovation to catalyse private sector finance and investment.

To meet the country's nationally determined contribution (NDC), Indonesia will need to mobilise approximately USD 220 billion of investments by 2030 in the clean energy and sustainable transport sectors. Both domestic and international public and private sources of finance are required to meet these goals. Well-functioning financial markets can strongly contribute to enhancing investment opportunities and lowering financing costs. Creating a clean energy finance ecosystem that can support Indonesia's clean energy transition will require broad reach across government, financial markets, industry and development cooperation.

To mobilise finance from the private sector, the Indonesian government has been working closely with the financial sector to develop sustainable finance products within the banking, capital market and non-bank financial institutions. The sustainable finance activities led by the Financial Services Authority (OJK) and the Ministry of Finance are commendable and Indonesia stands out among major emerging economies in its sustainable finance activities. This chapter looks at the current status and future requirement of clean energy finance in Indonesia; financial market regulation including the role of sustainable finance and targeted green finance instruments; and the role of development finance and opportunities for institutional innovation to catalyse private sector finance and investment.

Assessment and recommendations

A sustainable finance framework is in place and continues to evolve.

Central to these activities is OJK's Sustainable Finance Roadmap, which in Phase I (2015-2019) increased awareness amongst financial service institutions on the importance of sustainable finance and provided comprehensive regulatory frameworks and guidelines. The recently released Phase II (2020-2024) of the roadmap focuses on building the sustainable finance ecosystem by strengthening the implementation of environmental, social and governance (ESG) risks and supporting innovation and development of financial services and products. These efforts will help to reset Indonesia's financial system to help the country achieve its sustainable development goals (SDGs) and the Paris Agreement. Indonesia can learn from the experience of other countries as it develops its Sustainable Finance Taxonomy as part of its roadmap and considers how ambitious sustainable finance taxonomy in other countries will impact the attractiveness of Indonesia as a destination for foreign direct investment (FDI). The government could play a role via national public information campaigns on the importance of integrating ESG considerations in investment decisions to spur public pressure for a quicker adoption of sustainable finance activities within the country's financial services sector.

Prudential regulation may create barriers to renewable energy financing.

Prudential regulation governing Indonesia's financial services industry could be more accommodative to clean energy power projects. Current levels of the BMPK (Batas Maksimum Pemberian Kredit or Legal Lending Limit) could create barriers to the financing of renewable energy projects by financial institutions A number of financial institutions are already at or near the legal lending limits given significant exposure to PLN (Perusahaan Listrik Negara the State Electricity Company) in their loan portfolios. As the single buyer of electricity, PLN or its subsidiaries are involved in a significant number of renewable energy projects (including large hydro projects) and hence these projects are consolidated as part of PLN exposure in calculating this limit. Equally, relaxation of the current ATMR (Aset Tertimbang Menurut Risiko or Risk Weighted Asset) calculation formula for renewable energy could be considered to incentivise financial institutions to increase lending to these projects, although this should be done with careful consideration of potential systemic impact. Beyond addressing financial market regulation barriers to increasing access to domestic lending, to facilitate project evaluation and increase access to domestic debt for clean energy projects, OJK could consider implementing a "credit programme" aimed at unifying and standardising rules and other contractual provisions, which would help facilitate credit appraisal as successfully implemented in the palm oil sector.

Alignment with the Ministry of Energy and Mineral Resources (MEMR) is needed on sustainable finance categories to address inconsistencies that create confidence issues.

To support the development of sustainable finance in Indonesia, OJK issued Regulation No. 60/2017 that categorises activities that can be financed through green bonds. As of 2019, Indonesian financial institutions had financed approximately IDR 913 trillion (USD 64 billion) of investments meeting the green finance definitions outlined by the OJK Sustainable Finance roadmap (OJK, 2021[1]). While OJK's activities to promote the adoption of sustainable finance activities are to be commended, as the Ministry of Energy and Mineral Resources (MEMR) was not involved in setting these definitions, there are inconsistencies between the government's clean energy plans and its sustainable finance definitions. This has created confidence issues among financial institutions and a reluctance to finance certain clean energy projects under the Energy Plan (RUEN) and Electricity Plan (RUPTL), which are not covered by OJK regulation.

Indonesia is a leader in sovereign green bonds and is a fintech innovator.

A notable green finance development in Indonesia is the country's leadership role in the green bond market. Indonesia was the first country to issue a sovereign green Islamic bond (sukuk) in 2018. The country is also a fintech innovator, having completed the world's first retail green bond/sukuk in 2019. The government's retail green sukuk issuance aimed to develop a more sustainable investor base and help raise awareness, particularly among millennials on the importance of investing in climate solutions such as clean energy and other technologies to overcome various environmental challenges. The online subscription system attracted and allowed for investors from all 34 provinces to participate with millennials, accounting for 56% of first time investors, and provides useful lessons for other countries.

Capital markets hold significant potential to finance clean energy projects

Additional efforts could also be made to further develop capital market instruments for financing green projects. This will need to be accompanied by the development of regulation to help diversify financial products and efforts to further deepen Indonesia's capital markets which when compared to other Association of Southeast Asian Nations ASEAN countries such as Malaysia and Thailand, remain comparatively small given the size of the economy. Efforts to further develop capital market instruments would also help to increase the availability of long-term capital and should include both primary and secondary markets for infrastructure finance. Instruments should address issues of scale necessary to attract international capital and could include products such as asset backed securities, sustainability-linked bonds and clean energy funds.

The finance sector is lagging on clean energy, despite strong government action.

Recent developments in green and sustainable finance are promising, although Indonesia's financial institutions face a number of challenges when it comes to expanding their sustainable finance portfolios, particularly as they pertain to financing renewable energy and energy efficiency projects. These include a lack of familiarity with renewable and efficiency projects; insufficient information; high perceived risks; lack of suitable financing instruments and funds; and limited access to green finance to support projects. Government action is needed to improve data availability and in setting up monitoring and reporting protocols; support capacity building among financial institutions staff and to develop innovative finance schemes to help attract investors and corporations. A number of lessons can be learnt from countries in Europe, Australia and South Africa among others on how initiatives in these countries have supported an uptake of green finance for clean energy investments.

High collateral requirements makes access to finance challenging, particularly for smaller project developers.

Energy efficiency and some renewable energy projects, particularly those in the less developed eastern islands of Indonesia, tend to be developed by smaller project developers with limited balance sheets and experience in financial structuring of projects. With little or no credit history, these project developers often face additional challenges accessing finance including high collateral requirements from commercial banks that can exceed the value of the project and often beyond the means of these project developers. The sustainable development goal (SDG) Indonesia One Fund could be used to support guarantee schemes aimed at de-risking projects and help project developers overcome collateral requirements and build experience and confidence among financial institutions in both energy efficiency and renewable energy projects. These funds should target projects with good replicability structures that address risks which the market currently is not able to adequately evaluate so that in the future, as these projects demonstrate their financial viability, the market can take over without the need for de-risking.

Further capacity building and support is required to build investor confidence.

Efforts to engage financial actors in clean energy development are yielding some progress, but additional training and capacity building efforts are needed to familiarise those actors with institutional and operational aspects of clean energy projects, as well as to understand the risks of those projects and gain confidence in funding them. Lessons could also be drawn from financing facilities set up to support the biodiesel industry such as the crude palm oil fund, which has been successful in opening up financing to the biodiesel sector and created a growing market.

Lack of domestic project finance for clean energy drives up financing costs.

Another important financing challenge is the mismatch between project lifetimes, which range from 20 to 40 years for renewable energy assets, and the lack of available long-term financing, with tenures usually averaging 5 to 7 years. The absence of a domestic long-term debt market means that local currency non-recourse project finance is uncommon in Indonesia. This attractive means for financing clean energy projects, the norm in OECD countries and in some other major markets, is another factor attributing to significantly higher costs for clean energy projects.

Box 6.1. Main policy recommendations on financial market policy

- Review bank regulation and practices such as legal lending limits and high collateral requirements to identify options to overcome these hurdles. Clean energy projects could be treated as a special category to address issues around concentration limits linked to the high exposure of many financial institutions to PLN and could be supported by credit enhancement or off-taker insurance schemes. To help project developers access debt financing and meet equity requirements, options such as guarantee schemes, innovative structures or facilities should be considered. OJK can also work with banks to establish project finance structures for renewable energy and energy efficiency projects that could be standardised and widely replicated across various banks.
- Support corporate and sub-regional green bond (green sukuk) issuances as a way to take advantage of the rapid development of the global green bond (and green sukuk) market that offers an attractive financing vehicle for clean energy project developers to raise long-term debt finance. Indonesia can build upon its experience with sovereign green bond/green sukuk and

consider a number of measures to facilitate access to this market, including incentives to cover issuing costs, credit enhancements or guarantees, information campaigns to improve corporate and regional government awareness and aggregation of smaller projects under a larger structure.

- Align definitions on sustainable finance to ensure that targets outlined under the RUEN and the Planning Ministry's (Bappenas) upcoming 2020-24 mid-term development plan (RPJMN) are compatible with OJK's regulation to financial institutions. OJK should seek inputs from MEMR, Bappenas and other related institutions as it sets out the country's sustainable finance taxonomy, as it will influence capital needed to finance clean energy projects. These inputs can also help overcome current inconsistencies that hamper access to finance.
- Consider different design elements based on international experience (i.e. European Union (EU), France and Japan) in the development of Indonesia's Sustainable Finance Taxonomy, to identify economic activities and define environmental and other objectives linked to the taxonomy. The taxonomy should enable an adaptable framework to address changes in technology and innovation, and should consider usability by end users, issuers and investors. A simple-to-use taxonomy will make it easier for the market to adopt and apply, while data availability must also be factored in to facilitate verification.
- Co-ordinate across relevant ministries to ensure that tariffs and contract structures, for example power purchase agreement (PPA) terms, provide suitable long-term visibility on revenue streams necessary for banks to provide long term non-recourse lending directly to projects. De-risking mechanisms may also be needed for the first projects to help financial institutions gain confidence in these new financing structures. The government should consider the creation of an ecosystem that would help financial institutions increase lending portfolios to clean energy projects and could engage within the IKBI (Inisiatif Keuangan Berkelanjutan Indonesia or Indonesia's Sustainable Finance Initiative) network of financial institutions that support sustainable finance to help identify and implement solutions to overcome a variety of financing risks as well as help the market gain experience and confidence in financing both renewable energy and energy efficiency projects among other climate solutions such as waste management and clean water.
- Undertake a detailed market assessment of financing needs and challenges as well as opportunities to scale, to identify suitable financing instruments that meet the requirements of the market. This evaluation should inform considerations for the creation of a dedicated green finance facility that can help overcome current barriers to raising affordable finance for clean energy projects. Such a facility could be established within one of the existing public finance institutions that already have a mandate to support climate friendly investments, such as the environment fund management agency (BPDLH) or PT Sarana Multi Infrastruktur (PT SMI).
- Consider using the abovementioned facility as an intermediary to provide support and advisory services, to structure an aggregated portfolio of energy efficiency projects, and to manage the overall transaction process (e.g. through contract standardisation). The facility could include financial support, such as reimbursable grants for collateral, guarantees or insurance against energy savings risk, to help overcome barriers to financing of energy service models.

Strengthening and deepening local financial markets

Indonesia's private sector debt (as a share of GDP) is among the lowest in South East Asia, reflecting the relative underdevelopment of the country's financial sector as a whole (see Figure 6.1). As in many countries, commercial banks hold the bulk of the financial sector's aggregated assets and are the largest source of debt finance in the country, including for clean energy infrastructure (see Figure 6.2). The country's banking sector is also particularly fragmented with around 110 commercial banks (of which, eight are foreign-owned) and 1,512 rural banks, albeit rather concentrated given the country's four largest commercial banks own around a third of banks' aggregated assets.

The country's commercial banks are relatively healthy, with a high capital adequacy ratio (around 23% as of September 2020, largely above Basel III requirements of 8%) and a low level of non-performing loans (3.1%), despite a slight increase due to the COVID-19 crisis. Yet, commercial banks tend to be conservatively run as they rely mostly on short-term deposits (retail funding), constraining their ability to provide long-term financing for investments (due to risks of asset-liability mismatch) (IMF, 2018[2]). In September 2020, based on OJK's monthly Banking Statistics, roughly a quarter of the commercial banks' portfolio is used for financing investments.

Aside from commercial banks, the country's domestic institutional investor[1] base remains very small (see Figure 6.2) and has so far played a very limited role in financing infrastructure projects, let alone clean energy. In 2020, assets under management of pension funds and insurance companies were roughly 3% and 5% of GDP respectively (Bank Indonesia, 2020[3]; World Bank, 2020[4]).

Figure 6.1. Domestic credit to the private sector for selected regional peers, 2019

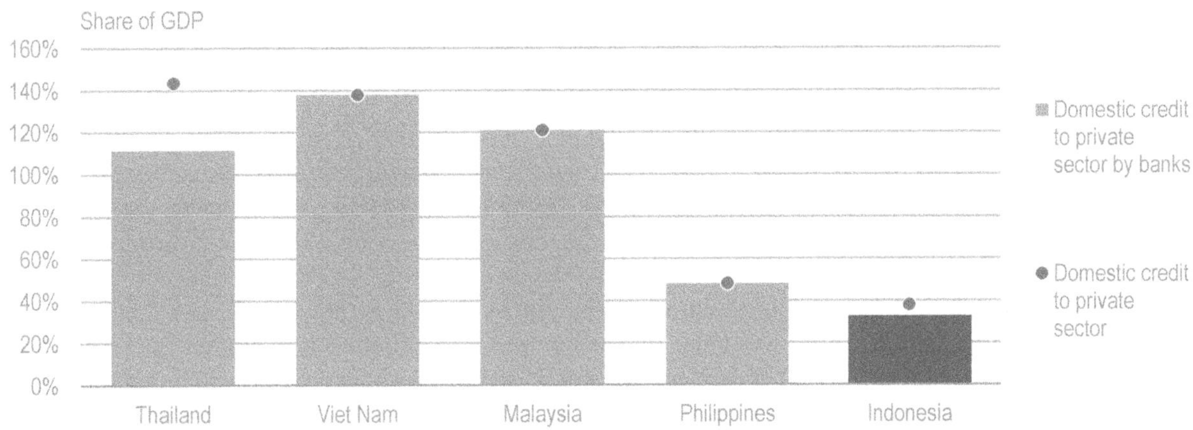

Source: World Bank(2020[5]), World Development Indicators.

StatLink https://stat.link/n6cmu4

Figure 6.2. Indonesia's financial assets by financial players, as of October 2020

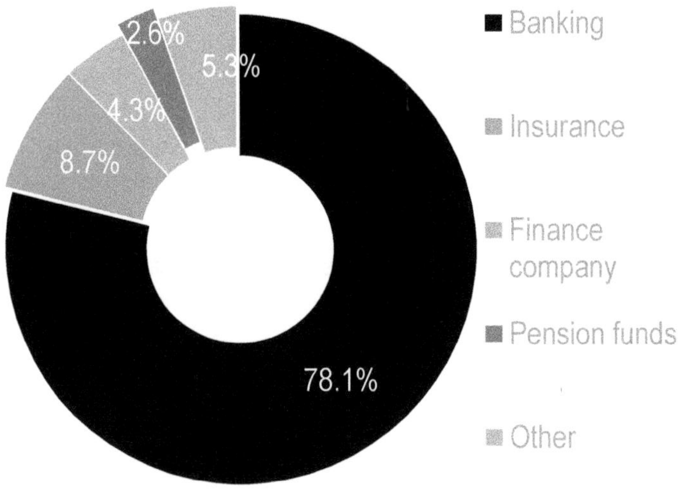

Notes: "Other" includes guarantee institutions, infrastructure finance companies, micro finance institutions and insurance brokers.
Source: Bank Indonesia (October 2020).

StatLink https://stat.link/sbkxg1

Indonesia's investment requirement for infrastructure over the next 5 years is estimated under the 2020-24 RPJMN at IDR 5,957 trillion (around USD 412 billion) ((Bloomberg, 2019[5]), representing more than half the assets of the country's financial sector which in 2020 was roughly IDR 11,357 billion (around USD 805 billion) (Bank Indonesia, 2020[3]). Investment needs for the clean energy sector over the next five years to meet the RUEN renewable energy generation targets are estimated at about USD 44.2 billion (IESR, 2019[6]). This highlights an important financing gap given that infrastructure is only one of many sectors that will be vying for this limited capital. Indonesia will need to attract foreign sources of capital to help fund its infrastructure development as well as continue to promote and implement policies to increase financial inclusion as well as step up efforts to deepen its financial sector. Given the size and importance of the economy, Indonesia's financial sector development is well behind those of its regional peers. There are few domestic institutional investors in Indonesia with insurance companies and pension funds accounting for just 11.32% of the country's financial assets (see Figure 6.2). Efforts are needed to develop this market and shift investment horizons towards longer-term investments as a way to support the development of more robust capital markets to fund Indonesia's economic development and sustainable development goals.

Shallow capital markets in Indonesia limit financing options for corporates

Few non-financial corporates (including clean energy developers) have so far tapped into Indonesia's (shallow) capital markets for financing. In 2018, the growing domestic corporate bond market accounted for less than 3%[2] of GDP, compared with 46.3% in Malaysia, for example. Close to 80% of the market's outstanding securities had a tenor inferior to five years (see Figure 6.3). Securitisation and project bonds represented a negligible share of outstanding debt securities. The bulk of issuers are financial institutions (around two thirds) with most of the remainder being state-owned enterprises (SOEs) (ADB, 2017[7]; IMF, 2018[2]). By contrast, Indonesia's sovereign bond market was much larger (accounting for 16% of GDP) and more liquid than the corporate bond market (albeit much less so than regional peers) and offered longer average maturity. The Indonesian government has also been much more active in tapping into sustainable finance products, being one of the world's largest issuers of green bond/sukuk (further discussion later in the chapter). As for the bond market, few corporates obtain primary financing through the stock market, as shown by the low number of annual initial public offerings. Partly as a result, Indonesia's stock market also has a smaller market capitalisation than its regional peers and has a far lower turnover.

Figure 6.3. Corporate bonds by term of maturity, 2019

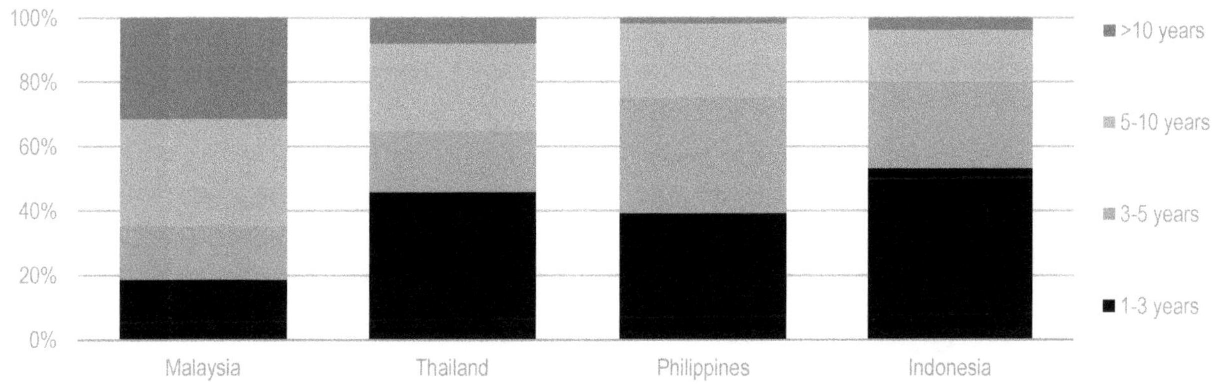

Source: ADB (2020[8]), Asian Bonds Online.

StatLink https://stat.link/ohtflg

Recognising the need to deepen its financial markets, the Government of Indonesia created a national council for financial inclusion and a high-level joint forum to promote interagency coordination. Chaired by the President, the national council adopted the National Strategy for Financial Inclusion in 2016 that covers the following five pillars: financial education, public property rights, expansion of financial productions, distribution of government transfers and consumer protection. The strategy set a goal for 75% of adults to hold a transaction account by the end of 2019. The results of the 2019 national inclusion survey reported 76.19% of adults held accounts, exceeding the set goal[3]. The high-level joint forum focuses on the development of the following six financial markets in parallel: money, foreign exchange, bond, equity, Sharia investments and structured products. The development of these markets will play an integral role in deepening Indonesia's financial sector and with it the country's ability to mobilise more domestic and international investment and finance for clean energy.

Indonesia's capital markets remain relatively under-developed when compared to its ASEAN peers with the country's stock and bond markets significantly less developed than its regional peers. Further development of the country's capital markets represents an opportunity to shift savings from short-term deposits towards longer-term investments in bonds, equity and other structured instruments. Diversification of the bond market to stimulate more corporate bond issuances could help to widen the bond market that is currently made up almost exclusively of government bonds, with corporate bonds representing just 13% of the market.

Access and status of finance for clean energy

An analysis undertaken by the International Energy Agency (IEA) of investment trends in power generation, showed the high reliance on foreign capital for financing Indonesia's electricity demand growth with domestic finance representing just a quarter of total investments (see Figure 6.4). The largest share at 40% came from development finance institutions and export credit agencies (40%), followed by the private sector accounting for over a quarter with the remainder from public sources. China is a key source of funding from both the public and export credit agencies, while other (ASEAN) investors representing an important share of private funding sources. International investors (excluding China and other ASEAN nations) account for about half of total funding split across all three segments with a relatively higher weighting in the Development Finance Institution (DFI) and Export Credit Agency (ECA) segment as well as private sector. Local funding sources are slightly tilted towards the public budget with private funding from commercial banks accounting for under half. Given the key role that DFIs and ECAs have played, the country relies heavily on concessional finance for its power generation expansion.

Figure 6.4. Sources of finance in the power generation sector, 2016 to 2019

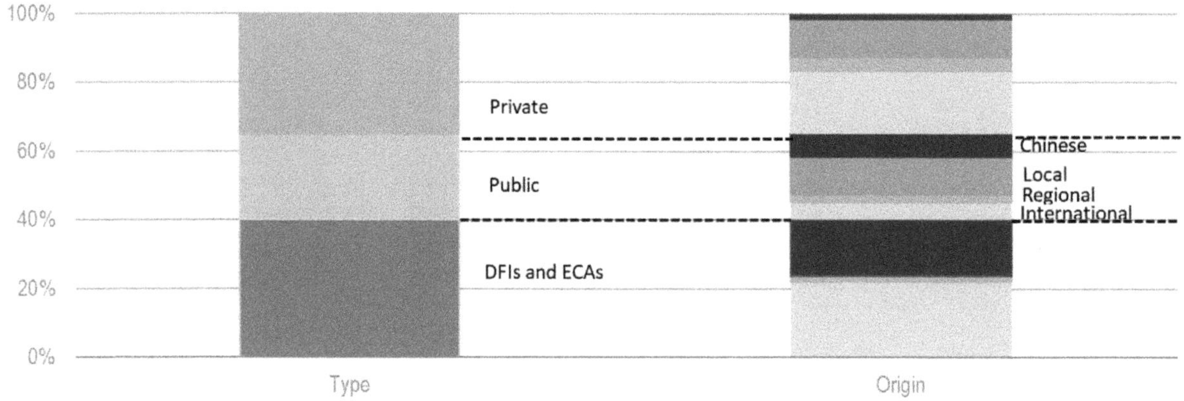

Source: IEA(2020[9]), Power investment trends in indonesia.

StatLink https://stat.link/4n2fbg

In contrast to fossil fuel power generation, where public funds represent about 40% of total funding, renewable energy projects have depended on financing from DFIs and ECAs as well as from private sources, mainly commercial banks (see Figure 6.5). While investments in fossil fuel plants continue to dominate the market, a growing share of investments in new power generation are being met by renewable energy sources with geothermal representing the largest share given the high potential of this technology in the country (**see Chapter 1**). The current high reliance on development finance and concessional funds to meet growing electricity demand is unsustainable and the Indonesian government will need to continue improving its policy frameworks to shift a greater portion of finance towards private sources.

Figure 6.5. Sources of finance by technology in the power generation sector, 2016 to 2019

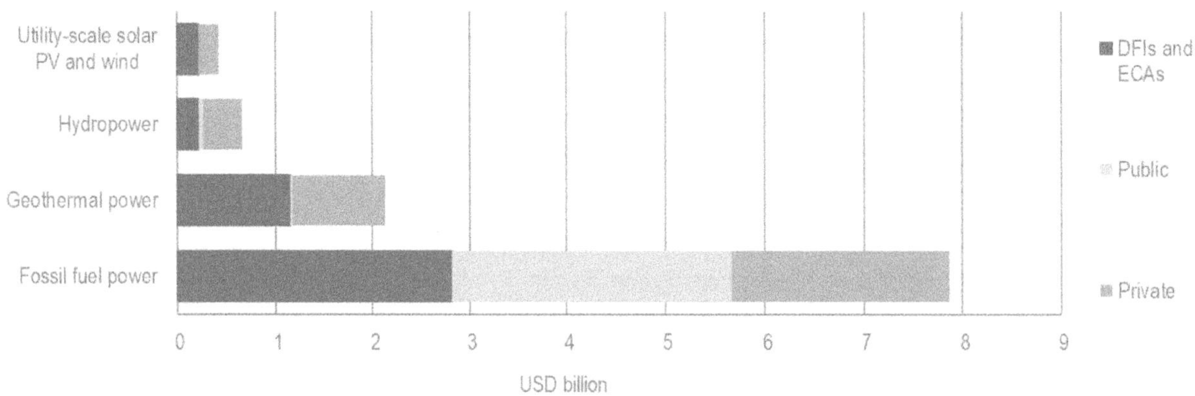

Source: IEA(2020[9]), Power investment trends in indonesia.

StatLink https://stat.link/xw3t9s

Currently in Indonesia, commercial banks' contribution to financing clean energy projects has so far been limited. Official data for 2019 show that commercial banks only allocated 3.5% of their loan portfolio to the electricity, gas and water sector, which compares with around 6.1% and 6.7% for the construction and agriculture sectors, respectively. There is no disaggregated data for clean energy, but its share is likely to be a small fraction of that aggregate figure. While as a whole, financing for clean energy projects among commercial banks in Indonesia remains a relatively new and uncertain market, positive signs are apparent from the sustainable finance action plans of the SOE banks that this is a sector with significant growth potential with a total financing estimated in September 2019 at IDR 20 trillion[4] (around USD 1.4 million).

Regulatory barriers and lack of adequate data and information pose challenges for banks to finance clean energy projects

Financial institutions in Indonesia face a number of challenges in financing renewable energy projects. These include a lack of familiarity with renewable projects among financiers and insufficient information; high-perceived risks due to insufficient availability of projects' track record given few operating projects; lack of suitable financing instruments and funds; and limited finance to support corporate sourcing of renewables[5]. Consequently, commercial banks have so far only provided financing to a handful of geothermal and bioenergy projects while none has yet done so for operating utility-scale solar and wind projects in the country.

Similar issues also constrain bank financing for energy efficiency projects. This can, in large part, be explained by the intangible nature of their cash flows, their limited deal size, as well as limited project and developer track records. Most commercial banks also have strict collateral rules often in the range of 80-120% of total loan value – as such rules preclude the use of projected energy savings as collateral. This, in turn, severely limits developers' borrowing capacity (APEC, 2017[8]).

To overcome these challenges the Indonesian government will evaluate additional incentives to support investments; improve availability of data and information by implementing monitoring and reporting protocols; support capacity building among financial institutions staff; and develop innovative finance schemes to help attract investors and corporations.

Regulation governing Indonesia's banking sector, namely BMPK (Batas Maksimum Pemberian Kredit or Legal Lending Limit) and the ATMR (Aset Tertimbang Menurut Risiko or Risk Weighted Asset) calculation formula for renewable energy could also create barriers to the financing of renewable energy projects by financial institutions. The BMPK or legal lending limit poses constraints on banks with significant exposure to PLN in their loan portfolios to expand lending to renewable energy projects. As the single buyer of electricity, PLN or its subsidiaries are involved in a significant number of renewable energy projects (including large hydro projects) and hence these projects are consolidated as part of PLN exposure in calculating this limit. An easing of BMPK regulation would require a review for all sectors and not merely just for energy making this regulatory barrier particularly difficult to overcome for some domestic banks.

The ATMR (or risk weighted asset) calculation formula for renewable energy provides a basis to determine the risks faced by financial institutions in lending to renewable energy projects. Financial institutions highlighted that a review of the ATMR formula could facilitate increased lending to the sector, although this should be done with careful consideration of potential systemic impacts. OJK has implemented a capacity-building programme to facilitate risk evaluation by financial institutions and improve knowledge of clean energy projects, which still faces high-perceived risks.

Beyond addressing financial market regulation barriers, to facilitate project evaluation and increase access to domestic debt for clean energy projects, OJK could consider implementing a "credit programme" aimed at unifying and standardising rules and other contractual provisions, which would help facilitate credit appraisal.

Where local commercial banks have provided finance for projects, long-tenor loans (above 10 years) are extremely rare and there is an absence of non-recourse project financing (the norm for most renewable energy projects in OECD and other major economies) and limited-recourse financing is virtually absent as well. Interest rates are also well above (around 7-12% in USD) international sources of funding (around 5-8%) (CPI, 2018[9]; IESR, 2019[10]). Estimates suggest that bringing down interest rates to 5% (in line with average rates generally practised in the electricity, gas and water sector) could help achieve a 40% reduction in current solar photovoltaics (PV) levelised cost of electricity (IESR, 2019[10]) The asset liability mismatch, present in many markets, also poses a major challenge to raising long-term capital for clean energy projects. This is due to an over-reliance on short-term deposits to fund lending operations that restricts typical loan tenors to just 5-7 years, in contrast to the long lifetime of projects which can be 15-20 years or more for clean energy projects.

Sustainable finance regulation, taxonomy development and green bonds

Mapping a path towards sustainable finance

Indonesia is one of the leading countries in the emerging markets to recognise and take action on the importance of integrating sustainability within the country's financial regulation. The central bank of Indonesia, Bank Indonesia, joined the International Sustainable Banking Network in 2012, which the OJK subsequently joined in 2013 after its establishment as an independent regulatory body. Bank Indonesia as the monetary authority is responsible for maintaining monetary stability as well as financial system stability. OJK was created in 2011 to replace Bank Indonesia as the supervisory authority for financial institutions and is responsible for ensuring that the financial system grows in a sustainable and stable manner.

OJK published Phase I (2015-2019) of its Sustainable Finance Roadmap that focused on increasing awareness amongst financial service institutions on the importance of sustainable finance and provided comprehensive regulatory frameworks and guidelines. This was followed by regulation in 2017 (OJK Regulation No. 51/2017) to operationalise the implementation of the roadmap, including a comprehensive reporting mechanism for financial institutions, issuers, and publicly listed companies.

The regulation includes guidelines for banks to implement its sustainable finance regulation however, no guidelines have been issued for other financial institutions. The guidelines for banks define activities and operations considered compliant with eight sustainable finance principles covering: 1) Responsible Investment; 2) Strategy and Practice of Sustainable Business; 3) Managing Social and Environmental Risks; 4) Governance; 5) Informative Communication; 6) Inclusivity; 7) Priority Superior Sector Development; and 8) Coordination and Collaboration. These eight principles serve as the basis for financial industry players to develop their activities. OJK also requires financial institutions to devise a strategy that contains the implementation of environmental, social and governance (ESG) principles in their business plan and to submit a public report that outlines the implementation of the ESG principles. OJK has also classified a number of Sustainable Business categories that will serve as a reference for the classification of green sectors and to facilitate the development of sustainable finance activities by financial institutions.

Guidelines covering the clean energy sector have also been released by OJK and include a broad Guidance for Clean Energy[6], Guidance for Financing Energy Efficiency[7] and Guidance for Green Buildings[8] with a guideline now under preparation for solar power plants. These guidelines include clean energy definitions, overview on related regulation, financing schemes and project evaluation methods.

The sustainable finance regulation requires financial institutions to submit to OJK annual and five-year sustainable finance action plans (RAKBs), which define their strategy and outline goals to mainstream sustainable finance activities within the institutions operations. The largest domestic banks and foreign banks are required to have issued their RAKBs by 2019 and to start publishing annual sustainability reports that outline progress by 2020. Other institutions (smaller banks, asset managers and institutional investors) are required to publish their RAKBs in 2020 and reporting progress in 2021. All banks have fulfilled their obligations and have submitted their RAKBs to OJK.

Phase II (2020-2024) of OJK's Sustainable Finance roadmap was issued in January 2021 and focuses on building the sustainable finance ecosystem needed to help the country achieve its SDGs and the Paris Agreement (OJK, 2021[1]). The roadmap identifies the following five priority areas that are expected to accelerate the transition of the financial sector: 1) the development of a green taxonomy; 2) implementation of ESG aspects into risk assessments; 3) real programme development through innovative finance schemes; 4) development of innovative financial products and services; and 5) a national sustainable finance campaign that helps to build awareness and capacity.

OJK will soon issue supervisory guidance outlining the process for addressing ESG risks. Current guidance does not include climate risk assessments and the adoption of mandatory climate risk assessments (as outlined in Task Force for Climate Related Financial Disclosure (TCFD) recommendations) could help to effect change in the system. A few Indonesian banks have already implemented ESG principles and in early 2020, BNI-AM issued an ESG themed Exchange Traded Mutual Fund under the name of BNI-AM Mutual Fund MSCI ESG Leaders Indonesia (XBES), which began trading on the Indonesian Stock Exchange on 9 January 2020.

To promote and implement sustainable finance practices, OJK established the "First Movers on Sustainable Banking" with a group of eight national banks (Bank Artha Graha Indonesia, BRI Syariah, Bank Central Asia, Bank Mandiri, Bank Muamalat, Bank Negara Indonesia, Bank BJB, and Bank Rakyat Indonesia). These eight banks together with WWF Indonesia established the Indonesia Sustainable Finance Initiative (ISFI) with cooperation from OJK that has now grown to include 14 banks and PT SMI, a non-bank financing institution. The ISFI is a market-led initiative which aims to support the financial services industry as it implements the sustainable finance and green bond regulations (OJK Regulation No. 51/2017 and No. 60/2017) and demonstrates the willingness of the financial sector to begin implementing more sustainable finance practices.

While this is encouraging, lack of experience, data gaps and policy related barriers have in practice led to slow implementation as bankable project pipelines, particularly for clean energy projects are lacking. Of the 15 banks within ISFI, four (BNI, Bank Mandiri, BCA and BRI) have dedicated clean energy units. Some have energy units that cover both clean and traditional energy projects. The creation of dedicated clean energy project teams within financing institutions would help to develop the expertise needed for project evaluation and help expand funding for projects. On a positive note, a number of ASEAN and Asian financial institutions active in Indonesia such as HSBC, CIMB Negra, and DBS are joining a growing movement among financial institutions to adopt clean energy policies that prohibit financing of new coal power plants among other policies to increase support for renewables.

Indonesia should also accelerate efforts to promote ESG considerations in the financial sector in line with international standards. This includes assessing in particular the extent of barriers for integrating these factors in the market, notably when it comes to long-termism and quality of reporting and rating frameworks (OECD, 2020[11]).

Considerations for the development of Indonesia's Sustainable Finance Taxonomy

The development of Indonesia's Sustainable Finance Taxonomy will be an important step in Phase II of OJK's Sustainable Finance Roadmap and help to complement the already existing green bond regulation as well as RAKB design guidelines for banks to create a list of eligible sectors. The taxonomy to be developed by OJK will be a national taxonomy, which will apply across sectors and not just for financial institutions. Indonesia can draw on lessons from other countries and regions such as France, the EU, Japan and China in their taxonomy development. Important considerations from international experience include defining the environmental and other objectives linked to the taxonomy, identification of economic activities as well as integration of changes in technology and innovation. A second set of considerations are the usability of the taxonomy for end users, issuers and investors. A simple to use taxonomy will make it easier for the market to adopt and data availability must be factored in to facilitate verification.

While the country's taxonomy should be ambitious, it will need to reflect the country's economic realities and recognise that Indonesia's transition to a green economy will not be achieved overnight. The taxonomy should help guide investors on how the transition to a decarbonised electricity sector can be achieved and should encourage an accelerated shift away from coal and diesel fired generators towards renewables and other low carbon electricity sources. Consultation across government ministries, key actors across all related economic sectors, as well as users, will be critical.

The taxonomy should facilitate a quicker transition and not create additional barriers to developing the countries financial sector. It will also need to consider the impact of regulation and taxonomies in other countries as more stringent environmental definitions in other countries or regions, such as in Europe, could limit the ability for firms in those countries to invest in Indonesia if these investments do not meet the more stringent taxonomy definitions in their home country.

As financial regulators around the world have been stepping up climate disclosure requirements and implementing stress testing of portfolios and greater scrutiny of climate risks and compliance to new sustainable finance regulation, countries and corporations that lag behind on the green transition could find themselves outside the universe of investible assets. As a member of the International Platform on Sustainable Finance, Indonesia could draw from the experience and lessons learned from this group in developing a taxonomy suited to the country's national circumstances and where possible consider harmonising principles and approaches to facilitate investments across different jurisdictions.

Box 6.2. Lessons from the development of the EU Sustainable Finance Taxonomy

While the focus of this box is on the EU taxonomy, other countries including China, Japan, Malaysia and many others have developed national taxonomies to help support the transition of their finance sectors. The EU taxonomy requirements are generally more developed than criteria in other frameworks because of the level of detail the European Commission (EC) requested from the Technical Expert Group (TEG) in its recommendations for technical screening criteria. A comparison and summary of the taxonomy for the EU, China, Japan, France and the Netherlands can be found in the OECD's Developing Sustainable Finance Definitions and Taxonomies 2020 report (OECD, 2020[12]).

The EU Taxonomy is designed to help reorient capital flows towards sustainable development, manage financial risks from climate change, environmental degradation and social issues, and to foster transparency and long-termism in financial and economic activity. It aims to provide a classification system and common language for defining what is a sustainable activity. This can help to address risks of green washing and can improve investor confidence when investing in sustainable finance products.

To assist in the development of the EU taxonomy, the European Commission nominated a Technical Expert Group made up of 35 members mainly from the financial services industry as well as development banks, trade associations and NGOs. The OECD is an observer to the TEG together with the European Bank for Reconstruction and Development, the Central Bank Network for Greening the Financial System and the United Nations Environment Programme Finance Initiative. Over a period of about 12 months, the TEG met regularly (on average two days per month) in four sub-groups (taxonomy, benchmarks for the asset management industry, climate related disclosures and future Standard for EU-labelled Green Bonds) to assist the EC in preparing the delegated acts which will contain the details for implementing the regulation.

The EU sustainable finance definitions move beyond green definitions to consider also social and governance aspects in addition to climate. The EU taxonomy covers the following six environmental objectives: 1) climate change mitigation; 2) climate change adaptation; 3) sustainable use and protection of water and marine resources; 4) transition to a circular economy; 5) pollution prevention and control; and 6) protection and restoration of biodiversity and ecosystems.

An activity must meet the following three criteria to be considered compliant with the EU taxonomy: 1) contribute substantially to one or more of the environmental objectives; 2) do no significant harm to any of the other environmental objectives; and 3) comply with minimum social and governance safeguards. The do no significant harm criteria ensures a comprehensive application of broader environmental considerations and is a particularly unique feature of the EU taxonomy compared to those of other countries. The Technical Screening Criteria or performance level required to meet the do no significant harm criteria are intended to be aligned with a net zero by 2050 goal and hence can be considered globally relevant.

Economic sectors are defined based on the NACE[9] industrial classification system and used to define the technical screening criteria for this sector. This approach has some limitations as certain technologies (i.e. carbon capture and storage) and economic activities may fall outside of the NACE codes. NACE codes do not exist for buildings or for natural capital preservation, restoration and creation. To overcome this, Classification of Environmental Protection (CEPA) and Classification of Resource Management Activities (CREMA) classifications are also used. In addition, the EU taxonomy applies a system approach to economic activities to better integrate aspects of production, impact of use and end of life are taken into consideration. For example, the mitigation impacts of an electric vehicle will depend on a number of other considerations such as the carbon intensity of electricity, related congestion and whether there is reuse or recycling of the battery at the end of its useful life. Metrics defining substantial contribution for mitigation and the do no significant harm criteria are a key component of the EU taxonomy.

Four principles have guided the development of the EU Taxonomy. It is designed to be technology neutral; dynamic and evolving; easy to understand and use; and should enable transition activities. Transition activities cover three kinds of economic activities: those that are already low carbon (i.e. renewables); those that contribute to a net zero economy in 2050 (i.e. electricity generation up to 100g CO2/kWh); and those that enable emissions reductions in the first two activities (i.e. installation of efficient boilers in buildings).

The EU taxonomy covers 72 economic activities, which make up over 93% of EU-28 greenhouse gas (GHG) emissions and additional activities may be included in the future. A review of the taxonomy regulation will take place two years after its entry into force and every three years after the first review. Financial products that are to be marketed as sustainable investments must comply with the sustainable finance taxonomy and will need to disclose how and to what extent the taxonomy was used. Asset management and insurance companies will also need to report the share of their portfolios, which are taxonomy-compliant and large corporates that are subject to the non-financial reporting directive, will need to disclose the taxonomy-compliant share of revenues, capital expenditure and operating expenses. The increase in disclosure requirements that are subject to the EU sustainable finance taxonomy is expected to facilitate a faster transition towards sustainable finance and investment practices across the economy.

Source: (OECD, 2020[12])

A market leader and innovator in sovereign green bonds (sukuk)

To support the implementation of the sustainable finance regulation and facilitate a shift towards sustainable finance products, OJK issued Regulation No. 60/2017 that outlines the conditions for green bond issuances in the domestic market. The regulation defines 11 eligible sectors (including renewable energy and energy efficiency) that qualify as a green project and is in line with both the Green Bond Principles and the ASEAN Green Bond Standards issued by ICMA. Issuers are also required to report on the use of proceeds and environmental benefits from the projects must be reported and verified by an independent third party. Coordination issues with MEMR have however been highlighted by banks on the setting of definitions as certain technologies such as biofuels, which MEMR have prioritised as part of their renewables development, are outside the scope of the green bond regulation which leads to some uncertainty for banks as to which renewable projects are considered sustainable by different authorities or ministries.

Indonesia was the first country to issue a sovereign green sukuk in 2018 raising USD 1.25 billion in the foreign bond market. While a green bond needs to meet certain environmental thresholds, a green sukuk must also comply with Sharia investment principles that go beyond environmental considerations to include other sustainability and well-being considerations as well as precluding certain investments that are not permitted under Sharia law. This first issuance was followed by subsequent issuances in 2019 and 2020 that raised a further USD 1.5 billion to fund green projects including energy efficiency and renewable energy projects. The 2020 Green Sukuk Issuance in the global market has made notable achievements including obtaining the lowest coupon rate for a 5 year tenor, oversubscription by 7.4 times and attracting a greater share of green investors (34% vs. 29% compared to the two previous issuances).

The Ministry of Finance has issued two green sukuk allocation and impact reports in 2019 and 2020 covering the 2018 and 2019 issuances respectively. Sustainable transport accounted for the largest share of proceeds in both years at 62% for the 2018 issuance and 48% for the 2019 issuance. Energy efficiency projects saw a large increase from 6% in the 2018 issuance to 27% in the 2019 issuance while renewables actually declined from 8% in the 2018 issuance to 4% in the 2019 issuance. Interestingly, according to CICERO's evaluation of the green shading of projects, the energy efficiency projects only received a light to medium shade of green, while the sustainable transport received a medium to dark green and the renewable energy projects received dark green[10] (Ministry of Finance, 2020[13]).

Indonesia has so far raised a total of USD 3.2 billion of green sukuk issuances, comprising USD 2.75 billion from the three global issuances and USD 490 million (IDR 6.88 trillion) from the two domestic issuances. In addition to the above mentioned sovereign issuances, the country has also issued corporate green bonds by PT SMI, PT BRI and OCBC NISP. In November 2019, the government of Indonesia also issued the world's first retail sovereign green sukuk raising IDR 1.46 trillion (USD 150 million) in the local market from retail investors. This success is followed by the second retail green sukuk issuance in December 2020, raising IDR 5.4 trillion – which achieved the highest purchase volume and attracted the largest number of investors in the history of savings sukuk issuance. Millennials also accounted for more than half (56.7%) of the new investors attracted from this issuance. While the amount was relatively small and the tenor short at just 2 years, it represents a number of important milestones in the transition towards more sustainable finance. First, it demonstrated that there is appetite for green bonds among retail investors and allows for a diversification of the investor base, particularly millennial investors who were the primary audience for this issuance; secondly, the issuance was completely done online using a platform developed in-house by the Ministry of Finance which paves the way for further issuances at relatively low costs demonstrating the capacity Fintech can play in helping to reduce financings costs as well as to increase financial inclusion; and thirdly, it helped to raise awareness of the importance of investing in solutions to address climate change and the role individuals can plan in being part of the solution as minimum subscriptions to the bond were fixed at just IDR 1 million (USD 70) making the bond widely accessible to a significant portion of the population.

Rapid development of the global green bond (and green sukuk) market offers an attractive financing vehicle for clean energy project developers to raise long-term debt finance. Indonesia is already a leader in the sovereign green bond/green sukuk market, but corporate and sub-regional sovereign issuances have yet to take off with just three corporate green bonds issued by financial institutions PT SMI, PT BRI and OCBC NISP and no sub-regional sovereign issuances to date. The first two being state owned enterprises and the third the only non-government corporate to raise capital via green bonds. Globally, non-financial corporates for the first time represented the largest share (23%) of the green bond market issuing USD 59.1 billion in green bonds in 2019 (doubling its issuances compared to 2018) pushing out financial corporates as the top issuer, while sub-regional governments accounted for over 5% of the market (Climate Bonds Initiative, 2020[14]). The government could consider implementing policies to facilitate the issuance of green bonds/sukuk by corporates and sub-regional governments including incentives to help with the cost of certification and capacity building to improve market awareness.

Additional efforts could also be made to further develop capital market instruments for financing green projects. This will need to be accompanied by the development of regulation to help diversify financial products and efforts to further deepen Indonesia's capital markets. There is a need to develop capital market instruments that can also help to increase the availability of long term capital and should include both primary and secondary markets for infrastructure finance. Instruments should address issues of scale necessary to attract international capital and could include products such as asset backed securities, sustainability-linked bonds and clean energy funds.

Role of development finance

Development finance institutions have played a key role in helping to kick-start the clean energy sector in Indonesia supporting a variety of energy efficiency and renewable energy projects. Combined with export credit agencies, as highlighted above, these are the single largest source of funding for renewable power generation projects. Multilateral development banks such as the World Bank and the ADB have been working closely with the government to provide technical assistants to policy makers, project developers and the financial sector to help strengthen the country's clean energy ecosystem. Other multilateral development banks active in the country with clean energy programmes include the Asian Infrastructure Investment Bank (AIIB) and the European Investment Bank (EIB). In addition, a number of bilateral development banks including KfW (Kreditanstalt für Wiederaufbau), AFD (Agence Française de Développement), IFU (International Fund for Developing Countries) and JBIC (Japan Bank for International Co-operation) among many others are also financing clean energy projects and an overview of development finance co-operation programmes is summarised in Table 6.2 below. The Green Climate Fund (GCF) and a number of philanthropic foundations are also present in Indonesia and support clean energy finance and investment.

Table 6.2. Selected renewable energy programmes with DFI support

	Selected programmes
ADB	USD 40 million bundled loan to four 7 MW solar PV projects (2017) USD 300 million loan to 110 MW Muara Laboh geothermal project (2017)
AFD	USD 100 million credit line to PT SMI (2015)
JBIC	USD 490 million loan to 330 MW Sarulla geothermal project as well as political risk guarantee to private financiers (2018)
OPIC	USD 160 million loan to 72-MW Jeneponto Wind Farm (2017)

Source: (ADB, 2020[15]); (AFD, 2020[16]); (US International Development Finance Corporation, 2019[17]) (JBIC, 2014[18]); OECD, Credit Reporting System (database).

Between 2003 and 2017, development finance institutions financed about USD 3.9 billion in renewable energy projects with hydropower and geothermal projects accounting for the largest share of funding over this period (Figure 6.6). More recently, DFI's funding has shifted towards solar and wind projects that are only beginning to be established in the market, while commercial banks in Indonesia, thanks to efforts by the DFIs to build experience and market confidence, are more comfortable financing hydropower and geothermal projects.

Figure 6.6. Renewable energy financing by development finance institutions

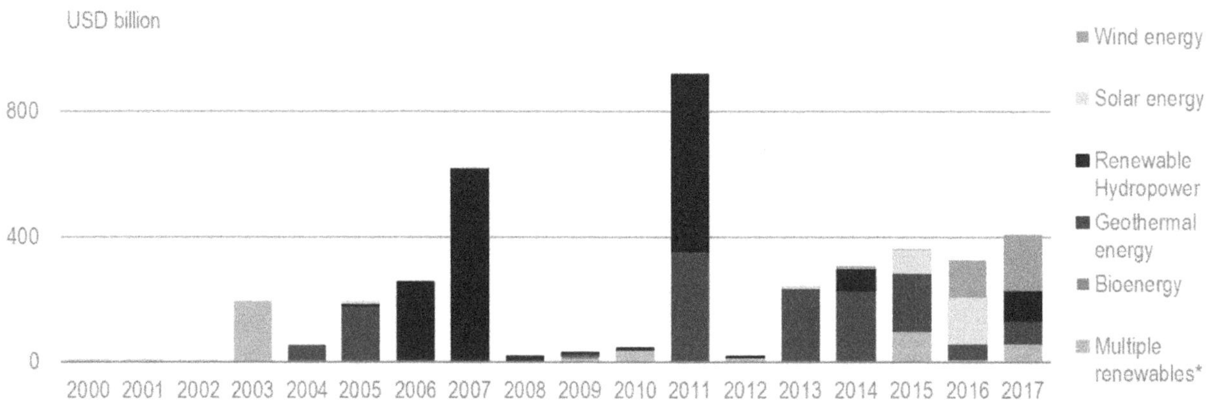

Source: IRENA(2020[20]), Renewable Energy Finance Flows (Database).

StatLink https://stat.link/yfobm1

The allocation of development finance to government institutions and SOEs is the responsibility of Bappenas, who publishes an official list of eligible projects and recipient institutions in what is known as the bluebook. The bluebook covers priority projects (usually those covered by presidential mandates) for the next five years and is updated annually. Bluebook projects tend to be relatively large infrastructure projects highlighting a potential mismatch in the process for allocating development finance that favours large centralised projects over the more characteristically smaller decentralised energy efficiency and renewable energy projects.

DFIs, like many other finance institutions, have steered away from financing smaller projects due to high transaction costs and limited project due diligence capacity. This raises the question of whether these institutions, given these practical constraints, are not actually pushing commercial banks out of the market with more attractive financing rates. This in turn could hinder the development of a commercial finance market for clean energy projects and create an unrealistic expectation on the appropriate cost of debt finance given the concessional nature of some of their funds. With DFIs in some cases fully funding or financing a large share of a project, it is difficult to evaluate whether they are helping to drive in private capital or actually holding it back. Discussions with financial institutions and international project developers alluded to potential competition between DFIs and private financial institutions in financing clean energy projects. More detailed project level and sectoral data for clean energy projects should be made publicly available to facilitate such analysis to help DFIs better target their funding allocations and recipient countries to set priorities[11]. DFIs also play a key role in providing technical assistance for project developers and financial institutions and could assist in the development of clean energy finance and investment databases.

Blended finance and the SDG One Indonesia Fund

Indonesia has been an active contributor to the development of blended finance mechanisms that use development funds to help catalyse private finance through various de-risking instruments including first loss and partial risk guarantees, co-investments and subordination among others[12]. The OECD defines blended finance as the strategic use of development finance for the mobilisation of additional finance towards sustainable development in developing countries, where additional finance refers to commercial finance that does not primarily target development outcomes in developing countries, while development finance is public and private finance that is being deployed with a development mandate (OECD, 2018[19]) (Figure 6.7).

In 2018, Indonesia showed its support for the Tri Hita Karana Roadmap for Blended Finance[13] that recognises that a common language and collective action is needed to deliver the financing needs to support the fulfilment of the SDGs. The development of blended finance mechanisms is led by OJK and the financial regulator has been active in collaborating with DFIs and commercial banks in creating appropriate structures and setting guidelines for the use of blended finance to meet the SDGs including for clean energy projects. The Coordinating Ministry of Maritime and Investment Affairs is the co-ordinator for the Blended Finance Programme in Indonesia.

In 2018, Indonesia launched the SDG One Indonesia Fund, which is a multi-donor blended finance platform with about USD 3 billion in funding commitments for supporting Indonesia's achievement of the SDGs. At the implementation level, PT SMI is responsible for managing the fund and working closely with development finance institutions in setting up a variety of financing facilities including those dedicated to supporting clean energy such as that of AFD. This dedicated USD 150 million loan facility will also include an additional grant component (EUR 5.6 million) for technical assistance to support project preparation (AFD, 2020[16]). Other clean energy related facilities under the SDG One Indonesia fund have also been set up by KfW to support project preparation for renewable energy and ClimateWorks for feasibility studies for solar rooftop development. The KfW grant facility of EUR 16 million under the Support for Infrastructure Investments in Indonesia programme (S4I), funded by the EU allows PT SMI to assist municipal governments and renewable energy developers in project preparation and environmental and social safeguards.

Figure 6.7. Understanding blended finance mechanisms

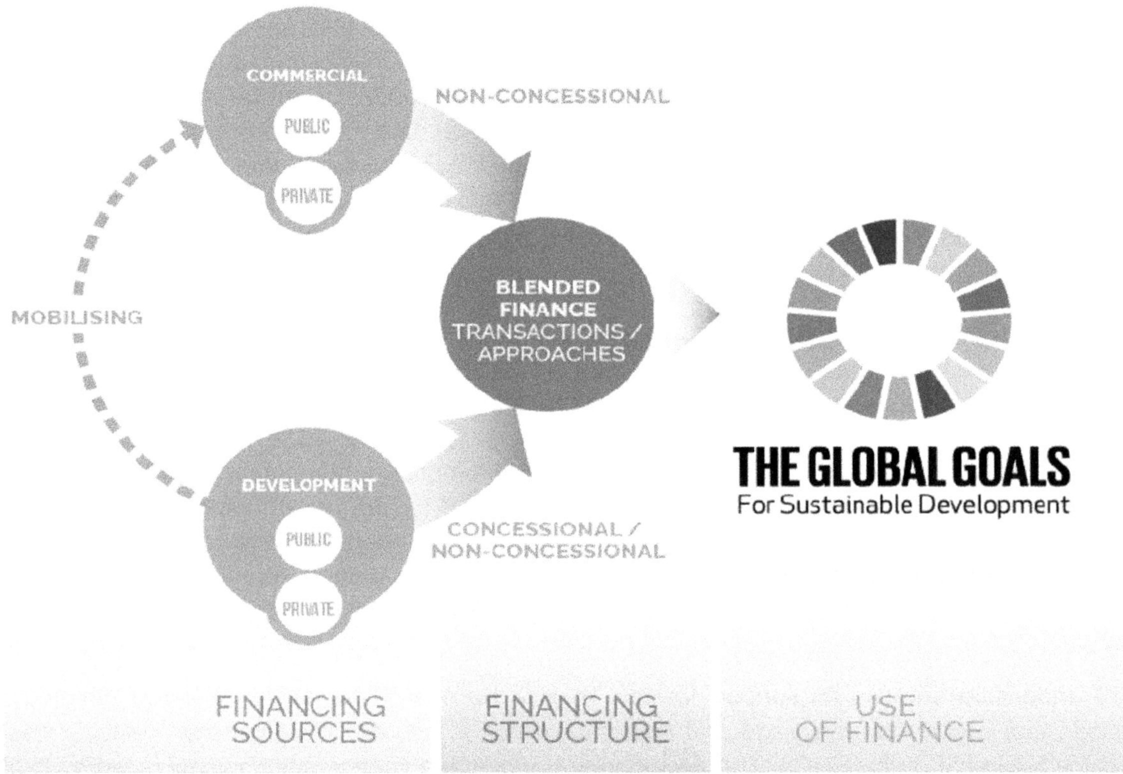

Source: OECD 2018.

The SDG One Indonesia fund is designed to use strategic development finance to crowd in private capital. One notable example for renewable energy includes the use of a grant from AFD to set up a first loss mechanism covering a maximum of 15% of the loan value for a mini-hydro plant that helped to de-risk and encourage other commercial banks to fund the project. PT SMI is working with MEMR to support the development of renewable energy as well as energy efficiency projects with the support of this fund including for combined solar Photovoltaics (PV) and light-emitting diode (LED) street lighting, various renewable electricity power plants and to establish minimum energy performance standards for a variety of appliances. For these funds to have the largest benefits, focus should be on projects with good catalytic potential that can help create markets, in particular, where there is opportunity for replicability and standardisation to help prove market viability and demonstrate new business and financing models for renewable energy or energy efficiency technologies that have yet to be established. As reflected in the OECD blended finance principles, blended finance should be deployed with a view to exit concessional finance and exit public development finance overall (OECD, 2018[19]).

Dedicated finance facilities and institutional innovation to promote clean energy

Indonesia has a variety of public finance options available to support climate finance through a number of different public institutions such as PT SMI, BPDLH and IIGF (Indonesia Infrastructure Guarantee Fund). Each of these institutions have different operational structures and mandates and could play an important role in helping to leverage private investments for clean energy. PT SMI and IIGF have already supported clean energy projects, while the BPDLH is still currently evaluating the possibility of financing clean energy projects.

In addition, as part of the Omnibus Law, Indonesia will establish a sovereign wealth fund as a new government investment body (known as Lembaga Pengelola Investasi or the Indonesia Investment Authority) to support investments in sustainable infrastructure and clean energy. The Indonesian government has already committed IDR 15 billion (USD 1 billion) as initial capital for the fund with another USD 4 billion to come from SOEs and is aiming for investments from foreign investors to reach USD 20 billion this year. Investors in the US, Japan, Canada, Denmark and the UAE have already reported investment interest (in the order of USD 10 billion) (Reuters, 2021[20]) (Reuters, 2021[21]). The fund which is expected to be operational later this year, will facilitate project development by managing the licensing process and co-investing in projects.

While Indonesia does not have a development bank, PT SMI could be considered as a quasi-development bank. It is the only national public finance institution with a mandate to support the finance of infrastructure projects and can do so via debt and equity finance and also provides capacity building and technical assistance. PT SMI also manages two funds relevant to clean energy: the Geothermal Resource Risk Mitigation fund and SDG Indonesia One. These have supported clean energy projects (though more frequently renewable energy development) through their de-risking and financing facilities. PT SMI plans to expand its financing of clean energy projects and the recently established SDG Indonesia One platform will be an important vehicle to meet this objective.

Renewable energy projects financed by PT SMI up to and through 2019 represented about IDR 3.2 trillion (about USD 224 million), consisting of IDR 2.12 trillion in mini-hydro and hydropower projects, IDR 735 billion in biomass, IDR 250 billion in geothermal and IDR 184 billion in wind projects. As an SOE, PT SMI is operated as a profit seeking entity with practical limitations on the scale and types of projects it finances, which generally are well above USD 20 million. As a result many smaller renewable energy and energy efficiency projects struggle to access PT SMI funding.

IIGF is another large public finance institution and specialises in providing guarantees for Public Private Partnership (PPP) projects in Indonesia. It provides guarantees to a range of infrastructure projects from toll roads and street lighting to coal fired power plants. Renewable energy is a priority sector for IIGF and a few renewable energy projects, mainly hydropower, were supported by IIGF guarantees. IIGF provides credit guarantees to SOEs; state guarantees as part of PPP arrangements; project preparation assistance; and also conducts policy advisory work (IIGF, 2020[22]). On energy efficiency, IIGF has announced intentions to step-up efforts to promote energy efficiency projects and is in the process of setting up a guarantee instrument with the Asian Development Bank specifically targeting energy efficiency projects.

BPDLH, the SDG One Indonesia Fund managed by PT SMI, GCF and the Climate Investor One fund (supported by FMO, the Dutch development bank) are seen as important financing vehicles to channel international climate finance with a goal of attracting private investors. With limited state budget, the Government of Indonesia is looking into how these funds could be used strategically to mobilise private finance. The biggest challenge Indonesia faces is the development of a scalable pipeline of bankable clean energy projects with additional technical assistance needed to support project development.

A green finance facility can play an important role in overcoming barriers to raising commercial finance for clean energy projects by using public funds to crowd in private finance. The green finance facility (or green bank) model is designed to address market constraints in finance for climate investments. It uses concessional funding to blend public funds with private capital to build investor confidence and help lower financing costs for new technologies that offer climate mitigation or adaptation solutions. It typically establishes products for repeatable financing of a target market and its objective is to mobilise finance from domestic finance institutions.

Box 6.3. Green Finance Facility: Lessons from Australia, Mongolia and South Africa

The experiences of Australia, Mongolia and South Africa in setting up a dedicated green finance facility or green bank highlighted a variety of different models that can be used to help catalyse private investments in clean energy and crowd in private capital for projects that would not otherwise be financed by the market. These examples showed how limited public funds can be used to pull in private capital and expand clean energy markets. Different blended finance models are available to de-risk projects and help the banking sector gain experience and confidence in financing clean energy projects. These include partial risk guarantees, subordinated debt, tenure extensions and other de-risking instruments. Such facilities have played an important role in providing local currency debt for projects that are not able to access affordable finance.

Financial instruments used by countries include the provision of debt and equity finance, investing in green bonds, investment and creation of funds to co-deliver projects, concessional finance, on-lending facilities, credit enhancement via first loss or subordinated funding and tenor extension, reimbursable grants to help smaller project developers meet collateral requirements and green mortgages. The use of grants and concessional finance varied across countries but all focused on projects with high social and/or environmental impact or with significant demonstration capacity and replicability to develop scalable project pipelines. Tools to evaluate the environmental and social impact of projects are also an important element; in the case of South Africa's Climate Finance Facility, a high impact committee was established to help evaluate project impacts.

In the case of both Mongolia and South Africa, the GCF is playing an important role in capitalising the facility or institution as well as providing technical assistance in its development and could be a partner for a facility in Indonesia. Different capitalisation models were used, e.g. a completely public funded model (Australia); a mix of state budget and GCF (South Africa); and a mix of state budget, GCF and consortium of private banks (Mongolia). The decision to create a new institution or house a facility inside an existing institution depended on whether a suitable existing institution already exists with appropriate governance structure and operational mandate.

An important first step in setting up a facility is a comprehensive understanding of the market needs to better tailor the design of financial instruments to overcome market barriers. The involvement of the local finance sector in identifying market gaps (and propose tailored solutions) and the importance of transparency and clear operational mandates is critical. Independence from the government and political interference in the funds operation are seen as important elements.

Strong technical capacity of staff and experience in financing clean energy or climate solutions is considered another important prerequisite for success. The staffing of a dedicated green finance facility requires expertise in project evaluation as well as project development and ideally experience evaluating energy efficiency, renewable energy projects and other climate related sectors such as water and waste management, international collaboration to support training and capacity building.

Source: (Muhammed Sayed, 2020[23]) (Sylvester, 2020[24]) (Bold Magvan, 2020[25])

A green finance facility should focus funding towards commercial or near commercial projects that have a strong demonstration impact or potential for replicability to help build investor confidence and develop knowledge and expertise among local financiers. Finance should focus on additionally and pull in commercial finance which would otherwise not have funded a project. Operational independence from the government can protect against political uncertainty that often comes with changes in government. Such independence can be achieved through the legal frameworks set up in the creation of the facility or institution. Through a programmatic approach such a facility could also help address capacity gaps (lack of clean energy expertise) within the financial sector, including for financial structuring that could also be supported with risk mitigation measures.

To help prove concepts and demonstrate viability of projects, such a facility could start with easy wins in more mature sectors, for example solar and wind projects that are already competitive in many countries but lack sufficient experience in Indonesia. Where grants or concessional funding is used, such projects should have significant social impacts, and benefits of low interest rates should be passed on directly to the project developer. Once a sector has reached maturity, the facility should phase out financing such projects and shift funding towards other promising sectors that are not able to access commercial funding. Given the number of different dedicated facilities for financing clean energy projects in Indonesia, a detailed assessment of market needs should be undertaken to ensure that any new facility is well targeted and designed. Financing challenges linked to regulatory or policy barriers cannot be overcome by such a facility and should not be used in such situations.

References

ADB (2020), *Asian Bonds Online*, https://asianbondsonline.adb.org/ (accessed on 22 December 2020). [28]

ADB (2020), *Projects and Tenders*, https://www.adb.org/projects (accessed on 22 December 2020). [15]

ADB (2017), "ASEAN+3 Bond Market guide 2017 - Indonesia", http://dx.doi.org/10.22617/TCS178908-2. [7]

AFD (2020), *Promoting renewable energy and climate investments through a green credit line to PT SMI, a key public financial institution of Indonesia*, https://www.afd.fr/en/carte-des-projets/promoting-renewable-energy-and-climate-investments-through-green-credit-line-pt-smi-key-public-financial-institution-indonesia (accessed on 22 December 2020). [16]

APEC (2017), *Energy Efficiency Finance in Indonesia Current State Barriers and Potential Next Steps*, https://apec.org/Publications/2017/10/Energy-Efficiency-Finance-in-Indonesia-Current-State-Barriers-and-Potential-Next-Steps (accessed on 8 April 2020). [8]

Bank Indonesia (2020), *Statistik Sistem Keuangan Indonesia (Indonesia's Financial System Statistics)*, https://www.bi.go.id/id/statistik/sski/default.aspx (accessed on 30 November 2020). [3]

Bank Indonesia (2019), *Indonesia Financial Statistics (Monthly Statistics - March 2019)*, https://www.bi.go.id/en/statistik/ekonomi-keuangan/seki/Default.aspx (accessed on 22 December 2020). [26]

Bloomberg (2019), *Indonesia Has a $412 Billion Plan to Rebuild the Country*, https://www.bloomberg.com/news/articles/2019-05-16/indonesia-has-a-412-billion-plan-to-rebuild-the-country (accessed on 27 November 2020). [5]

Bold Magvan (2020), *Mongolia Green Finance Corporation*, https://www.slideshare.net/OECD_ENV/bold-magvan-mgfc-mongolia-green-finance-corporation (accessed on 18 December 2020). [25]

Climate Bonds Initiative (2020), *Green bonds global state of the market 2019*, https://www.climatebonds.net/system/tdf/reports/cbi_sotm_2019_vol1_04d.pdf?file=1&type=node&id=47577&force=0 (accessed on 13 January 2021). [14]

CPI (2018), *Energizing Renewables in Indonesia: Optimizing Public Finance Levers to Drive Private Investment*, http://www.climatepolicyinitiative.org (accessed on 10 January 2019). [9]

IEA (2020), *Power investment trends in indonesia*, International Energy Agency. [29]

IESR (2019), *Kebutuhan Investasi Energi di Indonesia (English translation: Energy investment needs in Indonesia)*, http://iesr.or.id/pustaka/kebutuhan-investasi-energi-indonesia/ (accessed on 3 April 2020). [6]

IESR (2019), *Levelized Cost of Electricity in Indonesia - Understanding The Levelized Cost of Electricity Generation*, http://www.iesr.or.id (accessed on 6 April 2020). [10]

IIGF (2020), *PT Penjaminan Infrastruktur Indonesia (Persero)*, https://ptpii.co.id/en/ (accessed on 22 December 2020). [22]

IMF (2018), *Realizing Indonesia's Economic Potential*, INTERNATIONAL MONETARY FUND, http://dx.doi.org/10.5089/9781484337141.071. [2]

IRENA (2020), *Renewable Energy Finance Flows (Database)*, https://www.irena.org/Statistics/View-Data-by-Topic/Finance-and-Investment/Renewable-Energy-Finance-Flows (accessed on 18 December 2020). [30]

JBIC (2014), *Project Financing and Political Risk Guarantee for Sarulla Geothermal Power Plant Project in Indonesia*, https://www.jbic.go.jp/en/information/press/press-2013/0331-19526.html (accessed on 22 December 2020). [18]

Keuangan, I. (ed.) (2009), *Economic and fiscal policy strategies for climate change mitigation in Indonesia : Ministry of Finance green paper*, Ministry of Finance, Republic of Indonesia : Australia Indonesia Partnership. [31]

Ministry of Finance, I. (2020), *Green Sukuk: Allocation and Impact Report*, https://www.djppr.kemenkeu.go.id/page/loadViewer?idViewer=9468&action=download (accessed on 8 March 2021). [13]

Muhammed Sayed (2020), *Climate Finance Facility*, Development Bank of Southern Africa, https://www.slideshare.net/OECD_ENV/muhammed-sayed-dbsa-climate-finance-facility (accessed on 18 December 2020). [23]

OECD (2020), *Developing Sustainable Finance Definitions and Taxonomies*, Green Finance and Investment, OECD Publishing, Paris, https://dx.doi.org/10.1787/134a2dbe-en. [12]

OECD (2020), *OECD Investment Policy Reviews: Indonesia 2020*, OECD Investment Policy Reviews, OECD Publishing, Paris, https://dx.doi.org/10.1787/b56512da-en. [11]

OECD (2018), *Making Blended Finance Work for the Sustainable Development Goals*, OECD Publishing, Paris, https://dx.doi.org/10.1787/9789264288768-en. [19]

OJK (2021), *Sustainable Finance Roadmap Phase II (2021-2025)*, OJK. [1]

Reuters (2021), *Indonesia president says new sovereign fund targeting $20 billion within a few months | Reuters*, https://www.reuters.com/article/us-indonesia-swf-idUSKBN29K1M6 (accessed on 11 February 2021). [20]

Reuters (2021), *Indonesia says new sovereign wealth fund attracts $10 billion commitment | Reuters*, https://www.reuters.com/article/us-indonesia-swf-idUSKBN29V0UT (accessed on 11 February 2021). [21]

Sylvester, B. (2020), *About the Clean Energy Finance Corporation*, Clean Energy Finance Corporation, https://www.slideshare.net/OECD_ENV/bianca-sylvester-cefc-about-the-cefc-experience-setting-up-a-green-finance-facililty-in-australia (accessed on 18 December 2020). [24]

US International Development Finance Corporation (2019), *Information Summary for the Public PT Energi Bayu Jeneponto*. [17]

World Bank (2020), *World Development Indicators*, The World Bank Group, Washington, D.C., https://data.worldbank.org/products/wdi (accessed on 9 July 2018). [4]

World Bank (2020), *World Development Indicators (Database)*, https://datatopics.worldbank.org/world-development-indicators/ (accessed on 22 December 2020). [27]

Notes

[1] Institutional investors are usually synonymous with "intermediary investors", that is to say, an institution that manages and invests other people's money. The term institutional investor can be used to describe insurance companies, investment funds, pension funds, public pension reserve funds (social security systems), foundations and endowments among others.

[2] This does not include private placements, which are smaller than public offerings.

[3] https://www.idnfinancials.com/archive/news/29984/Financial-inclusion-index-target-has-been-reached.

[4] Based on an OJK survey in 2019 of action plans from the 8 first mover banks.

[5] A focused group discussion on Corporate Sourcing of Renewables was held on 13 October.

[6] https://www.ojk.go.id/id/Documents/Pages/Keuangan-Berkelanjutan/buku-energi-bersih.pdf.

[7] https://www.ojk.go.id/id/Documents/Pages/Keuangan-Berkelanjutan/Green%20Lending%20Model%20Final.pdf.

[8] https://www.ojk.go.id/id/Documents/Pages/Keuangan-Berkelanjutan/Pedoman%20Pembiayaan%20Isi.pdf.

[9] Nomenclature des Activités Economiques dans la Communauté Européenne (NACE) is a European industry standard classification system which feeds into several EC economic and statistical systems, e.g. at Eurostat level.

[10] https://www.djppr.kemenkeu.go.id/page/loadViewer?idViewer=9468&action=download.

[11] The OECD CEFIM programme is currently developing a clean energy finance and investment database to better understand the current state of clean energy finance, identify good practices and highlight where potential funding gaps exist at the regional or technology level.

[12] OECD Progress update on Approaches to Mobilising Institutional investment for Sustainable Infrastructure.

[13] Further details on the Tri Hita Karana Blended Finance Roadmap are available at https://www.oecd.org/dac/financing-sustainable-development/development-finance-topics/tri-hita-karana-roadmap-for-blended-finance.htm.

7 Cross-cutting issues

This chapter examines other key areas that can help improve Indonesia's clean energy finance and investment framework. It reviews Indonesia's efforts to accelerate regional grid integration with a view to facilitating the expansion of renewable electricity, as well as to promote innovation, research & development for clean energy, which can help bring down the cost of clean energy technologies and support the domestic clean energy industry's development. The chapter also examines existing training and education programmes that are essential to create and develop knowledge and skills for clean energy finance and investment as well as looks at efforts to promote gender equality in the clean energy sector.

Indonesia needs to accompany efforts to create a robust clean energy finance and investment framework with supporting policies targeted at a number of key cross-cutting areas. These cover key policy areas – such as regional grid integration, Research & Development (R&D) and innovation, gender equality as well as skill and capacity development – which are critical to realise the country's clean energy goals.

Indonesia's efforts to encourage further regional grid integration within the ASEAN region, for example, can help increase renewable energy deployment if done with careful consideration of both the interplay between national and regional power decarbonisation policies as well as other national grid investment priorities. In the same spirit, increased R&D support can boost clean energy innovation and industrial development while more targeted and integrated skill and development programmes can help ensure Indonesia's workforce is well equipped to support the growing needs in clean energy finance and investment. Mainstreaming gender issues in the process will not only be key to accelerate the clean energy transition but also to ensure such transition is inclusive and equitable.

Assessment and recommendations

Regional integration can be an enabler for renewable investment, but co-ordination between renewables investment and regional integration is key

Indonesia is part of the ASEAN (Association for Southeast Asian Nations) region, which has a target to promote the ASEAN Power Grid and Multilateral Power Trade in the region as part of the ASEAN Plan of Action on Energy Cooperation. Currently, Indonesia is lacking a physical cross-border transmission infrastructure and thus needs to invest in one to engage in regional power trading; possible options could be to connect Sumatra and Malaysia or different Bruneian, Indonesian and Malaysian parts of Borneo island. Allocating greater share of limited infrastructure budget to cross-border connections, however, might risk diverting public investment away from the national grid where needs are also considerable.

Stronger support is needed for renewable electricity and energy efficiency R&D

The Electricity and New and Renewable Energy R&D Centre (P3TKEBTKE, its Indonesian acronym) of the Ministry of Energy and Mineral Resources (MEMR) is the leading R&D agency for clean energy, although other public institutions such as the Agency for Assessment and Application of Technology (BPPT), the Indonesian Institute of Sciences (LIPI) and various universities have also been active, albeit to a lesser extent. Most notably, P3TKEBTKE has made commendable efforts to support the development of testing equipment and facilities to monitor and evaluate the implementation of minimum energy performance standards and green fuels, as well as to survey renewable energy potentials.

However, although clean energy R&D represented a considerable share of P3TKEBTKE's budget over 2015-18, it has been declining substantially since 2016 in absolute and relative terms. This reflects both a general decline in P3TKEBTKE's total budget, as the institution is planned to become an income-generating institution (also called BLU or Badan Layanan Umum), as well as an overall lower focus on clean energy – particularly energy efficiency that only received a fraction of the institution's clean energy R&D budget. Instead, much of P3TKEBTKE's R&D activities remained focused on fossil fuel technologies. This highlights a major challenge in breaking dependence on fossil fuels, which is needed to achieve the country's ambitious energy and climate targets.

Accelerating the clean energy transition requires stronger support to spur development of domestic supply chains and clean energy entrepreneurs for renewable electricity and energy efficiency innovation. This includes measures such as the recently implemented tax incentive to support private spending on R&D, allowing a 300% reduction in R&D spending to gross revenues. However, this incentive only benefits firms that are already profitable. Other incentives targeting early stage companies and supporting firms to overcome the “valley of death” are also needed. Strong policies and incentives have benefited the biodiesel industry and Indonesia is now one of the leading producers of biodiesel.

An integrated approach is needed to fill the clean energy finance and investment skill gap

Indonesia has been making great strides into developing skill and capacity for clean energy as well as sustainable finance. MEMR’s Training Centre for Electricity, Renewable Energy and Energy Conservation (PPSDM EBTKE) has been designing, developing and implementing a number of technical trainings, certification schemes and guidelines for energy efficiency and renewables; universities have also followed suit in creating clean energy curricula, although these are still limited. OJK (the financial market regulator) has been equally active in its efforts to develop skills and capacity for sustainable finance, including clean energy finance. While these efforts are important, there remains areas where further skill and capacity development are needed. Hitherto, much of the clean energy skill and capacity building efforts have tilted towards the technical and operational aspects, as is the case in many countries. While these are critical for the clean energy transition, stepping up efforts to develop project finance and de-risking skills, targeted at a range of key stakeholders (e.g. project developers, engineering firms, government, and utilities), will be equally important to enable a pipeline of investment-ready projects and ensure financial institutions are well-equipped to fund them. In the same spirit, much of the financial institutions’ trainings for clean energy have been focused on renewable project financing, often overlooking energy efficiency. Balancing focus on energy efficiency while developing the evidence base of the financial viability of energy efficiency and renewable energy projects, paired with targeted awareness-raising campaigns, will thus be important.

Empowering women and supporting female entrepreneurs can accelerate Indonesia’s clean energy transition

Empowering women and in particular women entrepreneurs can help to accelerate the clean energy transition. Indonesia recognises the crucial role women will play in meeting the Sustainable Development Goals although, as with most countries, women remain underrepresented in leadership roles in Indonesian government and industry. While female Ministers head up the key Ministries of Finance, Environment and Forestry, and Foreign Affairs, of the 30 ministers, just six are women. There is also an absence of targeted programmes in the clean energy sector to support women’s empowerment or help women entrepreneurs overcome certain gender biases and financing challenges. The Ministry of Finance has a microfinance programme that has benefited women-led enterprises, but it is not targeted specifically at women nor has it benefited women enterprises in the clean energy sector. Indonesia can draw lessons from the Clean Energy, Education and Empowerment (C3E) Collaboration Programme to work with other countries, industry and organisations to develop concrete solutions promoting women’s participation and leadership in the clean energy sector and Indonesia could draw lessons from this group and even consider joining the programme.

Box 7.1. Main policy recommendations on R&D and innovation, skill and capacity development, and women's empowerment

- Develop national renewable energy development and regional transmission network integration and power trading in tandem, carefully considering the interplay between regional and national power system decarbonisation policies, to lead to significant net carbon reductions.
- Substantially increase public funding for energy efficiency and renewable energy R&D and accelerate a shift in R&D spending from fossil fuels towards clean energy technologies in order to accelerate the development of the country's clean energy industry. Given limited budgets, consider targeting technologies that have a wide uptake potential across the economy and low or medium capital requirements such as energy management systems in industries and commercial buildings and renewable energy applications for Micro, Small & Medium Enterprises (MSMEs).
- Establish programmes targeting clean energy incubators to support innovation and assist the next generation of start-ups developing energy efficiency and renewable energy solutions.
- Continue building the financial sector's capacity to unlock clean energy finance through the implementation of training and capacity building programmes and the development of guidelines. As part of the second phase of the Sustainable Finance Roadmap, focus efforts on increasing the availability and disclosure of clean energy projects' performance and risk-return profiles that will help to increase transparency and build investor confidence. Usefully complement these efforts by awareness-raising campaigns on the opportunities provided by financing clean energy projects.
- Consider using a more integrated approach for clean energy training programmes, which goes beyond the technical and operational aspects of energy efficiency and renewable energy project development, targeting key stakeholders e.g. project developers, government institutions and utilities. As part of these capacity-building programmes, consider integrating the financial and business development aspects of project development and include the design of bankable and internationally-recognised PPAs as well as the development and implementation of PPP models.
- Consider the implementation of targeted programmes and financial support schemes to encourage and facilitate access to finance for women entrepreneurs in the clean energy sector, particularly as women are important contributors to achieve sustainable development.

Regional grid integration

Indonesia is part of the ASEAN Plan of Action on Energy Cooperation Phase II (2021-2025), which has been created under the ASEAN framework and sets out two outcome-based strategies:

- Accelerating the development and completion of ASEAN Power Grid projects identified by ASEAN Interconnection Masterplan Study III (AIMS III) by 2020.
- Expanding regional multilateral electricity trading, strengthening grid resilience and modernisation, and promoting clean and renewable energy integration.

The AIMS III study identified five potential cross-border transmission projects connecting Indonesia with its neighbouring countries. This includes a connection from Sumatra to mainland Malaysia as well as connections between the Malaysian and Indonesian parts of Borneo island. The identified interconnections are:

- Malaka (Malaysia) – Sumatera (Indonesia)
- Batam (Indonesia) – Singapore
- Sarawak (Malaysia) – Kalbar (Indonesia)
- East Sabah (Malaysia) – North Kalimantan (Indonesia)
- Singapore – Sumatera (Indonesia)

So far, only the Sarawak – Kalbar interconnection has reached commercial operation. Interconnection development is complicated and typically takes years; however, key enabling factors can speed up development such as clear budgets and clear frameworks for utilising interconnections once built.

Indonesia has often paid limited attention to transmission development due to budget constraints. For example, the latest RUTPL (the Electricity Business Plan) 2019-28 budget for national transmission is 10% lower than the previous RUTPLs. Similarly, Indonesia has often prioritised national transmission development over cross-border connection as part of its network development strategy, due to public budget constraints and private investment being virtually not allowed in network infrastructure (although this is expected to change in the upcoming RUTPL; **see Chapters 2 and 4**). In light of these issues, and as shown in an IEA study on ASEAN cross border power trade, Indonesia should consider allowing more private capital into the transmission and distribution segments of its power market as a way to ease the burden on public budget and accelerate transmission network development (IEA, 2019[1]).

While increased interconnection and multilateral power could help accelerate renewable penetration, it could also result in an actual increase of emissions within ASEAN countries, given current levels of fossil fuel (IEA, 2019[1]). If transmission and multilateral power trade were established with the current levels of renewables, there is a risk that (cheap) coal power from Indonesia could be exported to the rest of ASEAN countries, resulting in increased emissions. On the contrary, increasing transmission and multilateral power trade in tandem with higher shares of renewable energy, would enable the total emissions for ASEAN countries to fall. This shows that holistic energy system planning is crucial in order to achieve the emissions reductions targets of ASEAN countries.

Developing multilateral power trade is also one of the targets of the ASEAN Plan of Action for Energy Cooperation (APAEC). Indonesia is engaged in this work via the Heads of ASEAN Power Utilities/Authorities as well as the ASEAN Energy Regulatory Network. Indonesia should continue engagement at the regional level as developing multilateral power trade can have several benefits for the Indonesian power system. One of which is benefits that help integrate higher shares of renewables in the Indonesian system due to the security benefits of multilateral power trade as well as the opportunity to export power to other ASEAN countries.

R&D and innovation

Most of Indonesia's clean energy R&D and innovation efforts are led by MEMR's P3TKEBTKE, which has undertaken a range of clean energy R&D activities on both renewables and energy efficiency. These activities include renewable energy resource mapping, research on supply-side technologies and testing methods to improve the energy performance of various appliances (e.g. washing machines, water pumps and rice cookers) as well as compliance with regulation on Minimum Energy Performance Standards (MEPS). Other public institutions also conduct clean energy R&D, albeit to a far lesser extent (see Table 7.1). For example, the BPPT, a public, independent R&D institution, has played a leading role in the field of energy in Indonesia but has so far undertaken few clean energy R&D activities.

Table 7.1. Examples of clean energy-related R&D activities of different R&D institutions

	Energy efficiency	Renewable power	Other related areas
P3TKEBTKE	• Testing methods for energy efficiency across a range of appliances; • Policy support to develop MEPS and energy labels;	• Technology development and innovation (including geothermal, solar, micro hydro, waste to energy); • Renewable resources mapping	• Smart grid development.
BPPT	• Deployment of energy conservation technology for industry (including technical guidance for energy management).	• Technology transfer for small-scale geothermal power plants; • Innovation for bioenergy power plants.	• Study on Outlook of Energy Indonesia; • Study on Local Content Requirements; • Smart grid for urban and rural electrification; • Electric vehicles and battery testing.
LIPI	• Development of pico hydro technology to support energy efficiency; • Energy management system development.	• Hybrid power plant design.	• Microgrid system in remote areas; • DC-DC converter and DC-AC inverter.

Note: AC= Alternating Current. DC= Direct Current
Source: BPPT, LIPI and P3TKEBTKE.

The scattered nature of R&D activities in Indonesia (even beyond the clean energy sector) recently led the President to announce plans to consolidate economy-wide R&D efforts under the umbrella of the National R&D Agency (BRIN) (The Jakarta Post, 2020[2]). Although the implications this will bear on clean energy R&D are not yet entirely clear, this could possibly entail a rebalancing of clean energy R&D activities from P3TKEBTKE to the BRIN. In this regards, P3TKEBTKE has already started to re-focus its institutional mandate from being a government R&D body to that of an income-generating BLU providing laboratory and testing services to businesses and other stakeholders. This means that, as a BLU, most of P3TKEBTKE's budget would come from third parties (e.g. from the private sector, research funding and international cooperation) rather than from government budget.

P3TKEBTKE's R&D activities have traditionally focused on clean fossil fuels, although the institution allocated a bit less than a third of its total budget to clean energy over 2015-20 (see Figure 7.1). Over that period, more than half of the institution's clean energy R&D spending went to research on renewable energy technologies (particularly in the power sector) with energy efficiency only receiving a small fraction of the total allocation (see Figure 7.2).

Figure 7.1. P3TKEBTKE's R&D spending and share of clean energy R&D in total spending, 2015-20

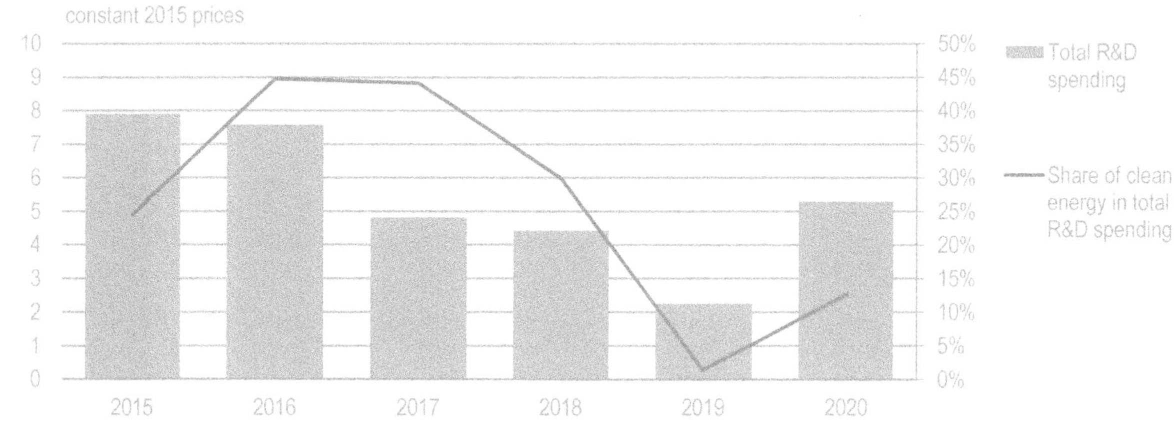

Source: P3TKEBTKE statistics.

StatLink https://stat.link/kt93y6

Figure 7.2. PT3KEBTKE's clean energy R&D budget per research areas, 2015-20

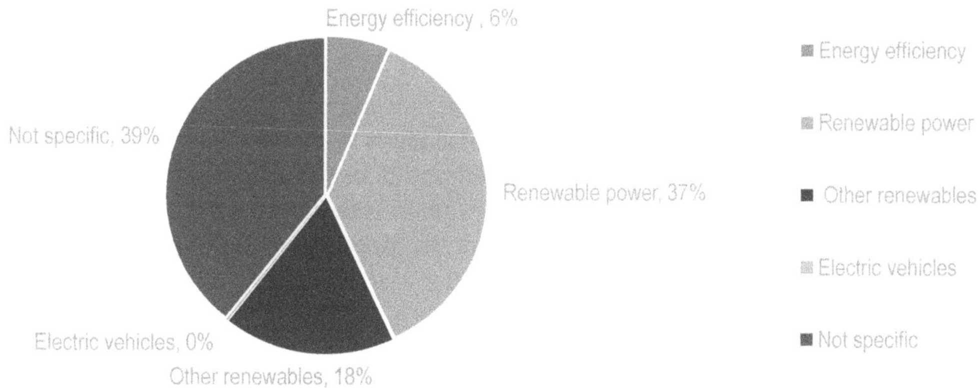

Note: "Other renewables" covers renewable energy activities not related to the power sector. "Not specific" covers research areas not specific to other categories or that are unspecified.
Source: P3TKEBTKE statistics.

StatLink https://stat.link/qyaeh9

Public clean energy R&D budget has been far too low to achieve Indonesia's clean energy goals. Total P3TKEBTKE R&D budget allocation for renewables and energy efficiency reached around USD 1.3 million annually on average over 2015-20. This is far below Indonesia's ambition under Mission Innovation, as part of which it pledged to increase the R&D budget allocated to clean energy to USD 150 million by 2020 or more than 80 times the average annual PT3TKEBTKE budget allocation over 2015-19 (see Figure 7.3). Even though total clean energy R&D budget would also include budgets from other research institutions (for which data is not publicly available), it is unlikely that the total would exceed the Mission Innovation's targets. Compounding this, P3TKEBTKE's clean energy R&D budget has been on a downward trend since 2016, with its share in total budget plummeting to 1.5% in 2019. On the one hand, this trend reflects a general decline in P3TKEBTKE's overall budget since 2015, due to plans to turn the institution into a BLU starting in 2020 (see Figure 7.1). On the other hand, this also reflects an overall lack of attention to clean energy technologies (particularly energy efficiency) compared to "clean" fossil fuel and other technologies, which remain a key focus area of R&D in the country's energy sector.

Figure 7.3. R&D budget allocation projection under Mission Innovation 2016-20 (Thousand USD)

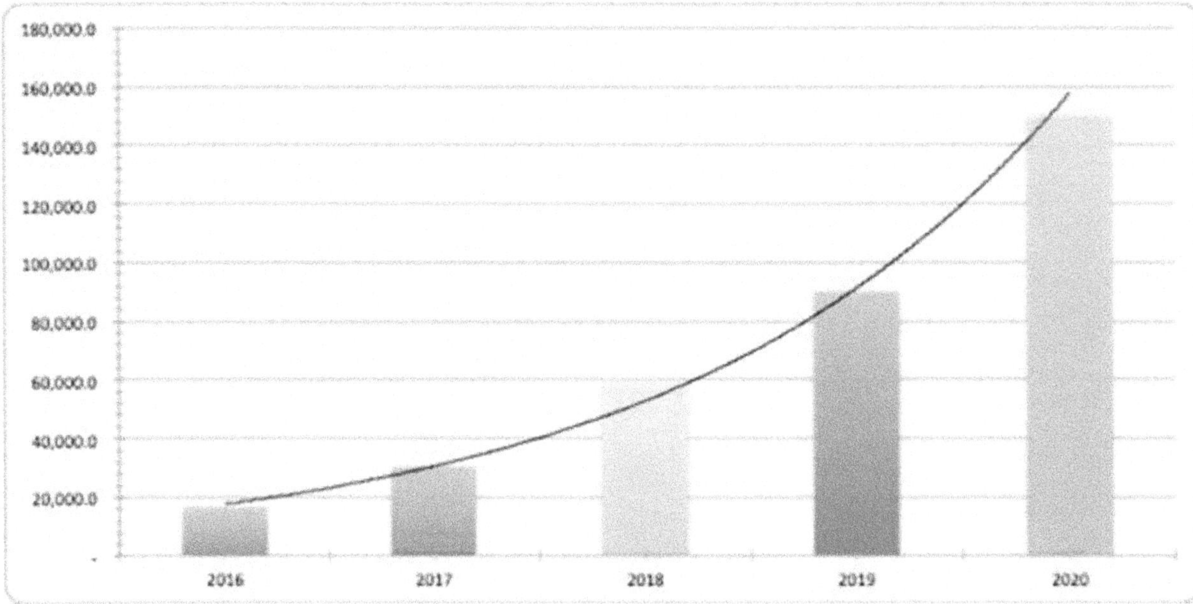

Source: Mission Innovation, 2016

P3TKEBTKE has received significant international support (IDR 32.18 billion in 2019) and has been involved in several international cooperation initiatives related to clean energy. This includes the following Mission Innovation challenges: smart grid, off-grid access to electricity, carbon capture, and sustainable biofuels. In addition, P3TKEBTKE has collaborated with Japan's New Energy and Industrial Technology Development Organisation, UNDP as well as the Korea Institute of Energy Technology Evaluation and Planning.

In addition to direct financial support for clean energy R&D, achieving the clean energy transition will also require policy support that can help to develop domestic supply chains and the innovation ecosystem more broadly and facilitate the development of clean energy entrepreneurs. One note-worthy policy implemented in Indonesia is the recently implemented tax incentive to support private spending on R&D, allowing a 300% reduction in R&D spending to gross revenues. While encouraging, this incentive only benefits firms that are already profitable and other incentives targeting early stage companies and supporting firms to overcome the "valley of death" are also needed.

Education, training and capacity building

MEMR's PPSDM EBTKE is responsible for developing and implementing training and capacity building activities for clean energy. In the energy efficiency sector, MEMR's PPDSM has notably put in place a number of trainings for green building and industry as well as a certification scheme for energy audit and energy management for energy auditors in both building and industry. In 2019 alone, PPSDM certified 79 energy managers and 175 energy auditors in the industry sector while the Ministry of Labour certified 775 energy auditors in total. These have been complemented by training and capacity building measures, such as Ministerial Regulation No. 41/2015, which established a national SKKNI (Standar Kompetensi Kerja Nasional Indonesia or Indonesia's national work competency standard) for building and industry energy managers designed to be the reference point for certified training agencies[1]. Ministerial Regulation No. 53/2018 also established a national working standard for energy audits, designed to be a reference for education and training, competency assessment and certification of energy auditors[2].

As for renewables, PPSDM developed a variety of trainings and competency certifications related to the feasibility study, construction, installation and maintenance of multiple renewable power technologies targeted at developers, installers and government staff. Furthermore, universities and vocational schools have also been following suit by developing renewable energy and energy efficiency curriculum, although these are still limited.

In the financial sector, OJK has made skill and capacity development one of the key pillars of its Sustainable Finance Roadmap. Hence, with support from international development cooperation, OJK has been putting considerable efforts into designing a number of guidelines for energy efficiency project financing as well as training modules on renewable energy and energy efficiency for banks, and conducting multi-level trainings (including a level for "training of trainers"). As of 2020, OJK implemented 53 training sessions, which supported capacity building on energy efficiency and renewable energy to around 1050 participants (including OJK staff).

Notwithstanding Indonesia's efforts, there remains a clean energy finance and investment skill gap. At present, the bulk of training programmes for clean energy has leaned towards the technical and operational aspects of clean energy projects, with a very limited integration of the business and financial aspects of project development. Yet, these skills are key to help project developers to develop bankable projects, whether through financially-robust business plans or solid loan applications, and bring projects towards financial closure. In energy efficiency, for instance, there is not yet an internationally-recognised certification for investment grade audit – although there have been attempts to develop such a certification with the TUV Rheinland University – which has affected the bankability of numerous energy efficiency projects. Similar efforts are also needed to ensure national and local governments and the utilities are well equipped to support and fund clean energy projects. For example, such efforts could focus on designing public-private partnerships (PPPs) and bankable Power Purchase Agreements (PPAs) for clean energy as well as on enhancing the flexibility of the network (looking at processes and forecasting) to allow for increased integration of renewables.

Additionally, training for financial institutions has so far primarily focused on renewable energy, often overlooking aspects of energy efficiency project financing. As a result, commercial banks continue to be relatively unfamiliar with and reluctant to fund energy efficiency projects, in large part due to their small size and the intangibility of their energy-savings-based cash flows. Developing the evidence base of the financial viability of energy efficiency and renewable energy projects (e.g., increasing the availability of projects' historical data), paired with targeted awareness-raising campaigns, will thus be important.

Gender diversity and supporting women entrepreneurs

There is global recognition that closing the gender gap in the energy sector can help to drive the clean energy transition as women play a vital role in innovation and the development of inclusive solutions. Supporting female entrepreneurship in the clean energy sector not only promotes social inclusion and empowerment, but can also be a driver of economic growth and a success factor for projects. Women can play a significant role in the successful deployment of clean energy to displace fossil fuel supply, but equally, as they are often the most affected, they have the biggest stake in expanding access to energy.

The sector depends on a range of activities along the supply chain, from research and development, manufacturing, installation, operation and maintenance, to finance, business development and many others. Eliminating barriers to entry for women creates more resources for a growing industry. Gender diversity at every level of the organisation from workforce to leadership has co-benefits in terms of growth, culture and sustainability. Studies show that increasing the diversity of leadership teams improved the quality of innovation and financial performance of businesses[3]. Removing barriers for women to take on leadership roles in the clean energy sector creates a virtuous cycle for more women to enter the sector.

In Indonesia, women are often less financially independent than men. On the demand side, female entrepreneurs generally have less knowledge of the available business opportunities, credit facilities and bank services. Most importantly, women are often at a disadvantage by having less capital to invest or collateral against which to borrow. On the supply side, an Asia Foundation study found that bank managers often lack confidence in business plans put forward by women, which they deem riskier by default[4]. Hence, the need for targeted support for women entrepreneurs to help overcome this bias and build a stronger track record of developing successful businesses.

While the Ministry of Finance has a microfinance programme that has benefited women-led enterprises, the programme is not targeted at women nor has it benefited women enterprises in the clean energy sector. Women-owned businesses need inclusive financing channels, but also training and mentoring programmes in technical, financial and leadership skills. Multilateral development banks (MDBs) have recognised the credit deficit for women entrepreneurs and have launched initiatives to scale up access to finance, markets, networks, mentors and information. A strong example of a collaboration to help women access financial and nonfinancial services is the *Women Entrepreneurs Finance Initiative (We-Fi)* launched by 14 governments and six MDBs[5].

An additional solution, which is fast developing across emerging economies, including in Indonesia, is fintech. Given the extremely high penetration of mobile phones, mobile solutions provide a unique opportunity to reach even the most vulnerable segments of the population. Mobile platforms can give women greater control over payments and savings, and for entrepreneurs it can provide information and access to financial services. The *Women's MSME Fintech Innovation Fund*, supports pilot solutions in Southeast Asia that improve access and usage of financial services for women-owned MSMEs, such as blockchain platforms to link entrepreneurs with investors, digital payments, automated bookkeeping and data-driven credit assessments (UNESCAP, 2021[3]). These solutions can provide a platform for businesses to raise seed capital, in the form of investment, credit, or even donations.

Gender responsive green financing for energy projects can have measurable impacts across sustainable development goals, empowering women, alleviating poverty, supporting economic growth and improving human health through reducing air pollution, whilst also supporting the expansion of clean energy to fight climate change. Gender-lens investors who want to improve the lives of women have a growing number of options across asset classes. Investors can benefit from a choice of fixed income and equity strategies in private and public markets to support women and clean energy in small-scale but also in utility-scale projects. In 2019, BBVA provided a 44 million USD loan for a 48 MW wind farm in Turkey, as a gender loan (BBVA, 2019[4]).

The Clean Energy, Education and Empowerment Collaboration Programme (C3E), an initiative of the Clean Energy Ministerial, provides a vehicle for countries, industry and organisations to work together to develop concrete solutions that promote women's participation and leadership in the clean energy sector[6]. Countries part of this initiative, such as Canada, Chile, Italy and Sweden among others, are making the promotion of women's leadership and participation in the energy transition a key priority. The C3E initiative launched in 2018 the Equal by 30 Campaign, which is a public commitment by governments and corporations to take action on reaching equal pay, equal leadership and equal opportunity for women in the clean energy sector by 2030. The campaign facilitates sharing of best practices and success stories in supporting women's empowerment in the clean energy sector and provides a platform to facilitate data collection and reporting on progress towards achieving the campaign's commitments. The Indonesian government could consider participating in the initiative and energy or energy-related companies in Indonesia could consider signing up to the campaign.

References

BBVA (2019), *Garanti BBVA finances wind farm in Turkey with gender loan to Polat Energy | BBVA*, https://www.bbva.com/en/garanti-bbva-finances-wind-farm-in-turkey-with-gender-loan-to-polat-energy/ (accessed on 11 February 2021). [4]

IEA (2019), *ASEAN Renewable Energy Integration Analysis*, https://www.iea.org/reports/asean-renewable-energy-integration-analysis (accessed on 9 December 2020). [1]

IEA (2015), *Energy Policies Beyond IEA Countries: Indonesia 2015*, Energy Policies Beyond IEA Countries, International Energy Agency, Paris, https://dx.doi.org/10.1787/9789264065277-en. [5]

The Jakarta Post (2020), *Jokowi wants BRIN to take center stage in research efforts*, https://www.thejakartapost.com/news/2020/01/31/jokowi-wants-brin-to-take-center-stage-in-research-efforts.html (accessed on 8 February 2021). [2]

UNESCAP (2021), *Catalyzing Women's Entrepreneurship | ESCAP*, https://www.unescap.org/projects/cwe (accessed on 11 February 2021). [3]

Notes

[1] Ministerial regulation no. 41/2015

[2] MINISTERIAL OF MANPOWER DECREE NO. 53 OF 2018

[3] https://www.bcg.com/en-us/publications/2018/how-diverse-leadership-teams-boost-innovation.aspx

[4] https://asiafoundation.org/2017/11/01/financial-inclusion-women-entrepreneurs/

[5] https://we-fi.org//

[6] http://www.cleanenergyministerial.org/initiative-clean-energy-ministerial/clean-energy-education-and-empowerment-c3e

www.ingramcontent.com/pod-product-compliance
Ingram Content Group UK Ltd.
Pitfield, Milton Keynes, MK11 3LW, UK
UKHW051503290926
15471UKWH00008B/1395